# HOME
# COMING

**Also by John Bradshaw:**

*Bradshaw On: The Family* (Health Communications/Airlift),
*Creating Love — The next great stage of growth* (Piatkus),
*Family Secrets: What you don't know can hurt you* (Piatkus),
*Healing the Shame That Binds You* (Health Communications/Airlift).

———

For information on John Bradshaw's audio and video cassette tapes,
write to:

Bradshaw Cassettes
8383 Commerce Park Drive, Suite 600
Houston, TX 77036
USA

or phone: 001 800 627–2374

For information about workshops and lectures, write to:

John Bradshaw
2412 South Boulevard
Houston, TX 77098
USA

Please send a stamped, self-addressed envelope.

# HOME COMING

## Reclaiming & Championing Your Inner Child

## JOHN BRADSHAW

PIATKUS

To the wounded inner child in my mother Norma. To my sister Barbara and my brother Richard. Our inner kids know better than anyone what it was like!

To my son John and my step-daughter Brenda. Forgive me for the wounds I've passed on to you.

Grateful acknowledgment is made for permission to reprint excerpts from the following previously published material:

"A Dream of My Brother" from *Selected Poems* by Robert Bly. Copyright © 1973 by Robert Bly. Reprinted by permission of Harper & Row, Publishers, Inc.

"Night Frogs" from *Loving a Woman in Two Worlds* by Robert Bly. Copyright © 1985 by Robert Bly. Reprinted by permission of Doubleday, a division of Bantam Doubleday Dell Publishing Group, Inc.

"For the Time Being" from *Collected Longer Poems* by W. H. Auden. Copyright © 1969 by W. H. Auden. Reprinted by permission of Random House, Inc.

"Four Quartets" from *The Complete Poems and Plays* by T. S. Eliot. Copyright 1943 by T. S. Eliot and renewed 1971 by Esme Valerie Eliot. Reprinted by permission of Harcourt Brace Jovanovich, Inc. and Faber and Faber Ltd.

This edition first published in
Great Britain in 1991 by
Judy Piatkus (Publishers) Ltd
5 Windmill Street, London W1P 1HF

Reprinted 1992, 1993 (twice), 1994, 1995 (twice)

First published in the United
States of America and Canada
by Bantam Books

Cover design by Jennie Smith
Book design by Barbara Cohen Aronica

*British Library Cataloguing in
Publication Data*
Bradshaw, John
Homecoming: Reclaiming and championing
your inner child.
I: Title
158.1

ISBN 0–7499–1054–2

Printed and bound in Great Britain by
Mackays of Chatham PLC, Chatham, Kent

# ACKNOWLEDGMENTS

To my Higher Power, who showers me with blessings and grace.

To Eric Berne, Robert and Mary Goulding, Alice Miller, Erik Erikson, Lawrence Kohlberg, David Elkind, Rudolf Dreikurs, Fritz Perls, and Jean Piaget, who taught me how the inner child develops and is wounded.

To Carl Jung and Robert Bly and Edith Sullwold, who taught me about the wonder child.

To Wayne Kritsberg, Claudia Black, Sharon Wegscheider-Cruse, Jane Middelton-Moz, Rene Fredrickson, Jean Illsley Clarke, Jon and Laurie Weiss, Bob Subby, Barry and Janae Weinhold, Susan Forward, Roxy Lerner, and above all Pamela Levin who deepened my understanding of the inner child.

To Father David Belyea, who loved me at my worst.

To Fran Y., Mike S., Harry Mac, Bob McW., Bob P., Tommy B., Warner B., and Lovable "Red," who were the first to accept my wounded inner child.

To Rev. Michael Falls, who has led me to discover the wonder of my inner child by experiencing his inner child. Our inner kids are best friends.

To Johnny Daugherty, George Pletcher, Kip Flock, and Patrick Carnes, my dearest friends, who often father my wounded child.

To Mary our Mother, to Sister Mary Huberta, to Virginia Satir, to my Aunt Millie, to Mary Bell and Nancy who have often mothered my wounded little boy.

To Sissy Davis, who loves him now.

To Toni Burbank, for her brilliant and insightful editing of this book. Her assistance was indispensible.

To the whole staff at Bantam who are second to none.

To Winston Laszlo and the whole staff at Bradshaw Events in Denver, especially Mary Lawrence. They make the Inner Child workshop happen.

To Karen Fertitta, my personal assistant and friend who takes care of my wounded inner child's anxiety.

To Marc Baker, Barbara Westerman and the staff at Life Plus for their nurturing committment.

And last, but not least, to my sister Barbara Bradshaw, who painstakingly typed and retyped this manuscript at all hours and at great personal sacrifice. She has been my support and unselfish friend.

# CONTENTS

# PROLOGUE

I know what I really want for Christmas. I want my
childhood back. Nobody is going to give me that.... I
know it doesn't make sense, but since when is Christmas
about sense, anyway? It is about a child of long ago and
far away, and it is about the child of now. In you and
me. Waiting behind the door of our hearts for something wonderful to happen.

—Robert Fulghum

As I walked among the participants in my workshop, I was struck
by their intensity. One hundred people, in groups of six or eight,
filled the room. Each group was self-contained, its members sitting
close together and whispering to one another. This was the second
day of the workshop, so a good deal of interaction and sharing had
already occurred. Still, these people had been total strangers when
they began.

I moved nearer to one group. They were listening with rapt attention to a gray-haired man. He was reading the letter his inner child
had written to his father.

Dear Dad,
I want you to know how you hurt me. You punished me more
than you spent time with me. I could have endured the welts and
cuts, if only you would have spent time with me. I wanted your
love more than I could ever tell you. If only you would have played
with me or taken me to a ball game. If only you could have told me
you loved me. I wanted you to care about me....

He put his hands over his eyes. The middle-aged woman beside him
began tenderly stroking his hair; a younger man reached out to take
his hand. Another man asked if he wanted to be held; the gray-haired
man nodded.

Another group was sitting on the floor with their arms around one another. An elegant woman in her seventies was reading her letter:

Mother, you were too busy with your charity work. You never had time to tell me you loved me. You paid attention to me only when I was sick or when I was playing the piano and making *you* proud. You only let me have the feelings that pleased you. I only mattered when I pleased you. You never loved me for *myself*. I was so alone. . . .

Her voice cracked and she began to cry. The wall of control that she had carefully maintained for seventy years began to fall with her tears. A teenage girl embraced her. A young man told her it was okay to cry. He praised her for her courage.

I moved to another group. A blind man in his mid-thirties was reading a letter he had written in braille:

I hated you because you were ashamed of me. You locked me in the garage apartment when you entertained your friends. I never got enough to eat. I was so hungry. I knew you hated me because I was a burden to you. You laughed and ridiculed me when I fell down. . . .

Now I *had* to move on. I was feeling the residual anger in my own wounded inner child, and I wanted to cry out in rage and indignation. The sadness and loneliness of childhood felt overwhelming. How could we ever recover from so much grief?

Yet, by the end of the day, the mood had changed to one of peace and joy. People sat together; some held hands; most were smiling as we did the closing exercise. One after another they thanked me for helping them find their wounded inner child. A bank president who had been openly resistant at the start of the workshop told me that he had cried for the first time in forty years. As a child, he had been cruelly beaten by his father, and had vowed never to be vulnerable or to show his feelings. Now he talked about learning to take care of the lonely boy inside him. His face had softened, and he looked younger.

At the beginning of the workshop I had urged the participants to put their masks aside and come out of hiding. I had explained that when they kept their wounded inner child in hiding, that wounded child contaminated their lives with temper tantrums, overreactions, marital problems, addictions, toxic parenting, and damaging and pain-ful relationships.

I must have touched a nerve, for they had really responded. I felt both excited and grateful as I looked at their open, smiling faces. This workshop took place in 1983. In the years since then I have become more and more fascinated with the healing power of the inner child.

Three things are striking about inner child work: the speed with which people change when they do this work; the depth of that change; and the power and creativity that result when wounds from the past are healed.

I began my inner child work more than twelve years ago, using a rather makeshift meditation with some of my therapy clients. But this meditation achieved some very dramatic results. When people first made contact with their inner child, the experience was often over-whelming. Sometimes they sobbed intensely. Later, they said things like "I've been waiting all my life for someone to find me"; "It feels like a homecoming"; "My life has been transformed since I found my child."

Because of this response, I developed an entire workshop to help people find and embrace their inner child. The workshop has evolved over the years, due mostly to an ongoing dialogue with those who have participated in it. This is the most powerful work I have ever done.

The workshop focuses on helping people finish their unresolved grief from childhood—griefs resulting from abandonment, abuse in all forms, the neglect of childhood developmental dependency needs, and the enmeshments that result from family-system dysfunction. (I'll discuss each of these in detail later on.)

In the workshop we spend most of the time on grieving our neglected childhood developmental dependency needs. That is also the major focus of this book. In my experience, a developmental approach is the most thorough and effective way to heal our emo-tional wounds. I believe that this focus on healing each developmen-tal stage is unique to my workshop.

During the workshop I describe the normal dependency needs of childhood. If those needs are not met, we tend to grow into adult-hood with a wounded inner child. Had our childhood needs been met, we would not have become "adult children."

After I have outlined the needs of a particular stage, the participants split off into groups. Taking turns at being the focus subject, each person listens as the others speak the affirmative words he or she needed to hear in infancy, toddlerhood, the preschool years, and so on.

Depending on the subject's boundaries, members of the group stroke, nurture, and offer validation for the person's childhood pain. When the subject hears a particular affirmation that he* needed to hear but was deprived of during childhood, usually he begins to weep, mildly to intensely. Some of the old, frozen grief begins to melt. By the end of the workshop, everyone has done at least some grief work. The amount depends on where a person is in the healing process. Some people have done a lot of work before coming to the workshop; others have done none.

Toward the end of the workshop, I give a meditation for embracing the inner child. At that time, many people feel an intense discharge of emotion. As the participants leave the workshop, I encourage them to spend some time each day in dialogue with their inner child.

Once people have claimed and nurtured their wounded inner child, the creative energy of their wonderful natural child begins to emerge. Once integrated, the inner child becomes a source of regeneration and new vitality. Carl Jung called the natural child the "wonder child"—our innate potential for exploration, awe and creative being.

The workshop has convinced me that the inner child work is the quickest and most powerful way to effect therapeutic change in people. This almost-immediate effect continues to amaze me.

Normally I'm skeptical about any type of quick fix, but this work seems to begin a process of lasting transformation. Writing one or two years after the experience, many participants claimed that the workshop had changed their lives. I was gratified but somewhat confused. I really didn't know why the work had such an impact on some people and only minimal effect on others. As I searched for an explanation, a picture slowly began to emerge.

I first turned to the work of Eric Berne, the creative genius behind Transactional Analysis. T.A. theory places major emphasis on the "child ego state," which refers to the spontaneous natural child we all once were. T.A. also describes the ways that the natural child *adapted* to the pressures and stresses of early family life.

*In this book, "he" and "his" refers to human beings of either sex. I have chosen to do this for grammatical consistency—no insensitivity is intended. Whenever I use an example pertaining to a person, it is based on my experience, either personal or with a client. Details of cases have been changed in order to honor boundaries and prevent identification.

The natural or wonder child is present when you meet an old friend; when you belly-laugh; when you're creative and spontaneous; when you are awed by a wondrous sight.

The adapted or wounded child is present when you refuse to go through a red light even though it is obviously stuck, or run a red light because there's no one around and you think you can get away with it. Other wounded child behaviors include throwing temper tantrums, being overly polite and obedient, speaking in a childlike voice, manipulating, and pouting. In chapter 1, I will outline the many ways that the wounded child contaminates our adult life.

Although I had used T.A. as my major therapeutic model for many years, I had never focused my work on the various developmental stages that the inner child goes through in adapting to survive. I now believe that the lack of developmental detail is a shortcoming in most T.A. work. Any part of our wonder child's early development can be arrested. As adults we can act infantile; we can regress to the behavior of a toddler; we can continue to believe in magic like a preschooler; and we can pout and withdraw like a first-grader who has lost a game. All these behaviors are childish and represent various levels of arrested childhood development. The major purpose of this book is to help you reclaim your wounded inner child at *each stage of development*.

A later influence on my work came from the hypnotherapist Milton Erickson. Erickson believed that every person has his own unique map of the world, an inner belief system that is unconscious and constitutes a kind of hypnotic trance. Using Ericksonian hypnosis, I learned natural ways to connect with the trance my clients *were already in* and to use that trance to aid expansion and change. What I did not see, until I started doing inner child work, was that it is the wounded inner child who forms the core belief system. By age-regressing into the inner child's trance, it is possible to change the core beliefs *directly and quickly*.

Therapist Ron Kurtz deepened my understanding of the dynamics of inner child work. Kurtz's system, called Haikomi therapy, focuses directly on the core material. Core material is the *way our internal experience is organized*. Composed of our earliest feelings, beliefs, and memories, our core material formed in response to the stresses of our childhood environment. This core material is nonlogical and primitive; it was the only way a magical, vulnerable, needy and boundary-less child knew how to survive.

Once the core material is formed, it becomes the filter through which all new experiences must pass. This explains why some people continually choose the same kind of destructive romantic relationship; why some experience their lives as a series of recycled traumas; and why so many of us fail to learn from our mistakes.

Freud called this urge to repeat the past the "repetition compulsion." The great modern therapist Alice Miller calls it the "logic of absurdity." It is logical when one understands how the core material shapes our experience. It's as if you were wearing sunglasses: No matter how much sunlight there actually is, it will be filtered the same way. If the glasses are green, the world will seem green. If the glasses are brown, you won't see bright colors very well.

Obviously, then, if we want to change, we have to change our core material. Since it was our inner child who first organized our experience, making contact with the inner child is a way to change our core material immediately.

Inner child work is an important new therapeutic tool and is vastly different from the way therapy was done in the past. Freud was the first to grasp that our neuroses and character disorders are the result of unresolved childhood conflicts that are repeated throughout our lives. He tried to cure the wounded child by setting up a safe environment that would allow the wounded inner child to emerge and transfer his unmet needs to the therapist. The therapist would then reparent the wounded inner child so that he could finish his unfinished business; the wounded child would be healed.

Freud's method required an enormous commitment of time and money, and it often set up an unhealthy dependency in the patient. One of my clients came to me after ten years of psychoanalysis. Even while I worked with her, she called her analyst two or three times a week to ask his advice on the most trivial decisions. The analyst had truly become her inner child's good parent. However, he was hardly nurturing her. She was miserably dependent on him. True nurturing would have helped her to claim and use her own adult powers to nurture her inner child.

In this book I will offer you a new way to contact, reclaim, and nurture your inner child. *You must do the work suggested* if you want to experience change. *It is up to the adult part of you to decide to do this work.* Even while you are in your child state, your adult self will still know exactly where you are and what you are doing. Your inner child will experience things the way you first experienced them in childhood, but this time your adult self will be there to protect and support your child as he completes important unfinished business.

The book has four parts. Part 1 looks at how your wonder child lost his wonder and how the wounds sustained in childhood continue to contaminate your life.

Part 2 takes you through each of your childhood developmental stages, showing you what you needed in order to grow in a healthy way. Each chapter contains a questionnaire to help you determine whether your inner child's needs were met during a specific stage. Then I will lead you through the experiences I use in my workshop to help you reclaim your child at each stage.

Part 3 presents specific corrective exercises for helping your child grow and flourish; for learning healthy ways to get other adults to meet some of your inner child's needs; and for building protective boundaries for your inner child as you work on intimacy in your relationships. This part shows how *you* can be the nurturing parent you never had in childhood. When you learn how to re-parent yourself, you will stop attempting to complete the past by setting up others to be your parents.

Part 4 shows how your wonder child emerges as the wounded child is healed. You will learn how to access your wonder child, and you will see that he is the most creative and transformative energy you possess. Your wonder child is the part of you that is most like your Creator and can lead to an immediate, personal relationship with your unique self and with God as you understand God. This is the deepest healing of all, promised by the great teachers of all faiths.

Along the way, I also tell my own story. When I first started this work twelve years ago, I couldn't have imagined the transformation in my thinking and behavior that have resulted from my own personal discovery of my inner child. Prior to this discovery, I minimized the impact of my childhood and was caught in the compulsion to idealize and protect my parents, especially my mother. As a child, I often used to say to myself, "When I grow up and get out of here, everything's going to be all right." As the years went on, I realized that things were not getting better; they were getting worse. I could see it in other members of my family more clearly than I could see it in myself. Ten years after I had won my victory over alcoholism, I found that I was still driven and compulsive.

One rainy Thursday afternoon I experienced what Alice Miller wrote about her own inner child: "I could not bring myself to leave the child alone.... I made a decision that was to change my life profoundly: to let the child lead me." On that day I made the decision to reclaim and champion my inner child. I found him frightened to the point of terror. At first he did not trust me and would not go with me. Only by persisting in my efforts to talk to him and insisting that I would not leave him did I begin to gain his trust. In this book I describe the stages of the journey that allowed me to become the guardian and champion of my inner child. That journey has changed my life.

# PARABLE

## The Double Tragedy of Rudy Revolvin
### (Based on *The Strange Life of Ivan Osokin*, by P. D. Ouspensky.)

Once upon a time, there was a man named Rudy Revolvin. He lived a painful and tragic life. He died unfulfilled and went to the dark place.

The Ruler of Darkness, seeing that Rudy was an adult child, felt he could add to the darkness by giving Rudy a chance to live his life over again. You see, the Ruler of Darkness had a mission to continue the darkness—even to make it darker if he could. He told Rudy that he had no doubt that Rudy would make *exactly the same mistakes all over again and experience the exact same tragedy as before*!

He then gave Rudy one week to make up his mind.

Rudy thought long and hard. It became obvious to him that the Ruler of Darkness was tricking him. Of course he would make the same mistakes, because he would be deprived of the memories of what he had gone through in his previous life. Without such memories he would have no way of avoiding his errors.

When he finally appeared before the ruler, he refused the offer.

The Ruler of Darkness, knowing the "secret" of the wounded inner child, was undaunted by Rudy's refusal. He told him that, contrary to the usual policy, Rudy would be permitted to remember everything about his past life. The Ruler of Darkness knew that even with such memories, Rudy would *still* make exactly the same mistakes and have to suffer his painful life all over again.

Rudy chuckled to himself. "Finally," he thought, "I'm getting a real break." Rudy knew nothing about the "secret" of the wounded inner child.

Sure enough, even though he could foresee in detail every disaster that he had formerly created, he did repeat his painful and tragic life. The Ruler of Darkness was pleased!

# 1

# THE PROBLEM OF THE WOUNDED INNER CHILD

The knowledge illuminated forgotten chambers in the dark house of infancy. I knew now why I could feel *homesick at home*.

—G. K. CHESTERTON

# INTRODUCTION

Buckminster Fuller, one of the most creative men of our time, loved to quote Christopher Morley's poem about childhood:

> The greatest poem ever known
> Is one all poets have outgrown:
> The poetry, innate, untold
> Of being only four years old.
>
> Still young enough to be a part
> Of Nature's great impulsive heart,
> Born comrade of bird, beast and tree
> And unselfconscious as the bee—
>
> And yet with lovely reason skilled
> Each day new paradise to build
> Elate explorer of each sense,
> Without dismay, without pretense!
>
> In your unstained transparent eyes
> There is no conscience, no surprise:
> Life's queer conundrums you accept,
> Your strange Divinity still kept. . . .
>
> And Life, that sets all things in rhyme,
> May make you poet, too, in time—
> But there were days, O tender elf,
> When you were Poetry itself!

What happens to this wonderful beginning when we were all "Poetry itself"? How do all those tender elves become murderers, drug addicts, physical and sexual offenders, cruel dictators, morally degenerate politicians? How do they become the "walking wounded"? We see them all around us; the sad, fearful, doubting, anxious, and depressed, filled with unutterable longings. Surely this loss of our innate human potential is the greatest tragedy of all.

The more we know about how we lost our spontaneous wonder and creativity, the more we can find ways to get them back. We may even be able to do something about preventing this from happening to our own children in the future.

# CHAPTER 1

# HOW YOUR WOUNDED INNER CHILD CONTAMINATES YOUR LIFE

> The person ... in the grip of an old distress says things
> that are not pertinent, does things that don't work, fails
> to cope with the situation, and endures terrible feelings
> that have nothing to do with the present.
>
> —HARVEY JACKINS

I couldn't believe I could be so childish. I was 40 years old and I had
raged and screamed until everyone—my wife, my stepchildren, and
my son—was terrified. Then I got in my car and left them. There I
was, sitting all alone in a motel in the middle of our vacation on
Padre Island. I felt very alone and ashamed.

When I tried to trace the events that led up to my leaving, I couldn't
figure out anything. I was confused. It was like waking up from a bad
dream. More than anything, I wanted my family life to be warm,
loving, and intimate. But this was the third year I had blown up on
our vacation. I had gone away emotionally before—but I had never
gone away physically.

It was as if I'd gone into an altered state of consciousness. God, I
hated myself! What was the matter with me?

The incident on Padre Island occurred in 1976, the year after my
father died. Since then I've learned the causes of my rage/withdrawal
cycles. The major clue came to me on the Padre Island runaway.

While I sat alone and ashamed in that crummy motel room, I began to have vivid memories of my childhood. I remembered one Christmas Eve when I was about 11 years old, lying in my darkened room with the covers pulled up over my head and refusing to speak to my father. He had come home late, mildly drunk. I wanted to punish him for ruining our Christmas. I could not verbally express anger, since I had been taught that to do so was one of the deadly sins, and especially deadly in regard to a parent. Over the years my anger festered in the mildew of my soul. Like a hungry dog in the basement, it became ravenous and turned into rage. Most of the time I guarded it vigilantly. I was a nice guy. I was the nicest daddy you've ever seen—until I couldn't take it anymore. Then I became Ivan the Terrible.

What I came to understand was that these vacation behaviors were *spontaneous age regressions*. When I was raging and punishing my family with withdrawal, I was regressing to my childhood, where I had swallowed my anger and expressed it the only way a child could—in punishing withdrawal. Now, as an adult, when I was finished with an emotional or physical withdrawal bout, I felt like the lonesome and shame-based little boy that I had been.

What I now understand is that when a child's development is arrested, when feelings are repressed, especially the feelings of anger and hurt, a person grows up to be an adult with an angry, hurt child inside of him. This child will spontaneously contaminate the person's adult behavior.

At first, it may seem preposterous that a little child can continue to live in an adult body. But that is exactly what I'm suggesting. I believe that this neglected, wounded inner child of the past is the major source of human misery. Until we reclaim and champion that child, he will continue to act out and contaminate our adult lives.

I like mnemonic formulas, so I'll describe some of the ways the wounded inner child contaminates our lives using the word *contaminate*. Each letter stands for a significant way in which the inner child sabotages adult life. (At the end of this chapter you'll find a questionnaire to help you ascertain how badly your own inner child was wounded.)

Co-Dependence
Offender Behaviors
Narcissistic Disorders
Trust Issues
Acting Out/Acting In Behaviors
Magical Beliefs
Intimacy Dysfunctions
Nondisciplined Behaviors
Addictive/Compulsive Behaviors
Thought Distortions
Emptiness (Apathy, Depression)

## CO-DEPENDENCE

I define co-dependence as a dis-ease characterized by a *loss of identity*. To be co-dependent is to be out of touch with one's feelings, needs, and desires. Consider the following examples: Pervilia listens to her boyfriend talk about his distress at work. She cannot sleep that night because she is fretting about *his* problem. She feels *his feeling* rather than her own.

When Maxmillian's girlfriend ends their six-month relationship, he feels suicidal. He believes that his worth depends on her loving him. Maxmillian truly has no *self*-worth, which is engendered from within; he has *others*-worth, which depends on other people.

Jolisha is asked by her jock husband if she wants to go out for the evening. She is wishy-washy and finally says yes. He asks where she wants to go. She says *it doesn't matter*. He takes her to the Viking Barbecue Stand and to see the movie *The Return of the Ax Murderer*. She hates the whole evening. She pouts and withdraws from him for a week. When he asks, "What's the matter?" she answers, "Nothing."

Jolisha is a "sweetheart." Everyone comments on how nice she is. Actually, she only pretends to be nice. She is continually in an act. For Jolisha, being nice is a *false* self. She's unaware of what *she* really needs or wants. She is unaware of her own identity.

Jacobi is 52 years old. He comes to counseling because he has been in an affair with his 26-year-old secretary for two months. Jacobi tells me he doesn't know how this happened! Jacobi is an elder in his church and a revered member of the Committee to Preserve Morality. He led the fight to clean up pornography in his city. Actually,

Jacobi is in a religious "act." He is completely out of touch with his sexual drive. After years of active repression, his sex drive has taken over.

Biscayne takes his wife's weight problem personally. He has greatly curtailed their social life because he is embarrassed to have his friends see his wife. Biscayne has no sense of where he ends and his wife begins. He believes his manhood will be judged by how his wife looks. His partner, Bigello, has a mistress. He periodically weighs her to be sure she is maintaining her weight. Bigello is another example of a person who has no sense of self. He believes his manhood depends on his mistress's weight.

Ophelia Oliphant demands that her husband buy a Mercedes. She also insists on keeping their membership in the River Valley Country Club. The Oliphants are heavily in debt; they live from payday to payday. They spend enormous amounts of energy juggling creditors and fashioning an image of upper-class wealth. Ophelia believes that her self-esteem depends on maintaining the proper image. She has no inner sense of self.

In all the above examples we find people who are dependent on something outside of themselves in order to have an identity. These are examples of the dis-ease of co-dependence.

Co-dependence is fostered in unhealthy family systems. For example, everyone in an alcoholic family becomes co-dependent on the alcoholic's drinking. Because the drinking is so life-threatening to each family member, they adapt by becoming chronically alert (hypervigilant). Adaptation to stress was intended by nature to be a temporary state. It was never intended to be chronic. Over time, a person living with the chronic distress of alcoholic behavior loses touch with his own internal cues—his own feelings, needs, and desires.

Children need security and healthy modeling of emotions in order to understand their own inner signals. They also need help in separating their thoughts from their feelings. When the family environment is filled with violence (chemical, emotional, physical, or sexual), the child must focus solely on the outside. Over time he loses the ability to generate self-esteem from within. Without a healthy inner life, one is exiled to trying to find fulfillment on the outside. This is co-dependence, and it is a symptom of a wounded inner child. Co-dependent behavior indicates that the person's childhood needs were unmet, and therefore he cannot know who he is.

## OFFENDER BEHAVIORS

We tend to think that all people who have a wounded inner child are nice, quiet, and long-suffering. But in fact, the wounded inner child is responsible for much of the violence and cruelty in the world. Hitler was chronically beaten in his childhood; he was humiliated and toxically shamed by a sadistic father who was the bastard son of a Jewish landlord. Hitler reenacted the most extreme form of that cruelty on millions of innocent people.

My client Dawson comes to mind. When he came to see me about a problem in his marriage, he was a bouncer in a nightclub. He spoke of breaking a man's jaw earlier in the week. He passionately described how the man had *made* him do it. He had aggravated Dawson by acting tough around him. Frequently in the course of my counseling with Dawson he spoke in this manner. Offenders take no responsibility for their behavior.

As we worked together, it became clear that often Dawson was actually scared. When he felt fear, it triggered memories of the little boy that he once had been. His father had been violent and physically abusive to him. As the little boy of long ago, trembling in the wake of his brutal father's rage, it wasn't safe to be his own terrified self. So Dawson identified with his father's self. He *became* his father. When anything resembling the childhood scenes of violence occurred, it triggered the old feelings of fear and powerlessness, and Dawson became his brutal father, inflicting the same wounds onto others that his father had inflicted on him.

Offender behavior, the major source of human destruction, is the result of childhood violence and the suffering and unresolved grief of that abuse. The once powerless wounded child becomes the offender adult. In order to understand this, we have to understand that many forms of child abuse actually set up the child to be an offender. This is especially true of physical abuse, sexual abuse, and severe emotional battering. The psychiatrist Bruno Bettelheim coined a phrase for this process: He called it "identifying with the offender." Sexual, physical, and emotional violence are so terrifying to the child that he cannot remain in his own self during the abuse. In order to survive the pain, the child loses all sense of his identity and identifies instead with the offender. Bettelheim conducted his studies primarily among survivors of German concentration camps.

In one of my recent workshops a therapist from New York raised her hand. She identified herself as Jewish and proceeded to tell our group the gruesome details of her mother's experience in a Nazi concentration camp. The most startling part of her story was that her mother had treated *her* as the Nazi guards had treated her mother. Her mother spat on her and called her a Jewish pig as early as 3 years old.

Perhaps even more disturbing are the sexual offenders. More often than not, they themselves were sexually violated as children. When they molest children, they are reenacting the abuse they experienced in their own childhood.

While most offender behavior is rooted in childhood, it is not always the result of abuse. Some offenders were "spoiled" by their parents through overindulgence and oversubmission, so that they learned to feel that they were *superior* to others. Such pampered children come to believe that they deserve special treatment from everyone and that they can do no wrong. They lose all sense of responsibility, believing that their problems are always someone else's fault.

## NARCISSISTIC DISORDERS

Every child needs to be loved unconditionally—at least in the beginning. Without the mirroring eyes of a nonjudgmental parent or caretaker, a child has no way of knowing who he is. Every one of us was a *we* before we became an *I*. We needed a mirroring face to reflect all the parts of ourselves. We needed to know that we mattered, that we were taken seriously, and that every part of us was lovable and acceptable. We also needed to know that our caretakers' love could be depended on. These were our healthy narcissistic needs. If we did not get them met, our sense of I AM was damaged.

The narcissistically deprived inner child contaminates the adult with an insatiable craving for love, attention, and affection. The child's demands will sabotage his adult relationships, because no matter how much love is forthcoming, it's never enough. The narcissistically deprived adult child cannot get his needs filled because they are actually a child's needs. And children *need their parents all the time*. They are needy by nature, not by choice. A child's needs are dependency needs, that is, needs that depend upon another to be filled. Only grieving the loss will provide healing. Until that is done, the insatiable child will voraciously seek the love and esteem he or she did not get in childhood.

The needs of narcissistically deprived adult children take various forms:

- They are disappointed in one relationship after another.
- They are always looking for the perfect lover who will fill all their needs.
- They become addicts. (Addictions are an attempt to fill the hole in one's psyche. Sex and love addictions are prime examples.)
- They seek material things and money to give them a sense of worth.
- They become performers (actors and athletes) because they need the continuous adulation and admiration of their audience.
- They use *their own children* to meet their narcissistic needs. (In their fantasy, their children will never leave them and will always love, respect, and admire them.) They try to get from their children the love and special admiration they could not get from their own parents.

## TRUST ISSUES

When caretakers are untrustworthy, children develop a deep sense of distrust. The world seems a dangerous, hostile, unpredictable place. So, the child must always be on guard and in control. He comes to believe, "If I *control* everything, then no one can catch me off guard and hurt me."

A kind of control madness emerges: control becomes an addiction. A client of mine had so much fear of being out of control that he worked as much as a hundred hours a week. He couldn't delegate any authority because he didn't trust others to do their jobs. He came to me when his ulcerative colitis had become so aggravated that he had to be hospitalized.

Another client of mine was distraught because her husband had just filed for divorce. His "last straw" came when she changed the brand of phone he had put in her car. Her husband complained that no matter what he tried to do for her, it was never right. She always had to change what he had done. In other words, she was not comfortable unless she controlled all outcomes.

Control madness causes severe relationship problems. There is no way to be intimate with a partner who distrusts you. Intimacy demands that each partner accept the other *just the way* he or she is.

Trust disorders also engender extremes in trusting others. One either gives up all control and trusts in a gullible and naïve way, clinging to others and overinvesting esteem in them, or one withdraws into isolation and loneliness, building protective walls that allow no one to come in.

As addiction specialist Patrick Carnes has pointed out, a person who never learned to trust confuses intensity with intimacy, obsession with care, and control with security.

The first developmental task in life is to establish a basic sense of trust. We must learn that the other (Mom, Dad, the world out there) is safe and trustworthy. This basic sense of trust is a deep holistic feeling. If we can trust the world, we can learn to trust ourselves. Trusting yourself means that you can trust your personal powers, perceptions, interpretations, feelings, and desires.

Children learn trust from trustworthy caretakers. If Mom and Dad are consistent and predictable, if Mom and Dad trust themselves, the child will trust them and learn to trust himself.

## ACTING OUT/ACTING IN BEHAVIORS

### Acting Out

In order to grasp how our wounded inner child acts out unmet childhood needs and unresolved trauma, we have to understand that *the primary motivating force in our lives is emotion.* Emotions are the fuel that moves us to defend ourselves and get our basic needs met. (I like to write the word *E-motion:* energy in motion.) This energy is fundamental. Our anger *moves* us to defend ourselves. When we are angry, we take a stand, we become "fighting mad." With anger we protect and fight for our rights.

Fear moves us to take flight in the face of danger. Fear gives us discernment. It protects us by letting us know that danger is at hand and is too large to fight; it moves us to run and take refuge.

Sadness moves us to tears. Our tears are cleansing and help us resolve our distress. With sadness we grieve our losses and free up our energy to be used in the present. When we are unable to grieve, we cannot finish the past. All the emotional energy relating to our distress or trauma becomes frozen. Unresolved and unexpressed, this energy continually tries to resolve itself. Since it cannot be expressed in healthy grieving, it is expressed in abnormal behavior. This is called "acting out." My former client Maggie provides a good example of acting out.

Maggie saw her father, a rageful and violent alcoholic, verbally and physically abuse her mother. This scene was repeated continually throughout her childhood. From the age of 4, Maggie was her mother's comforter. After being beaten by her husband, her mother would get into bed with Maggie. Trembling and moaning, she would cling to Maggie. Sometimes her father would come after her mother and scream at her. This terrified Maggie. Any kind of violence to a family member terrifies the other members. *A witness to violence is a victim of violence.*

What Maggie needed in childhood was to express her terror and discharge her sadness. But there was no one she could go to for the necessary nurturing to resolve her unexpressed grief. As she grew up, she continually tried to find men and women who would act the role of nurturing parents for her. When she came to see me she had been through two brutal marriages and many other abusive relationships. And what was her profession? She was a counselor who specialized in treating *abused women*!

Maggie was acting out her childhood trauma. She took care of abused women and got into relationships with abusive men. She took care of people, but no one took care of her. The unresolved emotional energy from the past was being expressed in the only way it could—by "acting it out."

Acting out, or reenacting, is one of the most devastating ways in which the wounded inner child sabotages our lives. Maggie's story provides a dramatic example of the compulsion to repeat the past. "Maybe this time I can get it right," says Maggie's wounded inner child. "Maybe if I'm perfect and give Dad everything he needs, I'll matter to him and he'll show me love and affection." This is the magical thinking of a child, not the rational thinking of an adult. Once we understand it, it makes sense. Other examples of acting-out behavior are:

- Reenactment of violence on others
- Doing or saying to our children what we said we'd never say or do

- Spontaneous age regression—temper tantrums, pouting, etc.
- Being inappropriately rebellious
- Carrying on idealized parental rules

## Acting In

Acting out *on ourselves* the abuse from the past is called "acting in." We punish ourselves the way we were punished in childhood. I know a man who abuses himself whenever he makes a mistake. He taunts himself with criticisms, such as, "You idiot, how could you be so dumb?" On several occasions I've seen him hit himself in the face with his fist (his mother had hit him in the face with her fist when he was a child).

Unresolved emotion from the past is often turned against the self. Joe, for example, was never allowed to express anger when he was a child. He felt great anger at his mother because she never allowed him to do anything for himself. Just when he'd start a task, she would jump in and say something like, "Mom needs to help her little slow poke," or, "You're doing swell, but let Mama give you a helping hand." Joe allowed that even now, in adulthood, she did things for him that he could do for himself. Joe had been taught to be perfectly obedient and that to express his anger was sinful. So, Joe turned his anger inward, against himself. As a result, he felt depressed, apathetic, inept, and powerless to achieve his life goals.

Emotional energy that is *acted in* can cause severe physical problems including gastrointestinal disorders, headaches, backaches, neck aches, severe muscle tension, arthritis, asthma, heart attacks, and cancer. Being accident prone is another form of acting in. One inflicts punishment on oneself through accidents.

## MAGICAL BELIEFS

Children are magical. "Step on a crack, break your mother's back." Magic is the belief that certain words, gestures, or behaviors can change reality. Dysfunctional parents often reinforce their children's magical thinking. For example, if you tell children that their behavior is directly responsible for someone else's feelings, you are teaching them magical thinking. Some common statements are: "You're killing your mother"; "See what you've done—your mother is upset"; "Are you satisfied—you've made your father angry." Another form of magical reinforcement is the statement, "I know what you're thinking."

I remember one client who had been married five times by the age of 32. She thought marriage would solve all her problems. If she could just find the "right" man, everything would be fine. Such a belief is magical. It implies that some event or person could change her reality without her doing anything to change her behavior.

It's natural for a child to think magically. But if a child is wounded through unmet dependency needs, he does not really grow up. The adult he becomes is still contaminated by the magical thinking of a child.

Other contaminating magical beliefs are:

* If I have money, I'll be okay.
* If my lover leaves me, I'll die or I'll never make it.
* A piece of paper (a degree) will make me smart.
* If I "try hard," the world will reward me.
* "Waiting" will bring about wonderful results.

Little girls are taught fairy tales that are filled with magic. Cinderella is taught to wait in the kitchen for a guy with the right shoe! Snow White is given the message that if she waits long enough, her prince will come. On a literal level, that story tells women that their destiny depends on waiting for a necrophile (someone who likes to kiss dead people) to stumble through the woods at the right time. Not a pretty picture!

Boys too are taught magical expectations by fairy tales. Many stories contain the message that there is *one right woman,* whom they must search for and find. In his search the man must travel far, traversing dark woods and conquering dangerous and frightening dragons. Finally, he will *know,* without a doubt, when he finds her. (This is why many men are so anxious standing at the altar.)

Often the male's destiny is shaped by arcane things like magical beans or miraculous swords. He may even have to hang around with a frog. If he can muster the courage to kiss it, the frog may turn into a princess. (Women have their own version of the frog story.)

For women, the magic consists of *waiting* for the right man; for men, it is *searching* endlessly for the right woman.

I am aware that fairy tales operate on a symbolic and mythical level. They are nonlogical, and, like dreams, they speak through imagery.

Many fairy tales are symbolic statements about finding our male or female identity. When the developmental process is running smoothly, we eventually outgrow our inner child's literal understanding of these stories and come to grasp their symbolic significance.

But when our inner child is wounded, he continues to take these stories literally. As adult children, we magically wait and/or search for that perfect ending where we will live happily ever after.

## INTIMACY DYSFUNCTIONS

Many adult children move back and forth between the fear of abandonment and the fear of engulfment. Some are permanently isolated because of their fears of being smothered by another person. Others refuse to leave destructive unions due to their terror of being alone. Most fluctuate between the two extremes.

Herkimer's relationship pattern is to fall madly in love with a woman. Once he becomes intimate and close, he begins to pull away and distance himself from her. He does this by slowly gathering a "list of criticisms." The items on the list are usually about small, idiosyncratic behaviors. Herkimer initiates small squabbles over these behaviors. His partner usually withdraws and pouts for a day or two. Then they are reunited intensely, making wild passionate love and experiencing deep sharing. This lasts until Herkimer feels smothered again and creates distance by starting another fight.

Athena, age 46, has not dated in fifteen years. Her "true love" died in a car wreck. She claims that when he died, she vowed she would never touch another man in loyalty to his memory. In fact, Athena went with her deceased lover for only three months. She has never slept with a man during her adult life. Her only sexual experience was five years of abuse by her stepfather during her childhood. Athena has put steel walls around her wounded inner child. She uses the memory of her deceased boyfriend as a defense against being intimate with anyone.

Another woman I worked with has remained in a passionless marriage for thirty years. Her husband is a womanizing sex addict. She knows of six affairs he has had (she caught him in bed in one of them). When I asked her why she stayed in her marriage, she replied that she "loved" her husband. This woman confuses dependency with love. She was deserted by her father when she was 2 years old and she never saw him again. Her "dependency parading as love" is rooted in her deep fear of abandonment.

In all the cases cited above, the core problem is the wounded inner child.

The wounded inner child contaminates intimacy in relationships because he has no sense of his authentic self. The greatest wound a child can receive is the rejection of his authentic self. When a parent cannot affirm his child's feelings, needs, and desires, he rejects that child's authentic self. Then, a false self must be set up.

In order to believe he is loved, the wounded child behaves the way he thinks he is supposed to. This false self develops over the years and is reinforced by the family system's needs and by cultural sex roles. Gradually, the false self becomes who the person really thinks he is. He forgets that the false self is an adaptation, an act based on a script someone else wrote.

*It is impossible to be intimate if you have no sense of self.* How can you share yourself with another if you do not really know who you are? How can anyone know you if you do not know who you really are?

One way a person builds a strong sense of self is by developing strong boundaries. Like the borders of a country, our physical boundaries protect our bodies and signal us when someone is too close or tries to touch us in an inappropriate way. Our sexual boundaries keep us safe and comfortable sexually. (People with weak sexual boundaries often have sex when they don't really want to.) Our emotional boundaries tell us where our emotions end and another's begin. They tell us when our feelings are about ourselves and when they are about others. We also have intellectual and spiritual boundaries, which determine our beliefs and our values.

When a child is wounded through neglect or abuse, his boundaries are violated. This sets the child up for fears of being either abandoned or engulfed. When a person knows who he is, he doesn't fear being engulfed. When he has a sense of self-value and self-confidence, he doesn't fear being abandoned. Without strong boundaries, we cannot know where we end and others begin. We have trouble saying no and knowing what we want, which are crucial behaviors for establishing intimacy.

Intimacy dysfunction is greatly potentiated by sexual dysfunction. Children who grow up in dysfunctional families are damaged in their sexual development. Such damage is caused by poor sexual modeling in the family; a parent's disappointment in the child's gender; contempt for and humiliation of the child; and neglect of the child's developmental dependency needs.

Gladys's father was never home. His work addiction had taken over his life. In his absence, Gladys created a fantasy father. She is currently in her third marriage. Because her ideas about men are unrealistic, no man has ever measured up to her expectations.

Jake saw his father verbally abuse his mother. She always made the best of it. Jake has no idea how to be intimate with women. He tends to pick passive, complying women, then quickly loses interest in them sexually because he disdains them, as he did his mother. His most satisfying sexual experiences are when he masturbates, during which he fantasizes about women in demeaning sexual situations.

Many children know that their parents are disappointed in their gender—Dad wanted a boy and got a girl; Mom wanted a girl and got a boy. The child comes to feel ashamed of his gender, which may later lead to varying degrees of submissive sexual acting out.

A child victimized by parental contempt and humiliation is often set up for sadomasochistic sexual behavior. Jules's mother, an untreated incest victim, had never worked through her sexualized rage about her abuse. Jules bonded with her and internalized her anger at men. He later became a sex addict. He owns a large collection of pornographic books and videos. He is turned on by imagining himself being demeaned and humiliated by a dominant, mothering-type woman.

Children need firm guidelines to master the tasks of each stage of development. If a child cannot get his age-appropriate developmental needs met, he will be arrested at that stage of development. Children who fail to get their infancy needs met become fixated on oral gratification. This may manifest sexually with a fixation on oral sex.

Children arrested in the toddler stage are often fascinated by buttocks. Fascination with a genital part is called "sexual objectification," and it reduces others to genital objects.

Sexual objectification is the scourge of true intimacy. Intimacy requires two whole persons who value each other as individuals. Many co-dependent couples engage in intensely objectified and addicted sex. It is the only way their wounded inner kids know how to be close.

## NONDISCIPLINED BEHAVIORS

Discipline comes from the Latin word *disciplina*, which means "teaching." By disciplining children we teach them how to live more productively and lovingly. As M. Scott Peck has said, discipline is a way to reduce life's suffering. We learn that telling the truth, delaying gratification, being honest with ourselves, and being self-responsible can enhance life's joys and pleasures.

Children need parents who model self-discipline rather than preach it. They learn from what their parents *actually* do; not from what they *say* they do. When parents fail to model discipline, the child becomes undisciplined; when parents rigidly discipline (and don't walk what they talk), the child becomes overdisciplined.

The undisciplined inner child dawdles, procrastinates, refuses to delay gratification, rebels, is self-willed and stubborn, and acts impulsively without thinking. The overdisciplined child is rigid, obsessive, overly controlled and obedient, people pleasing, and ravished with shame and guilt. However, most of us who have a wounded inner child fluctuate between undisciplined and overdisciplined behavior.

## ADDICTIVE/COMPULSIVE BEHAVIORS

The wounded inner child is the major cause of addictions and addictive behavior. I became an alcoholic at an early age. My father, also an alcoholic, physically and emotionally abandoned me when I was a child. I felt worth-less than his time. Because he was never there to model behaviors for me, I never bonded with him, never experienced what it was like to be loved and valued by a man. Therefore, I never truly loved myself *as a man*.

In my early teens I ran with other fatherless guys. We drank and whored to prove our manhood. From ages 15 to 30, I drank and used drugs in an addictive manner. On December 11, 1965, I put the cork in the bottle. My addiction to chemicals was stopped, yet my addictive behavior continued. I smoked, worked, and ate addictively.

I have no doubt that my alcoholism was predisposed by my genetic inheritance. There seems to be ample evidence that alcoholism is rooted in genetics. But the inheritance factor isn't sufficient to explain alcoholism. If it were, all children of alcoholics would become alcoholic. Clearly, this is not the case. Neither my brother nor my sister is alcoholic. I have spent twenty-five years working with alcoholics and drug addicts. This includes fifteen years of working with teenage drug abusers. I never once found a person whose addiction was purely chemical, despite the fact that some chemicals addict very quickly— I've seen teenagers get severely hooked on crack in just two months. The common factor I always found was the wounded inner child. It is the insatiable root of all compulsive/addictive behavior. My proof of that was when I stopped drinking addictively. I turned to other forms of mood alteration. I worked, ate, and smoked compulsively, due to my wounded inner child's insatiable needs.

Like all children of alcoholic families, I was emotionally abandoned. To a child, abandonment is death. In order to meet my two most basic survival needs (*my parents are okay* and *I matter*), I became Mom's emotional husband and my younger brother's parent. To *help* her and others made me feel that I was okay. I was told and believed that Dad loved me but was too sick to show it and that Mom was a saint. All of this covered up my sense of being worth-less than my parents' time (toxic shame). My core material was composed of selected perceptions, repressed feelings, and false beliefs. This became the filter through which I interpreted all new experiences in my life. That primitive child's adaptation allowed me to survive childhood, but it was a poor filter for adult survival. At age 30 I wound up in Austin State Hospital at the tail end of seventeen years of alcoholism.

Being aware of the wounded inner child as the core of compulsive/ addictive behavior helps us to see addiction in a much broader context. An addiction is a pathological relationship to any form of mood alteration that has life-damaging consequences. The *ingestive* addictions are the most dramatic mood alterers. Alcohol, drugs, and foods have an inherent chemical potential for mood alteration. But there are many other ways feelings can be changed. I like to speak of *activity* addictions, *cognitive* addictions, *feeling* addictions, and addiction to things.

Addictive activities include work, shopping, gambling, sex, and religious rituals. In fact, any activity can be used to alter feelings. Activities alter feelings through *distraction*.

Cognitive addictions are a powerful way to avoid feelings. I *lived in my head* for years. I was a university professor. *Thinking* can be a way to avoid feelings. All addictions have a thinking component, which is called obsession.

Feelings themselves can be addictive. I was a rageaholic for a number of years. Rage, the only boundary I knew, covered up my pain and shame. When I raged, I felt strong and powerful, rather than vulnerable and powerless.

Probably everyone knows someone who is addicted to fear. Fear addicts tend to catastrophize and awfulize. They become worry warts and drive other people crazy.

Some folks get addicted to sadness and/or grief. They seem no longer to *have* sadness; they *are* it. For a sad addict, sadness has become a state of being.

The people I dread the most are the joy addicts. They are the good boys and girls who were forced to smile and be cheery. It's as if the smile got frozen on their faces. Joy addicts never see anything bad. They'll smile while telling you that their mother died! It's eerie.

Things can also be addictions. Money is the most common "thing" addiction. However, anything can become a preoccupation and, as such, a source of mood alteration.

At the core of most addictions, no matter what the genetic factors, is the wounded inner child, who is in a constant state of craving and insatiable neediness. One does not have to be around an addict very long to see these qualities in him.

## THOUGHT DISTORTIONS

The great developmental psychologist Jean Piaget called children "cognitive aliens." They do not think like adults.

Children are absolutizers. This quality of a child's thinking is manifested by an "all or nothing" polarity. If you don't love me, you hate me. There is no in between. If my father abandons me, *all men* will abandon me.

Children are nonlogical. This is manifested in what has been described as "emotional reasoning." I feel a certain way, therefore it must be this way. If I feel guilty, I must be a rotten person.

Children need healthy modeling in order to learn to separate thought from emotion—to think about feelings and to feel about thinking.

Children think egocentrically, which is manifested in their personalizing everything. If Dad has no time for me, it must mean that I'm not okay, that something is wrong with *me*. Children interpret most abuse in this way. Egocentricity is a natural condition of childhood, not a sign of moral selfishness. Children are just not fully capable of taking another person's point of view.

When a child's developmental dependency needs are not met, in adulthood he is contaminated by his inner child's mode of thinking. I often hear adults expressing these childish contaminated ways of thinking. "America right or wrong" is a good example of absolutist thinking.

I know several people who have serious financial problems because of *emotional* thinking. They think that *wanting* something is sufficient reason to buy it. When children don't learn how to separate thoughts from emotions, in adulthood they often use thinking as a way to avoid their painful emotions. They separate their heads from their hearts, as it were. Two common patterns of such thought distortion are *universalizing* and *detailing*.

Universalizing is not in itself a distorted form of thinking. All abstract sciences demand that we know how to universalize and think abstractly. Universalizing becomes a distortion when we use it to distract us from our feelings. There are many people who have a kind of academic genius yet can barely manage their everyday lives.

A truly distorted form of universalizing is called awfulizing. We awfulize when we make abstract hypotheses about the future. "What if there is no money left in the Social Security system when I retire?" is an awful thought. To think it triggers fear. Since the thought is not fact but pure hypothesis, the thinker literally scares himself. The wounded inner child frequently thinks this way.

As with universalizing, detailing can be an important intellectual ability; there is nothing wrong with thinking in a detailed and thorough way. But when detailing is used to distract us from our painful feelings, it distorts the reality of our lives. Compulsive perfectionistic behavior is a good example of this—we become absorbed in detail as a way to avoid our feelings of inadequacy.

You will hear examples of egocentric thinking everywhere once you start listening for them. I recently overheard a couple talking on an airplane. The woman was looking at the airline's vacation-planning magazine. She innocently remarked that she had always wanted to go to Australia. The man responded angrily, "What the hell do you expect from me; I'm already killing myself with work!" His wounded inner child believed that she was judging him as an inadequate financial provider simply because she wanted to go to Australia.

## EMPTINESS (APATHY, DEPRESSION)

The wounded inner child also contaminates adult life with a low-grade chronic depression experienced as emptiness. The depression is the result of the child's having to adopt a false self, leaving the true self behind. This abandonment of the true self amounts to having an empty place inside. I've referred to this as the "hole in one's soul" phenomenon. When a person loses his authentic self, he has lost contact with his true feelings, needs, and desires. What he experiences instead are the feelings required by the false self. For example, "being nice" is a common false self component. A "nice woman" never expresses anger or frustration.

To have a false self is to be in an *act*. One's true self is never present. A person in recovery described it this way: "It's like I'm standing on the sidelines watching life go by."

Feeling empty is a form of chronic depression, as one is perpetually in mourning for one's true self. All adult children experience low-grade chronic depression to some degree.

Emptiness is also experienced as apathy. As a counselor, I often hear adult children complain that their lives seem dull and meaningless. They find life characterized by a kind of absence and cannot understand why other people get so excited about things.

The great Jungian analyst Marion Woodman tells the story of a woman who went to see the Pope when he visited Toronto. The woman brought a menagerie of complicated camera equipment so that she could get a picture of the Pope. She became so absorbed with her equipment that she got only one picture of him as he passed by. She actually missed seeing the Pope! When she developed her picture, the man she went to see was there, but she wasn't in it. She was *absent from the experience*.

When our inner child is wounded, we feel empty and depressed. Life has a sense of unreality about it; we are there, but we are not in it. This emptiness leads to loneliness. Because we are never who we really are, we are never truly present. And even if people admire and hang on to us, we feel alone. I felt this way most of my life. I always managed to be the leader of whatever group I was in. I had people all around me, admiring and praising me. However, I never felt truly connected with any of them. I remember a night when I was lecturing at the University of St. Thomas. My topic was Jacques Maritain's understanding of the Thomistic doctrine of evil. I was especially eloquent and sharp that evening. As I walked out, the crowd rose in an ovation. I remember vividly how I felt: I wanted to end my emptiness and loneliness. I felt suicidal!

This experience also explains how the wounded inner child contaminates with self-centeredness. Adult children are self-absorbed. Their emptiness is like a chronic toothache. When one is in chronic pain, all one can think of is himself. As a therapist, it is often exasperating to deal with the egocentricity of such clients. I have remarked to my fellow counselors that I could walk out of my office on fire and someone would say, "Have you got a minute?"

These categories of contamination cover most of the areas of human bondage. *My hope is that you can see what serious issues your wounded inner child continues to present in your adult life.* To help you further determine the damage your wounded inner child may be causing, answer the following questions yes or no.

## WOUNDED CHILD QUESTIONNAIRE

The questions in this section will give you an overall view of the extent to which your inner child is wounded. In part 2, I will give you a more specific index of suspicion for each developmental stage.

### A. IDENTITY

1. I experience anxiety and fear whenever I contemplate doing anything new. Yes _____ No _____

2. I'm a people pleaser (nice guy/sweetheart) and have no identity of my own. Yes _____ No _____

3. I'm a rebel. I feel alive when I'm in conflict. Yes _____ No _____

4. In the deepest places of my secret self, I feel there is something wrong with me. Yes _____ No _____

5. I'm a hoarder; I have trouble letting go of anything. Yes _____ No _____

6. I feel inadequate as a man/woman. Yes _____ No _____

7. I'm confused about my sexual identity. Yes _____ No _____

8. I feel guilty when I stand up for myself and would rather give in to others. Yes _____ No _____

9. I have trouble starting things. Yes _____ No _____

10. I have trouble finishing things. Yes _____ No _____

11. I rarely have a thought of my own. Yes _____ No _____

12. I continually criticize myself for being inadequate. Yes _____ No _____

13. I consider myself a terrible sinner and I'm afraid I'm going to hell. Yes _____ No _____

14. I'm rigid and perfectionistic. Yes _____ No _____

15. I feel like I never measure up; never get anything right. Yes _____ No _____

16. I feel like I really don't know what I want. Yes _____ No _____

17. I'm driven to be a superachiever. Yes _____ No _____

18. I believe I don't really matter except when I'm sexual. I'm afraid I'll be rejected and abandoned if I'm not a good lover. Yes _____ No _____

19. My life is empty; I feel depressed a lot of the time. Yes _____ No _____

20. I don't really know who I am. I'm not sure what my values are or what I think about things. Yes _____ No _____

## B. BASIC NEEDS

1. I'm out of touch with my bodily needs. I don't know when I'm tired, hungry, or horny. Yes _____ No _____

2. I don't like being touched. Yes _____ No _____

3. I often have sex when I don't really want to. Yes _____ No _____

4. I have had or currently have an eating disorder. Yes _____ No _____

5. I am hung up on oral sex. Yes _____ No _____

6. I rarely know what I feel. Yes _____ No _____

7. I feel ashamed when I get mad. Yes _____ No _____

8. I rarely get mad, but when I do, I rage. Yes _____ No _____

9. I fear other people's anger and I will do most anything to control it. Yes _____ No _____

10. I'm ashamed when I cry. Yes _____ No _____

11. I'm ashamed when I'm scared. Yes _____ No _____

12. I almost never express unpleasant emotions. Yes _____ No _____

13. I'm obsessed with anal sex. Yes _____ No _____

14. I'm obsessed with sado/masochistic sex. Yes _____ No _____

15. I'm ashamed of my bodily functions. Yes _____ No _____

16. I have sleep disorders. Yes _____ No _____

17. I spend an inordinate amount of time looking at pornography. Yes _____ No _____

18. I have exhibited myself sexually in a way that violates others. Yes _____ No _____

19. I am sexually attracted to children and I worry that I might act it out. Yes _____ No _____

20. I believe that food and/or sex is my greatest need. Yes _____ No _____

## C. SOCIAL

1. I basically distrust everyone, including myself. Yes _____ No _____

2. I have been or am now married to an addict. Yes _____ No _____

3. I am obsessive and controlling in my relationship. Yes _____ No _____

4. I am an addict. Yes _____ No _____

5. I'm isolated and afraid of people, especially authority figures. Yes _____ No _____

6. I hate being alone and I'll do almost anything to avoid it. Yes _____ No _____

7. I find myself doing what I think others expect of me. Yes _____ No _____

8. I avoid conflict at all cost. Yes _____ No _____

9. I rarely say no to another's suggestions and feel that another's suggestion is almost an order to be obeyed. Yes _____ No _____

10. I have an overdeveloped sense of responsibility. It is easier for me to be concerned with another than with myself. Yes _____ No _____

11. I often do not say *no* directly and then refuse to do what others ask in a variety of manipulative, indirect, and passive ways. Yes _____ No _____

12. I don't know how to resolve conflicts with others. I either overpower my opponent or completely withdraw from them. Yes _____ No _____

13. I rarely ask for clarification of statements I don't understand. Yes _____ No _____

14. I frequently guess at what another's statement means and respond to it based on my guess. Yes _____ No _____

15. I never felt close to one or both of my parents. Yes _____ No _____

16. I confuse love with pity and tend to love people I can pity. Yes _____ No _____

17. I ridicule myself and others if they make a mistake. Yes _____ No _____

18. I give in easily and conform to the group. Yes _____ No _____

19. I'm fiercely competitive and a poor loser. Yes _____ No _____

20. My most profound fear is the fear of abandonment and I'll do anything to hold on to a relationship. Yes _____ No _____

If you answered yes to ten or more of these questions, you need to do some serious work. This book is for you.

# CHAPTER 2

# HOW YOUR WONDERFUL INNER CHILD GOT WOUNDED

There was a time when meadow, grove and stream
The earth, and every common sight,
   To me did seem
   Apparelled in celestial light,
The glory and the freshness of a dream.
It is not now as it hath been of yore;—
   Turn wheresoe'er I may,
      By night or day,
The things which I have seen I now can see no more.
                                    —WILLIAM WORDSWORTH

Almost everyone brightens up in the presence of a baby. Even the sourest puss can be moved by the giggling of a child.

Children, naturally filled with wonder, are spontaneous and live in the now. In a sense, they are exiled in the now. Using the word *wonderful*, I'll give you a profile of the wonder child. Each letter stands for one of the natural traits.

**W**onder
**O**ptimism
**N**aïveté
**D**ependence
**E**motions
**R**esilience

Free Play
Uniqueness
Love

## WONDER

Everything is interesting and exciting to the natural child. He feels
wonder with all his senses. This is a manifestation of every child's
innate need to know, to experiment and explore, to look and to
touch. Curiosity leads the baby to the discovery of his hands, nose,
lips, genitals, fingers, and toes; ultimately it leads to the discovery of
his self.

Experimentation and exploration can also get the child in trouble.
If the parents had to repress their natural sense of wonder in childhood, they will inhibit their children in the same way. This causes the
child to close up and to fear exploration and risk taking. For him, life
becomes a problem to be solved rather than an adventure to be lived,
and he becomes dull and plays it safe.

Wonder and curiosity are crucial for normal growth and adaptation.
They push the child to acquire a basic knowledge of the world and to
learn the nuts and bolts of survival.

Wonder and curiosity are also the life energy that moves us toward
ever-expanding horizons. We *need* this life spark—it is indispensable
to our continued growth and essential to the work of the poet, the
artist, and the creative thinker. Our wonder and curiosity forge a kind
of exalted interest that triggers the expectation that there is "more to
come." Both Charles Darwin and Albert Einstein were filled with
childlike wonder and curiosity about the mysteries that lay beyond
the mystery of the world.

## OPTIMISM

The child's natural life spark pushes him to explore in an *optimistic*
manner. If his caretakers are even the least bit predictable, the child
comes to trust what is outside of him to get his needs met. Children
naturally believe the world is friendly; they have hope; all is possible
and lies ahead. This innate optimism and trust form a core part of our

natural endowment and are the pillars of what is referred to as "childlike faith."

It is due to this natural state of optimism and trust that children can be so wounded by their caretakers. When a child trusts completely, he is *vulnerable* to violation and abuse. Unlike the other animals, the human infant has no "instinct computer system" that tells him what to do. Children need to learn, and their learning depends on their caretakers. Children develop inner strengths as a result of their interactions with their adult caretakers. Nature's blueprint predisposes children to age-appropriate readiness for development of each inner strength.

When a child is abused and shamed, his openness and trust are deadened. The bond that allowed him to trust and move forward optimistically is severed. No longer able to rely on the safety of his caretaker, he becomes more vigilant and anxious. If the rupture is chronically repeated, he becomes *pessimistic*. He loses his sense of hope and comes to believe that he must manipulate in order to get his needs met. Instead of using his energy in direct interaction with the world, he uses it to entice his caretakers to do for him what he could actually do for himself.

Optimism and trust are the soul of intimacy. We must risk being vulnerable if we want to be intimate. However, since we can never gather enough data to trust anyone absolutely, we must take the risk of trusting them at some point. We also need optimism in our lives; with it we see all reality as ultimately having positive value. Optimism allows us to look at the bright side—to see the doughnut rather than the hole.

## NAÏVETÉ

Children's naïveté is part of their charm and attraction, and it is the core of their innocence. Children live in the now and are oriented to pleasure. They accept life's "queer conundrums," as Christopher Morley says. Their "strange Divinity" results from their lacking any sense of right or wrong, good or bad.

Children are life-oriented. At first, their movements lack direction, because they are so interested in everything that it's hard to choose any one thing. Due to this lack of direction, every child gets into forbidden places, touches things that are unsafe, and tastes things that are noxious. This is why they need constant attention and care, and why caretakers need to "child-proof" the house. This requires the time and attention of the caretakers, and even the healthiest among them will be exasperated at times. Of course, the child is surprised and confused when his caretaker is upset; what he was doing seemed so exciting and delicious.

Caretakers need to be patient and understanding. Lacking these qualities, the parent will expect far too much from the child. In most of the physical abuse cases that I'm familiar with, the abusing parent believed that the child was deliberately being malicious. They expected him to be much more mature than was possible for his age.

The tendency to venture into forbidden territory has often been cited as evidence of a natural perversity in the child. It has been argued that this innate perversity is the result of the original sin committed by Adam and Eve. The doctrine of original sin has been a major source for many repressive and cruel child-rearing practices. However, there is no clinical evidence to support any kind of innate depravity in children.

The opposite side of this is parental overprotection of the child's naïveté and innocence, which fosters troublesome naïveté in adulthood. I remember a seminarian, one year away from ordination, who expressed the belief that women had three openings in their genitalia! I also know of many women who were given no sexual information while growing up and who panicked when they began to menstruate.

Children can also learn to manipulate with a false naïveté and innocence. Playing dumb is a form of this. The "dumb blonde" act is a classic form of false innocence in adulthood. In children who fear abandonment, hysterical crying or begging are ways of playing dumb. Such behavior enables the child to avoid growing up, being responsible, and taking risks.

The naïveté and innocence of your wonder child can be a great asset to your recovery process. Naïveté is a major ingredient of docility— the state of being teachable. As you champion your wounded inner child, the wonder child emerges. You and your wonder child can cooperate in learning to create new and empowering experiences.

## DEPENDENCE

Children are dependent and needy by nature, not by choice. Unlike an adult, a child cannot meet his needs through his own resources, so he must depend on others to fill these needs. Unfortunately, this dependence on others is the child's greatest vulnerability. The child doesn't even know what he needs or what he feels. For better or for worse, his life is shaped from the beginning by the ability of his primary caretakers to know and to meet his needs at each stage of development.

If our caretakers have a wounded inner child, their neediness will prevent them from meeting their own children's needs. Instead, they will either be angry at their child's neediness or will try to get their own needs met by making their child an extension of themselves.

The wonder child is dependent because he is in a *process* of maturing, or "ripening." Each stage of development is a step toward the full ripening of adulthood. If the child's needs are not met at the proper time and in the proper sequence, he moves on without the resources necessary to meet the tasks of the next stage. A small mistake in the beginning has far-reaching consequences later on.

Healthy human life is characterized by continual growth. The very characteristics of childhood I am describing—wonder, dependency, curiosity, optimism—are crucial to the growth and flowering of human life.

In one sense, we remain dependent all our lives. We always are in need of love and interaction. No one is so self-sufficient that he does not need anyone else. Our wonder child's dependency allows us to form attachments and to make commitments. As we grow older, we need to be needed. At some point in healthy growth we become generative and care for life itself. This is our evolutionary vocation, if you will. It's really a matter of balance between dependency and undependency. When the inner child has been wounded through neglect of his developmental dependency needs, he either isolates and withdraws or clings and becomes enmeshed.

## EMOTIONS

Two emotions are unique to human infants—laughter and weeping. The anthropologist Ashley Montagu writes, "It is natural for children to laugh and to see the humor in all sorts of things, whether they be

real, imagined or of their own creation. They revel in the comic."
Humor is one of our earliest and greatest natural resources. Philoso-
phers have long pointed out that man alone has the "gift of risibility"
(the ability to laugh).

A sense of humor has *survival* value; life is more endurable when
one has a sense of humor. As a counselor, I could always mark the
moment my clients began to get well. It came with a sense of humor
about themselves. They quit taking themselves so seriously.

According to Montagu, children have a sense of humor from about
12 weeks of age. Look into the face and eyes of a baby who has
been loved and caressed, and you will see this natural joyfulness.
Watch a group of children romping and playing together and you'll
hear the sheer delight in their laughter.

A child's happiness and excitement can be quickly curtailed. If the
wounded inner child in our parent had his laughter squashed, he will
squash it in his own children. Such a parent will counsel his children
with statements like, "Don't laugh so loud," "Stop that noise in there,"
"Stop being so rambunctious," "We've had enough fun," and so on.
I've often wondered why I found it so hard to really laugh, dance, or
sing. I could do these well when I was drinking. But sober, my
muscles froze.

Children who are repressed when they are laughing and joyful
learn to be somber and stoic. Typically, they become the uptight
parents, teachers, or preachers who cannot tolerate children's excitement and loud laughter.

The other side of laughter is weeping. "Your joy is your sorrow
unmasked," the poet Kahlil Gibran told us. "The self same well from
which your laughter rises was oftentimes filled with tears."

Humans are the only animals who weep. (Other animals cry, but
do not shed tears.) According to Ashley Montagu, weeping serves us
socially and psychologically in much the same way as laughter. Just as
laughter and joy draw us to others, so weeping elicits our nurturing
and compassion. This has a special survival value for the human
infant. His coos of joy and gurgling laughter draw us closer, establishing the symbiotic bonding every infant needs. His tears are his
distress signals, which move us to aid and comfort him.

As emotional expressions that evoke a response from others, laughter and weeping have probably had a strong influence on the development of human communities across time. Weeping especially has
played a powerful role in our evolution as compassionate creatures.

The "freedom to weep," writes Montagu, "contributes to the health of the individual and tends to deepen our involvement in the welfare of others."

Children who are shamed for weeping are severely damaged in their development. In the majority of families, the child's weeping touches the unresolved sadness in the parent's wounded inner child. Most adult children had their weeping curtailed.

Parents have systematically repressed weeping in their children, believing that they were making their children strong. This is blatantly false. This book would be unnecessary had most of us been allowed to fully express our tears. What I call "original pain" work is primarily grief work, which is the key to reclaiming your wounded inner child.

## RESILIENCE

Resilience is the ability to bounce back from distress induced by the environment. Children are naturally resilient; and the younger they are, the more resilient they are. Just watch a child learning to eat or to walk and their resilience is apparent. I watched a 20-month-old try to get up on a couch. Each time she almost made it, she fell back. A couple of times she cried for a moment, then started back to work on the task at hand—getting up on the couch. After at least five tries, she made it. She sat there for a few minutes enjoying her achievement. When my large dog walked into the room, she observed him cautiously and dropped down off the couch to investigate this strange creature. As she approached, he playfully nudged her. This upset her, so she popped him on the nose! Here was an animal three times her size and she popped him on the nose! That's courage any way you look at it. Indeed, all children are courageous. We adults are giants compared to them. Instead of viewing their stubbornness as depravity or misbehavior, we need to see it as courageous. Children are resilient and courageous. The word *courageous* comes from the Latin word, *cor* (heart). Children have heart. They are courageous adventurers. The great Adlerian psychologist Rudolf Dreikurs believed that all misbehaving children are *dis-couraged*. Having lost heart, they believe they must manipulate in order to get their needs met.

Closely related to resilience is behavioral flexibility, which allows a child to learn behaviors in response to any pattern of socialization to which he is exposed. Such flexibility is a specific characteristic of humans, as opposed to most animals, and is a strong sign of mental health.

The same resilience and flexibility also account for our ability to adapt in unhealthy ways. All the behaviors I've ascribed to the wounded inner child are adapted behaviors. Our inner child's resiliency and flexibility allowed him to survive disease, disorders, and emotional abandonment. But it's unfortunate that we had to use our dynamic and resilient energy for survival rather than for growth and self-actualization.

Since resilience is a core trait of our authentic self, we can welcome it back as we reclaim and champion our wounded inner child. This will take time, because the wounded child must learn to trust our adult protection. As he feels protected and safe, his natural wonder and resilience will begin to emerge and then will be present in full bloom.

## FREE PLAY

Children have a natural sense of freedom, and when they feel safe, they move with great spontaneity. These qualities—freedom and spontaneity—form the structure of play. Plato saw the model of true play in children's need to *leap,* which involves testing the limits of gravity. Free play is the way a child transcends the repetition of mere habit. As we grow older we often lose sight of this quality of play and come to judge it as frivolous: it's okay for the very young, but not for adults. In fact, many adults see play as idleness, and idleness as the proverbial "devil's workshop."

Unfortunately, we in the United States have corrupted free and spontaneous play into an aggressive drive to win. Authentic free play is an activity of pure pleasure and delight. In later stages of development, it can be done for the pleasure that results from the skill and sportsmanship required by a specific game.

Free play is part of our essential nature. All animals play, but the play of children has a much wider range. Ashley Montagu writes, "Child's play is a leap of the imagination far beyond the capabilities of any other creature." Imagination has an essential role in children's playfulness. I remember my imaginative creations in childhood: most often they were preparations for adult life—we played "grown-up" and imagined what it would be like to be like Mom and Dad.

For children, free play is serious business; it is part of the foundation for later life. Perhaps if we were allowed the security and
comfort of play as children, we would not have to resort to noncre-
ative play as adults. Such play is really a substitute for unmet childhood needs and amounts to the accumulation of "adult toys." Perhaps
you've seen the bumper sticker HE WHO HAS THE MOST TOYS WHEN HE
DIES—WINS. Such a transformation of child's play prevents us from
seeing life as a free and spontaneous adventure.

If we view childhood as a time of free and creative play, we can
realize that to be human is to be playful. Our greatest human achieve-
ments are the "leaps of imagination" that account for our greatest
inventions, discoveries, and theories. As Nietzsche once remarked, to
become mature we must recover the sense of earnestness which we
had as a child in play.

## UNIQUENESS

Although a child is immature, he still has an organismic sense of
wholeness, of I AMness. In other words, he feels connected and
unified within himself. The feeling of unified wholeness and complete-
ness is the true meaning of perfection, and in this sense every child is
perfect.

Unified wholeness is also what makes each child *special, unique,*
and *wonderful.* No one else is *exactly* like him. This specialness
makes every child truly precious. Precious means "rare and valuable."
Gemstones and gold are precious, but every child is far more precious than that. The child has a gut-level sense of this at birth. Freud
spoke of "His Majesty the Baby."

The child's natural sense of his value and dignity is very precarious,
as it demands immediate mirroring and echoing from a nurturing
caretaker. If the caretaker doesn't accurately and lovingly reflect the
child as he is, he will lose the sense of being special and unique.

Children are also naturally spiritual. As far as I'm concerned, wholeness and spirituality are synonymous. Children are naïve mystics.
Christopher Morley's poem points out how their "strange Divinity" is
"still kept." But it's a naïve and uncritical spirituality. Later, it will be
the core of mature, reflective spirituality.

Spirituality involves what is deepest and most authentic in us—our
true self. When we are spiritual, we are in contact with our unique-

ness and specialness. It is our fundamental beingness or I AMness. Spirituality also involves a sense of connection and grounding in something greater than ourselves. Children are natural believers— they know there is something greater than themselves.

My belief is that our I AMness constitutes our core godlikeness. When a person has this sense of I AMness, he is one with himself and is self-accepting. Children have this naturally. Look at any healthy child and you will see him saying, in effect, "I am who I am." Interestingly, in the theophany of the burning bush, God told Moses that his name was *I am that I am* (Exod. 3:14). The deepest sense of human spirituality is this I AMness, which incorporates the qualities of being valuable, precious, and special. The New Testament is filled with Jesus reaching out to the "single one": the one lost sheep, the prodigal son, the person who is worthy of full wages even at the last hour. The "single one" is the one who is who he is; he has never been before and never will be again.

It is the spiritual wound more than anything else that sets us up to become co-dependent shame-based adult children. The story of every man's and every woman's fall is how a wonderful, valuable, special, precious child lost its sense of "I am who I am."

## LOVE

Children are naturally predisposed to love and affection. However, *the child must first be loved before he can love*. He learns to love by being loved. Montagu writes: "Of all purely human needs the need to love is ... the most basic. ... It is the humanizing need; beyond all others it makes us human."

No infant has the ability to love in a mature, altruistic sense. Rather, he loves in his own age-specific fashion. A child's healthy growth depends on someone loving and accepting him unconditionally. When this need is met, the child's energy of love is released so that he can love others.

When a child is not loved for his own self, his sense of I AMness is severed. Because he is so dependent, his egocentricity sets in, and his true self never really emerges. The childish contaminations I ascribe to the wounded inner child are the consequences of this egocentric adaptation. The failure to be loved unconditionally causes the child to suffer the deepest of all deprivations. Only faint echoes of the world of others ever truly reach the adult who has a deprived and wounded inner child. The need for love never leaves him. The hunger remains and the wounded inner child tries to fill this void in the ways I've described.

In reclaiming and championing your wounded inner child, *you* give him the positive, unconditional acceptance that he craves. That will release him to recognize and love others for who they are.

## THE SPIRITUAL WOUND

I believe that all the ways in which the wonder child is wounded can be summed up as the loss of I AMness. Every child needs desperately to know that (a) his parents are healthy and able to take care of him, and (b) that he *matters* to his parents.

Mattering means that the child's specialness is reflected in the eyes of his parents or other significant caretakers. Mattering is also indicated by the amount of time they spend with him. Children know intuitively that people give time to what they love. Parents shame their children by not having time for them.

Any child from a dysfunctional family will receive this spiritual wound—this loss of I AMness—to some degree. An alcoholic mother and co-dependent enabling father cannot be there for their children. The alcoholic is absorbed in drinking and the co-dependent is absorbed with the alcoholic. They simply cannot be present for their children emotionally. The same is true when the parental coalition is under any chronic distress, including addictions to work or religious activities; eating disorders; addictions to control or perfectionism; or mental or physical illness. Whatever the disorder, when the parents are absorbed in their own emotional issues, they can't be there for their children. The psychiatrist Karen Horney wrote:

> But through a variety of adverse influences a child may not be permitted to grow according to his individual needs and possibilities. ... When summarized they all boil down to the fact that the people in the environment are *too wrapped up in their own neuroses to be able to love the child,* or even conceive of him as the particular individual he is. (Italics added.)

The frustration of a child's desire to be loved as a person and to have his love accepted is the greatest trauma that a child can experience.

No parents in a dysfunctional family can give their child what he needs, because they are too needy themselves. In fact, *most children from dysfunctional families have been hurt the most when they were the most needy.* I think of Joshua, who had an alcoholic father. By age 7 Joshua never knew whether his father was going to be there. By age 11 his father had abandoned him emotionally and financially. A boy needs a father; in order to love himself as a man, he needs the love of a man. He needs to bond with a man. But Josh never had this father bonding. He was terrified most of the time and felt the deep insecurity of a child who has no protection. Father represents protection. Added to this, his mom unconsciously hated men. On three occasions at the dinner table she humiliated Joshua by making fun of the size of his penis. Apparently she thought this was a joke, and she shamed him for being so sensitive. This was his most vulnerable masculine area. As crazy as it actually is, penis size *is* a symbol for manliness in our culture. Here was a boy who desperately needed to have his manliness affirmed, being betrayed by the only significant parent he had. His mother, an untreated incest victim, acted out on her son her deep contempt and rage against men.

## SEXUAL, PHYSICAL, EMOTIONAL ABUSE

### Sexual Abuse

In sexual abuse a child is *used* by adults for their sexual pleasure. This teaches the child that the only way he can matter is by being sexual with the adult. The consequence of such violation is that the child grows up to believe that he must be a great sexual partner or be sexually attractive in order for anyone to truly care about him. There are many forms of sexual abuse. The nonphysical forms are the most misunderstood and can be the most crazymaking.

To clearly understand nonphysical, or emotional, sexual abuse we need to understand that a family is a social system governed by its own laws. The most important laws of family systems are: (1) The whole system reflects everyone in such a way that the family can be defined only by the interrelationship of its members, not by the sum of its parts. (2) The whole system operates on a principle of balance, so that if one member gets out of balance another member will compensate for the imbalance. For example, a drunken, irresponsible father might be balanced by a teetotaling, superresponsible mother; a raging, hysterical wife might be balanced by an even-tempered, mild-mannered, soft-spoken husband. (3) The whole system is governed by rules. In healthy systems the rules are negotiable and open; in unhealthy systems the rules are rigid and inflexible. (4) The members of the system play roles to keep its needs in balance. In healthy family systems the roles are flexible and shared; in unhealthy systems the roles are rigid and frozen.

The family system also has components, the chief of which is the marriage. When the marriage has an intimacy dysfunction, the family system principle of balance and complementarity takes over. The family needs a healthy marriage in order to be balanced. When that balance is lacking, the system's dynamic energy will push the children to create it. If Dad is dissatisfied with Mom, he may turn to his daughter to get his emotional needs met. A daughter may become her dad's Baby Doll or his Little Princess. A boy might become his mom's Little Man, or her significant man, in the place of Dad. There are many variations and they are not limited by gender. A girl can become Mom's caretaker in the place of Dad; a boy can be Dad's emotional wife. In all cases, a vertical or cross-generational bonding is set up. The children are there to take care of their parents' marriage and are used to take care of their parents' loneliness. Often a parent is shut down sexually but his sexual needs are still present. The child may feel uncomfortable with that parent's icky kisses or touching. *The rule of thumb is that whenever a child is more important to a parent than the parent's spouse, the potential for emotional sexual abuse exists.* This constitutes abuse because the parent is using the child for his own needs. Such behavior reverses the order of nature. Parents need to give their children time, attention, and direction, not *use* them to fill their own need. Use is abuse.

Sexual violation inflicts spiritual wounding more intensely than any other kind of violation. Recently we've come to understand sexual violation in new ways. The horror stories concerning physical penetration are only the tip of the iceberg. We now know a great deal about the impact of exhibitionism and voyeurism within the family. The key factor in such abuse seems to be the internal state of the parents—that is, whether they are turned on by their own nudity or by looking at their children's bodies.

A lot of sexual violation in families comes from boundary infringement. The child may have no place where he can be private and safe. Perhaps his parents barge into the bathroom while he is using the toilet. They may interrogate him endlessly about every detail of his sex life. Young children may be forced to bend over and be inflicted with unnecessary enemas.

Sexual violation also comes from parents' lack of appropriate sexual boundaries with their children. This is often characterized by inappropriate remarks and discussions. My client Shirley was often uncomfortable around her father. He frequently patted her on the buttocks and talked about her "sexy ass" and how he wished he were the right age to get "some of her." Shirley was upset by these remarks. She later sought out older men who were turned on by her buttocks.

Lolita's mother shared her sex life with her, telling her what a lousy lover her father was and what a little penis he had. By making her a "sorority sister," she severely violated her daughter's boundaries. Lolita was so enmeshed with her mother that she had no sexual identity of her own. She had numerous affairs with married men, but in the end she would always refuse them sex and reject them. She reported that in order to have an orgasm she had to fantasize that she was her mother!

Another form of sexual abuse stems from a lack of parental instruction about sex. June's parents gave her *no* information about her sexuality. When she began to menstruate, she was terrified that she was seriously ill.

Sexual violation can also come from older siblings. The rule of thumb here is about two years' age difference. Same-age kids often engage in sexual exploration, which usually is part of normal development. However, if a child acts out on a same-age kid a behavior that is inappropriate for their age level of understanding, it is often considered a symptom that the aggressor child has been violated and is sexually violating the other child.

Consider the case of Sammy, who was "buggered" several times by his same-age best friend at the age of 6½. It turned out that his best friend had been anally violated by an uncle. The friend then acted out his abuse on Sammy.

Children believe in their parents and will create fantasy bonds to maintain that belief. I denied and deluded myself to the bitter end— maintaining that my alcoholic father really loved me. I created a fantasy that he really thought about me a lot; but he was so sick, he just didn't have time to love me. No one likes to be used. As adults, when we know we're being used, we get furious. Children cannot know they are being used. But the inner child carries this wound. When we are sexually abused, we feel we're not lovable as we are, and we become antisexual or supersexual in order to feel that we matter.

## Physical Abuse

Physical abuse also inflicts the spiritual wound. A child getting beaten, a child getting jerked by the neck, a child being told to get his own weapons of torture can hardly believe that he is special, wonderful, and unique. How can he when he is being hurt physically by his caretaker? Physical punishment severs the interpersonal bond with a parent. Imagine how you would feel if your best friend walked over and slapped you.

We have no idea how many violent families there are. Those stats get hidden in hospital emergency rooms, in family shame, and, above all, in the terror of being hurt more if you talk about it.

The physical beating of women and children is an ancient and pervasive tradition. We still believe in corporal punishment. I was still condoning it in modified form three years ago. There is *no* true evidence that spankings and corporal punishment have no lasting side effects. Only in some perverted sense can a child believe he matters while being spanked, slapped, or threatened. Furthermore, children who witness violence are victims of violence. I still feel a physical reaction in my body when I think of my friend Marshall. I watched a nun at my elementary school hit him across the face at least a dozen times; obviously, she had lost control. Marshall was a tough kid and certainly needed guidance. His father was a violent alcoholic who beat him. But I vividly remember sitting there wincing with every blow from that nun, knowing at some level that this could also happen to me. Any school that permits corporal punishment runs the risk of a teacher's losing control in this abusive way.

I'll never forget the night, thirty years later, when Marshall called me from the locked ward at a V.A. hospital begging me to help him with his alcoholism. Where was the beautiful child who had come into this world with a sense of specialness, a sense of being unique and irreplaceable?

## Emotional Abuse

Emotional abuse also inflicts the spiritual wound. Screaming and yelling at children violates their sense of value. Parents who call their children "stupid," "silly," "crazy," "asshole," and so on wound them with every word. Emotional abuse also comes in the form of rigidity, perfectionism, and control. Perfectionism produces a deep sense of toxic shame. No matter what you do, you never measure up. All shame-based families use perfectionism, control, and blame as manipulating rules. Nothing you say, do, feel, or think is okay. You shouldn't feel what you feel, your ideas are crazy, your desires are stupid. You are continuously found to be flawed and defective.

### ABUSE AT SCHOOL

Toxic shaming continues when you enter school. You are immediately judged and graded. You compete to be okay. Children stand at the blackboard being publicly shamed. Grading itself can be shaming. I recently comforted the little boy of a friend of mine who got an F on a drawing he did *the first day at school*.

Schools also allow peer-group shaming. Children are cruel in their teasing of other children. Weeping is especially shamed. Because of peer-group shaming, school can be a true double bind for many children. They are urged by their parents and teachers to work hard and do well academically, but when they do well, they are made fun of by the other children.

In school we began to be aware of things like ethnic background and socioeconomic status. My Jewish friends have told me horror stories concerning the pain they experienced for being Jewish. School is also the place where many black children are told they don't "talk right." When I went to school in Texas, Mexican children were still being punished for speaking their "mother tongue" in school.

I remember the personal shame I felt because we did not have a car and I had to walk to school and later ride the bus. This was aggravated by the fact that I went to a school where most of the kids came from great wealth. School-age children learn very quickly about social status.

### ABUSE AT CHURCH

A child may also be shamed in Sunday school or in church by hearing a fire-and-brimstone sermon. I heard a preacher recently on TV who said, "You can't be good enough to be acceptable in the eyes of God." What a terrible affront to God the Creator. But how could a child know that this man was covering up his own shame with his toxic ranting? I can remember being taught the prayer of Saint Catherine of Genoa in elementary school. If my memory serves me, the prayer went like this: "Straining to leave this life of woe with anguish sharp and deep I cry. I die because I do not die." That's a happy little hummer to start the day with! This is a mystic's prayer that makes sense at the highest level of spirituality. But for fifth-graders it inflicts a spiritual wound.

## CULTURAL SHAME

Our culture has its own system of perfection that spiritually wounds us. We have perfect 10s. We have men with big penises and women with big breasts and firm buttocks. If your genitals are not big, you're considered inferior. I remember how painful it was to shower in the locker room after football practice. The big boys would tease the younger ones and make fun of them. I prayed that they would not decide to pick on me. I nervously laughed and joined them when they started on someone else.

I also remember the fat and ugly kids; they lived a daily nightmare just coming to school. The awkward kids, the ones who were nonathletic, also took a shaming at recess and during games.

These times leave lifelong scars. Growing up poor, I still feel shame when I go to a country club or any other exclusive place. Often I know that I'm better off financially than the people around me, but I still feel the toxic pang of cultural shame.

Children realize very early in life that there are real economic and social differences between themselves and their friends. They become acutely aware of dress styles and rich neighborhoods. The peer-group pressure in these areas gets increasingly worse as the years go by. Always there's a measure of your worth—and more often than not you don't measure up. The message is: *The way you are is not okay. You must be the way* **we** *want you to be.*

## TOXIC SHAME

All these kinds of abuse create toxic shame—the feeling of being flawed and diminished and never measuring up. Toxic shame feels much worse than guilt. With guilt, you've done something wrong; but you can repair that—you can do something about it. With toxic shame there's something wrong with *you* and there's nothing you can do about it; you *are* inadequate and defective. Toxic shame is the core of the wounded child.

I recently reworked a powerful meditation originally written by Leo Booth, adding to it some aspects of toxic shame explored in my book *Bradshaw On: Healing the Shame That Binds You*. I'd like to share it with you here.

### *My Name Is Toxic Shame*

I was there at your conception
In the epinephrine of your mother's shame
You felt me in the fluid of your mother's womb
I came upon you before you could speak
Before you understood
Before you had any way of knowing
I came upon you when you were learning to walk
When you were unprotected and exposed
When you were vulnerable and needy
Before you had any boundaries
MY NAME IS TOXIC SHAME.

I came upon you when you were magical
Before you could know I was there
I severed your soul
I pierced you to the core
I brought you feelings of being flawed and defective
I brought you feelings of distrust, ugliness, stupidity, doubt,
    worthlessness, inferiority, and unworthiness
I made you feel different
I told you there was something wrong with you
I soiled your Godlikeness
MY NAME IS TOXIC SHAME.

I existed before conscience
Before guilt

Before morality
I am the master emotion
I am the internal voice that whispers words of condemnation
I am the internal shudder that courses through you without any
    mental preparation
MY NAME IS TOXIC SHAME.

I live in secrecy
In the deep moist banks of darkness
    depression and despair
Always I sneak up on you I catch you off guard I come through
    the back door
Uninvited unwanted
The first to arrive
I was there at the beginning of time
With Father Adam, Mother Eve
Brother Cain
I was at the Tower of Babel the Slaughter of the Innocents
MY NAME IS TOXIC SHAME.

I come from "shameless" caretakers, abandonment, ridicule, abuse,
    neglect—perfectionistic systems
I am empowered by the shocking intensity of a parent's rage
The cruel remarks of siblings
The jeering humiliation of other children
The awkward reflection in the mirrors
The touch that feels icky and frightening
The slap, the pinch, the jerk that ruptures trust
I am intensified by
A racist, sexist culture
The righteous condemnation of religious bigots
The fears and pressures of schooling
The hypocrisy of politicians
The multigenerational shame of dysfunctional
    family systems
MY NAME IS TOXIC SHAME.

I can transform a woman person, a Jewish person, a black
    person, a gay person, an oriental person, a precious child into
A bitch, a kike, a nigger, a bull dyke, a faggot, a chink, a selfish
    little bastard

I bring a pain that is chronic
A pain that will not go away
I am the hunter that stalks you night and day
Every day everywhere
I have no boundaries
You try to hide from me
But you cannot
Because I live inside of you
I make you feel hopeless
Like there is no way out
MY NAME IS TOXIC SHAME.

My pain is so unbearable that you must pass me on to others
    through control, perfectionism, contempt, criticism, blame,
    envy, judgment, power, and rage.
My pain is so intense
You must cover me up with addictions, rigid roles, reenactment,
    and unconscious ego defenses.
My pain is so intense
That you must numb out and no longer feel me.
I convinced you that I am gone—that I do not exist—you
    experience absence and emptiness.
MY NAME IS TOXIC SHAME.

I am the core of co-dependency
I am spiritual bankruptcy
The logic of absurdity
The repetition compulsion
I am crime, violence, incest, rape
I am the voracious hole that fuels all addictions
I am insatiability and lust
I am Ahaverus the Wandering Jew, Wagner's Flying Dutchman,
    Dostoyevski's underground man, Kierkegaard's seducer, Goethe's
    Faust
I twist *who you are* into what you do and have
I murder your soul and you pass me on for generations
MY NAME IS TOXIC SHAME.

This meditation sums up the ways that the wonderful child got
wounded. The loss of your I AMness is spiritual bankruptcy. The
wonder child is abandoned and all alone. As Alice Miller writes in

*For Your Own Good,* it is even worse than being the survivor of a concentration camp.

> The abused inmates of a concentration camp ... are inwardly free to hate their persecutors. The opportunity to experience their feelings—even to share them with other inmates, prevents them from having to surrender their self.... *This opportunity does not exist for children.* They must not hate their father ... they cannot hate him.... They fear losing his love as a result.... Thus children, unlike concentration camp inmates, are *confronted by a tormentor they love.* (Italics added.)

The child continues to live in his torment, passively suffering or lashing out, acting out, acting in, projecting and expressing himself in the only ways he knows how. Reclaiming that child is the first stage of our homecoming journey.

# PARABLE

## The Almost Tragic Story of a Tender Elf

Once upon a time there was a tender little elf. He was a very happy elf. He was bright and curious and knew the secrets of life. For example, he knew that love was a choice; that love involved hard work; that love was the only way. He knew that he could do magic things and that his unique form of magic was called creativity. The little elf knew that as long as he truly created, there would be no violence. And he knew the greatest secret of all—that he was something rather than nothing. He knew he was *being* and that *being was everything*. This was called the secret of "I AMness." The creator of all elves was the Great I AM. The Great I AM always was and always will be. No one knew how or why this was true. The Great I AM was totally loving and creative.

Another most important secret was the secret of balance. The secret of balance meant that all life is a marriage of opposites. There is no life without physical death; no joy without sorrow; no pleasure without pain; no light without darkness; no sound without silence; no good without bad. True health is a form of wholeness. And wholeness is holiness. The great secret of creativity was to balance a wild creative unfocused energy with a form that allows that energy to be.

One day our tender elf, whose name by the way was Joni, was given another secret. This secret scared him a little. The secret was that he had a mission he must do before he could create forever. He had to share his secrets with a ferocious tribe of non-elves. You see, elf life was so good and wonderful that the secret of that wonder needed to be shared with those who didn't know anything about the wonderment. Goodness always wants to share itself. Each elf was assigned to one family of the ferocious non-elf tribe. The non-elf tribe was called Snamuh. The Snamuh knew no secrets. They often squan-

dered their *beings*. They worked endlessly and seemed to feel alive
only when they were doing something. Some elves referred to them
as DOs. They also killed one another and engaged in war. Sometimes
at sporting events and music concerts they trampled one another to
death.

Joni entered his Snamuh family on June 29, 1933, at 3:05 A.M. He
had no idea what was in store for him. He didn't know that he would
have to use every ounce of his creativity in order to tell his secrets.

When he was born, he was given the Snamuh name Farquhar. His
mother was a beautiful 19-year-old princess who was ravished by a
need to perform. She had a strange curse on her. The curse was a
neon bulb that rested in the middle of her forehead. Whenever she
tried to play, have fun, or just be, the light blinked on and a voice
said, *"Do your duty."* She could never just do nothing and be.
Farquhar's father was a short but handsome king. He also carried a
curse. He was haunted by his wicked witch mother, Harriet. She lived
on his left shoulder.

Anytime he tried to just *be,* she screamed and yelled. Harriet was
always telling him to *do* something.

In order for Farquhar to tell his parents and others his secrets, they
needed to be quiet and stop *doing* long enough to see and hear him.
This they could not do; his mom because of the neon bulb, and his
dad because of Harriet. From the moment he was born, Farquhar was
all alone. Since he had the body of a Snamuh, he also had the feelings
of a Snamuh. And because of his abandonment, he felt furious, deeply
frustrated, and hurt.

Here he was a tender elf who knew the great secrets of I AM and
no one would listen to him. What he had to say was life-giving, but his
parents were so busy doing their duty, they could not learn from him.
In fact, his parents were so confused, they thought that it was their job
to teach Farquhar to do *his* duty. Anytime he failed to do what they
thought was his proper duty, they punished him. Sometimes they
ignored him by putting him in his room. Sometimes they hit him or
screamed at him. In fact, Farquhar hated the screaming the worst. He
could take the isolation; and the hitting was over with quickly; but the
screaming and endless telling him about his duty went so deep that it
even threatened his elf soul. Now, you cannot kill an elf's soul,
because it is part of the Great I AM; but it can be so badly wounded
that it seems like it isn't there anymore. This is what happened to
Farquhar. In order to survive, he stopped trying to show his mother

and father his secrets and instead pleased them by performing and doing his duty.

His mom and dad were very unhappy Snamuhs. (Actually, most Snamuhs are unhappy unless they learn the secret of the elves.)

Farquhar's dad was so tormented by Harriet that he used all his energy to find a magic potion that took away all his feelings. But the magic was not creativity. It actually took away his creativity. Farquhar's dad became like a "walking dead man." After a while, he stopped even coming home. Farquhar's Snamuh heart was broken. You see, every Snamuh needs both his father's and his mother's love in order to let the elf in him tell his secrets.

Farquhar was overwhelmed by his father's abandonment. And, since his father could no longer help his mother, her neon bulb blinked more intensely. Consequently, Farquhar was yelled at and cajoled even more. By the time he reached his twelfth birthday, he'd forgotten he was an elf. A few years later, he learned about the magic potion that his father used to kill Harriet's voice. At 14 he started using it often. By his thirtieth year he had to be carried away to a Snamuh hospital. While in this hospital he heard an inner voice urging him to wake up. The voice that moved him to wake up was the "being" voice of his elf soul. *For you see, no matter how bad it gets, the elf voice will always call a Snamuh to celebrate his being.* Joni never gave up; he never stopped trying to save Farquhar. If you're a Snamuh and you're reading this, please remember this: You have an elf soul in you that is always trying to call you to your being.

When Farquhar was lying in the hospital, he finally heard Joni's voice. That made all the difference. And that is the beginning of another, better story. . . .

# PART

# 2

# RECLAIMING YOUR WOUNDED INNER CHILD

In fantasy and myth homecoming is a dramatic event: bands play, the fatted calf is killed, a banquet prepared, and there is rejoicing that the prodigal has returned. In reality exile is frequently ended gradually, with no dramatic, external events to mark its passing. The haze in the air evaporates and the world comes into focus; seeking gives way to finding; anxiety to satisfaction. Nothing is changed and everything is changed.

—SAM KEEN

Sam Keen sums up the work you are about to do. When you are finished, no band will play, calling you to a banquet. However, if you've done your work well, you can take your inner child to dinner and listen to a good band. You will be more serene and peaceful.

Reclaiming your wounded inner child is a Zenlike experience. Children are natural Zen masters; their world is brand-new in each and every moment. For the unwounded child, wonder is natural. Life is a mystery to be lived. Homecoming is the restoration of the natural. Such a restoration is not grandiose or dramatic; it is simply the way life ought to be.

*Reclaiming your inner child involves going back through your developmental stages and finishing your unfinished business.* Imagine that you are about to come upon a wonderful little child who has just been born. You can be there as a wise and caring adult to help this child come into the world. You can be there when you were born, when you learned to crawl and walk, when you learned to talk. Your child will also need *your* nurturing support as he grieves his losses. Ron Kurtz suggests that you can be a "magical stranger" to the child—magical because you were not *actually there* the first time your inner child went through these stages. I collect wizards, so I reclaimed my wounded inner child as a gentle and wise old wizard. You can be whatever you like, as long as you are there in a loving and nonshaming way.

Each of those stages demanded very specific kinds of nourishment. As you understand what your needs were at each stage, you can learn to give yourself that kind of nourishment. Later, as you learn to champion your inner child, you can find nurturing people who will give you what you needed then, and what your inner child needs now in order to grow.

The most important first step is to help your wounded child grieve its unmet developmental dependency needs. Most of the contaminations I described in the first part of this book result from unmet needs that are unresolved because they have never been grieved. The emotions that needed to be expressed were never expressed.

Getting these needs met at the proper time and in the proper sequence is nature's way. Lacking that, you become an adult with a hurt child inside of you clamoring to get those needs met. And the child tries to get them met *as a child*—the only way he knows how. What this amounts to is letting an immature, emotionally starving child run your life. To understand the impact of this, go through your daily routine and visualize how your life would be with this 3-year-old at the helm. This scenario can help you see how your wounded inner child complicates your life.

Childhood consists of four major developmental stages. In presenting these stages, I have relied primarily on the map of psychosocial development provided by Erik Erikson's classic book *Childhood and Society*. I have added bits and pieces from Jean Piaget, Pam Levin, and Barry and Janae Weinhold. According to Erikson, each developmental stage results from an interpersonal crisis—primarily with our parents, but also with our peers and schoolteachers. The crisis is not a catastrophic event, but a time of heightened vulnerability and increased potential. The resolution of each stage creates a new crisis. Erikson believes that the result of each crisis is an internal strength that he calls an ego strength. He posits four basic ego strengths as the necessary components of a healthy childhood. They are hope, willpower, purpose, and competence. Hope is the product of the infant's coming to feel a greater sense of *trust* than of *mistrust* in his caretakers. Willpower results when the toddler, in his struggle to separate and be born psychologically, gains a greater sense of *autonomy* than of *shame* and *doubt*. Purpose accrues when the preschooler's sense of *initiative* is stronger than his sense of *guilt*. And competence results from the school-age child's developing a greater sense of *industry* than of *inferiority*.

According to therapist Pam Levin, when these ego strengths are present, four basic powers are available to us—the power of being, the power of doing, the power of identity, and the power of having basic survival skills.

The very same powers and ego strengths you needed to develop in childhood will need to be strengthened in the later stages of life. The very same quality and kinds of needs will recur all through your later life. Pam Levin has suggested that the basic childhood needs get recycled every thirteen years. I'm not aware of any empirical data that support this thirteen-year-cycle theory, but I like to use it as a guideline.

At 13 puberty awakens the life spark in a new way. A new mental structure unfolds as the biological changes of sexual maturity take place. We begin the process of forming our own identity and leaving home. This necessitates challenging and testing our parents' view of us. At puberty we begin the process of deciding who we *think* we are. To *be* ourselves, we must slowly leave our parents. We need all our developed ego strengths in order to do this. We need to rely on the trust we developed as infants—a trust that the world is safe enough for us to actualize our potential. In addition, we must be autonomous enough to trust *ourselves* as we venture out and leave the security of our parental home. Our success in this depends on how well we negotiated our first counterdependency stage during the toddler years and on how well we established a beginning identity in the preschool stage, which calls for independence. If we accomplished those developmental tasks, our power to initiate this new transition will be easier.

If we learned well in school, we can use our social skills (interdependency) to make friends. We can rely on the survival skills we learned in school to be industrious. These school-age ego strengths will help us create our adult identity, which rests on the pillars of interpersonal love and gainful work.

In our middle to late twenties a new cycle begins. By 26, many of us are getting married and creating a family of our own. Once again, we need to rely on our senses of trust, autonomy, initiative, and interdependent cooperation in order to love well and be intimate. Each stage of childhood will be recycled in our quest for intimacy.

We will move from a kind of boundaryless dependence (in-love stage) to counterdependence (power-struggle stage as we work out our differences), to independence (self-actualization stage), and then to interdependence (cooperation and partnership stage). These stages mirror our childhood stages. Therefore, a great deal of our relationship success or failure depends on how we negotiated our childhood stages.

At 39 we begin another cycle as we enter middle age. This is a very dramatic stage in the life cycle. Someone coined the phrase "middle-age crazies" to express the drama and difficulty of this life transition. If you have a wounded inner child, this stage can be disastrous.

By middle age the arch of life has slowly flattened out. Our youthful idealism has been tempered by betrayal, disillusionment, and the death of someone near to us. As W. H. Auden expressed it:

> In the meantime
> There are bills to be paid, machines to keep in repair,
> Irregular verbs to learn, the Time Being to redeem
> From insignificance.

Life itself becomes like an irregular verb. Sam Keen says, "We move from the illusion of certainty to the certainty of illusion." Out of this disillusionment we must decide to hope and trust that it all makes sense. If we choose to trust, we will have to use our willpower to make new decisions about every aspect of our lives—our work, our relationships, our spirituality. We must grow up and stand on our own two feet. Whatever sense of autonomy and initiative we have will be challenged to create a new sense of purpose. And we may need to develop new skills to support our newfound purpose.

The next cycle of older adulthood is a time to deepen our hope and strengthen our new commitments. This is very often a peaceful time as well as a time of productivity. Hopefully, we have our wonder child available to us because we will need his spontaneity and resilience.

The beginning of old age demands renegotiation and coming to terms with aging and retirement. In old age we need to enter a second childhood! We need a childlike hope that there is something more, a faith in something greater than ourselves that will help us to see a larger picture. We will need all our accrued ego strengths to see the whole against its parts. When we achieve that vision, we have wisdom.

Each stage builds on the preceding one. *The foundation for it all is childhood.*

A small mistake in the beginning is a great mistake in the end. We had no say about the beginning of our lives; we were completely dependent on our caretakers for survival. Our needs were *dependency* needs—that is, they could be met only by our caregivers.

The accompanying charts show the various stages of human development with its transitions and recycling. The first chart outlines the various ego strengths and powers we needed to develop at each stage of personal growth. The second gives you an overview of the thirteen-year cycles of regeneration. The third gives you a picture of how your *being* expands and develops over the life cycle.

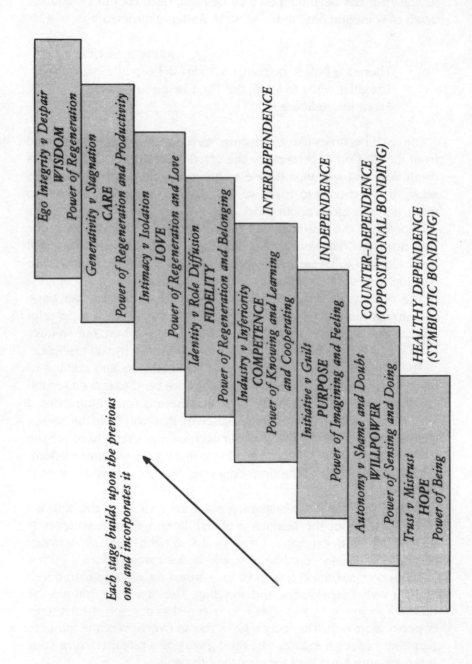

Ego Integrity v Despair
**WISDOM**
*Power of Regeneration*

Generativity v Stagnation
**CARE**
*Power of Regeneration and Productivity*

Intimacy v Isolation
**LOVE**
*Power of Regeneration and Love*

Identity v Role Diffusion
**FIDELITY**
*Power of Regeneration and Belonging*

Industry v Inferiority
**COMPETENCE**
*Power of Knowing and Learning and Cooperating*

Initiative v Guilt
**PURPOSE**
*Power of Imagining and Feeling*

Autonomy v Shame and Doubt
**WILLPOWER**
*Power of Sensing and Doing*

Trust v Mistrust
**HOPE**
*Power of Being*

*INTERDEPENDENCE*

*INDEPENDENCE*

**COUNTER–DEPENDENCE**
(OPPOSITIONAL BONDING)

**HEALTHY DEPENDENCE**
(SYMBIOTIC BONDING)

*Each stage builds upon the previous one and incorporates it*

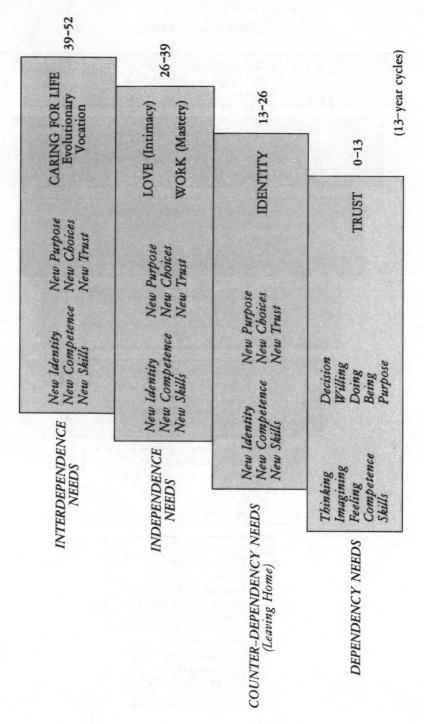

REGENERATIVE CYCLES

INTERDEPENDENCE NEEDS

New Identity
New Competence
New Skills

New Purpose
New Choices
New Trust

CARING FOR LIFE
Evolutionary
Vocation

39–52

INDEPENDENCE NEEDS

New Identity
New Competence
New Skills

New Purpose
New Choices
New Trust

LOVE (Intimacy)

WORK (Mastery)

26–39

COUNTER–DEPENDENCY NEEDS
(Leaving Home)

New Identity
New Competence
New Skills

New Purpose
New Choices
New Trust

IDENTITY

13–26

DEPENDENCY NEEDS

Thinking
Imagining
Feeling
Competence
Skills

Decision
Willing
Doing
Being
Purpose

TRUST

0–13

(13-year cycles)

## EXPANDING BEING

*I have wisdom*
*I can accept myself completely*
*I am one with all*

*I have personal power*
*I can create and produce*
*I can take care of the next generation*
*I am committed to life*

*I have another person who affirms*
*  my inner sense of self*
*I can love*
*I can be totally close and totally separate*
*I am intimate with self and another*

*I have an inner sense of who I am*
*I can regenerate*
*I can be faithful to a person or cause*
*I am unique*

*I have competence*
*I have limits*
*I can be skillful*
*I can think and learn*
*I am capable*

*I have conscience*
*I have purpose and value*
*I can imagine and feel*
*I am sexual*
*I am someone*

*I have limits*
*I have willpower*
*I can be separate*
*I can be curious and*
*  explore and do*
*I am me*

*I have hope*
*I can just be*
*I can trust you*
*I am you*

In addition to the natural recycling of childhood developmental tasks in later stages of life, there are other ways the stages can be recycled. Parenting our own children will trigger our earlier developmental issues. At each stage of our children's development, our own unresolved developmental issues and unmet childhood needs will come up. Often the result is toxic parenting. This is why it's so difficult for untreated adult children from dysfunctional families to be consistently effective parents. Parent/child conflict often reaches a climax during adolescence, which is a difficult time in the life cycle. Adding to the difficulty is that during adolescence, the parents are in the "middle-age crazies." This is not a pretty picture.

Childhood developmental stages can also be triggered whenever we encounter distress or trauma in adulthood. The death of a parent will definitely precipitate our childhood issues. The death of a friend or other loved one usually throws us back into our being needs. In the face of death, we are, as Tennyson said, "an infant crying in the night . . . and with no language but a cry."

Any new situation can trigger our infancy needs: a new job, a new house, a marriage, a baby. The way we handle new beginnings depends on how well we were handled in our first beginning.

To sum it up, our early childhood stages provide the foundation for our adult life. Those of us who are adult children from dysfunctional families lack this foundation. In part 1 you saw how your developmental deficits have had life-damaging consequences. If you want to change these damaging patterns you must reclaim your childhood.

Reclaiming our childhood is painful because we must grieve our wounds. The good news is that we *can* do this. Grief work is the legitimate suffering we've been avoiding with our neuroses. Jung said it well: "All our neuroses are substitutes for legitimate suffering." Grief work, which has been called original pain work, demands that we reexperience what we could not experience when we lost our parents, our childhood, and, most of all, our sense of I AMness. The spiritual wound *can* be healed. But it must be done by grieving, and that is painful.

In the following chapters I will describe the elements of original pain work and the kinds of nourishment you needed at each of the four primary childhood stages of development. I will suggest several exercises for each stage. If you are currently in therapy, please get your therapist's approval before starting the work. You *can* do it by yourself, using your own adult as a gentle and wise old wizard, but you still need your therapist's approval.

There are also meditation exercises for each developmental stage. In these meditations *your adult* will nurture your wounded inner child. This is the best I can offer you in book form. You can do the exercises alone, but it would be better to do them with a nurturing and supportive friend. It would be best if you did them with a support group.

**These exercises are not intended to replace any therapy or therapy group that you might be involved in. They are not intended to replace any 12 Step group that you belong to.** In fact, they should enhance your therapy or 12 Step work. **If you are an adult victim of sexual abuse or severe emotional battering,** or if you have been diagnosed as **mentally ill** or have a **history of mental illness** in your family, **professional help is essential for you.** If, as you experience these exercises, you start to **experience strange or overwhelming emotions, *stop immediately*.** Obtain the help of a qualified counselor before you proceed.

While this work can be extremely powerful and has been highly therapeutic for many people, it is not intended as a magical kind of "how-to potion."

Another caution: **If you are in an active addiction, you are out of control and out of touch with your true feelings.** You must modify that behavior if you want to benefit from this work. The 12 Step groups have proven to be the most effective agents in arresting addictions. Join one today. They are the best deal in town. The work I'm presenting here requires that you have at least one year of sobriety under your belt. In the early days of recovery from an addiction, especially ingestive addictions, your emotions are raw and undifferentiated. They are like the hot lava inside a volcano. If you explore painful childhood experience, you run the risk of being overwhelmed. Your boundaryless and insatiable wounded inner child is at the core of your addiction, and you drink, drug, sex, work, gamble, and so on precisely to avoid your inner child's spiritual wound. The Twelfth Step in the 12 Step programs talks about a "spiritual awakening" as a result of the Steps. This clearly indicates that addiction is about a spiritual bankruptcy.

For you to delve immediately into the core reasons why you've been addicted is to run the grave risk of **slipping back into your addiction.**

HOMECOMING                    65

Having said all this, I want to reiterate what I said in the prologue. You must actually *do* the exercises in the book if you want to reclaim and champion your inner child.

One final note. One way adult children avoid their legitimate suffering is by *staying in their heads.* This involves obsessing about things, analyzing, discussing, reading, and spending lots of energy in trying to figure things out. There is a story about a room with two doors. Each door has a sign on it. One says HEAVEN; the other says LECTURE ON HEAVEN. All the co-dependent adult children are lined up in front of the door that says LECTURE ON HEAVEN!

Adult children have a great need to figure things out because their parents were unpredictable adult children themselves. Sometimes they parented you as adults; sometimes they parented you as wounded and selfish children. Sometimes they were in *their* addictions, sometimes not. What resulted was confusion and unpredictability. Someone once said that growing up in a dysfunctional family is like "getting to a movie in the middle and *never* understanding the plot." Someone else described it as "growing up in a concentration camp." This unpredictability caused your continual need to figure things out. And until you heal the past, you will continue to try to figure it out.

Staying in one's head is also an ego defense. By obsessing on things, one does not have to *feel.* To feel anything is to tap in to the immense reservoir of frozen feelings that are bound by your wounded child's toxic shame.

So, I repeat, you must actually *do* the original pain work if you wish to heal your wounded inner child. The only way out is to go through it. "No pain no gain," as we say in the 12 Step programs.

My belief is that recovery from childhood abandonment, neglect, and abuse is a process, not an event. Reading this book and *doing* the exercises will not make all your problems disappear overnight. But I guarantee that you'll discover a delightful little person within yourself. You will be able to listen to that child's anger and sadness and to celebrate life with your inner child in a more joyous, creative, and playful way.

# CHAPTER 3

# ORIGINAL PAIN WORK

Neurosis is always a substitute for legitimate suffering.
—C. G. JUNG

Problems cannot be solved with words, but only through
experience, not merely corrective experience but through
a reliving of early fear (sadness, anger).
—ALICE MILLER

I believe that if the theory behind original pain work were better
understood, it would revolutionize the treatment of neuroses in
general and compulsive/addictive behaviors in particular. So often
patients who desperately need to do their feeling work are drugged
with tranquilizers. In our Life Plus treatment center in Los Angeles we
have run into obstacles from some mental-health professionals who
cannot understand why we don't want to medicate our patients. We
believe that the only way to cure compulsive/addictive disorders is
through the feeling work.

We specialize in treating co-dependence, which is rooted in toxic
shame—the internalized feeling of being flawed and defective as a
human being. In the internalization process, shame, which should be
a healthy signal of limits, becomes an overwhelming state of being, an
identity if you will. Once toxically shamed, a person loses contact
with his authentic self. What follows is a chronic mourning for the
lost self. The clinical description of this state of affairs is dysthymia or
low-grade chronic depression. In my book *Bradshaw On: Healing the
Shame That Binds You,* I showed how toxic shame was the master

emotion. It binds all our feelings in shame so that whenever we feel anger, distress, fear, or even joy, we also feel shame. Likewise with our needs and drives. The parents in dysfunctional families are adult children themselves; their own wounded inner child is needy. Whenever their children feel needy, which they do naturally, the adult-child parent gets angry and shames them. Subsequently, anytime the child's wounded inner child feels needy, he feels shamed. For a large part of my adult life I felt ashamed whenever I needed help. Finally, no matter how appropriate the context, the shame-based person feels shame when he is sexual.

Once one's feelings are bound in shame, one numbs out. This numbing out is the precondition for all addictions, because the addiction is the only way the person is able to feel. For example, a chronically depressed man who becomes a superachieving executive through his work addiction can feel only when he is working. An alcoholic or drug addict feels high with mood-altering drugs. A food addict feels a sense of fullness and well-being when his stomach is full. Each addiction allows the person to feel good feelings or to avoid painful ones. The addiction mood alters the hurt and pain of the spiritually wounded inner child. The spiritual wound inflicted by toxic shame is a rupture of the self with the self. One becomes painfully diminished in *one's own eyes;* he becomes an object of contempt to himself.

When a person believes that he cannot *be* himself, he is no longer at-one with himself. The ecstatic mood alteration of an addiction gives him a sense of well-being, of being one with self. Whenever a shame-based person feels his real feelings, he feels ashamed. So, to avoid that pain he numbs out.

Numbing our pain is achieved through various ego defenses we use when reality becomes intolerable. Some of the most common defenses are: denial ("it's not really happening"); repression ("it never happened"); dissociation ("I don't remember what happened"); projection ("it's happening to you, not to me"); conversion ("I eat or have sex when I feel it happening"); and minimizing ("it happened, but it's no big deal").

Basically, our ego defenses are ways to distract us from the pain we are feeling.

## THE PRIMACY OF EMOTIONS

Silvan Tomkins, a research psychologist, made a major contribution
to our understanding of human behavior by arguing for the primacy
of emotions. Our emotions are forms of *immediate* experience. When
we are experiencing our emotions, we are in direct contact with our
physical reality. Because our emotions are forms of energy, they are
physical; they are expressed in the body even before we are consciously aware of them.

Tomkins distinguishes nine *innate* emotions that are manifested in
various facial expressions. Every human child is born with these
expressions "preprogrammed" into his facial muscles, and researchers have shown that people everywhere in the world, in every culture, identify these emotions the same way. They are the basic
communications we need for biological survival.

As we develop, emotions form the basic blueprint for thinking,
acting, and decision making. Tomkins sees emotions as our innate
biological motivators. They are the "energy that moves us"—like the
fuel we use to drive our cars. Emotion intensifies and amplifies our
lives. Without emotion, nothing really matters; with emotion, anything
can matter.

In Tomkins's theory, the six primary motivators are interest, enjoyment, surprise, distress, fear, and anger. He sees shame as an auxiliary
emotion that is experienced on the primal level as an interruption.
Characterized by a sudden, unexpected exposure, it stops or *limits*
what is going on.

Dissmell and disgust are innate defensive responses. When we
smell something noxious, dissmell causes the upper lip and nose to
be raised and the head drawn back. When we taste or swallow a
noxious substance, disgust makes us spit it out or vomit it up. Like
our other reflexes, dissmell and disgust have evolved biologically to
protect us from dangerous substances, but we use them to express
nonphysical aversions as well.

To put it very simply, our emotions are our most fundamental
*powers*. We have them in order to guard our basic needs. When one
of our needs is being threatened, our emotional energy signals us.

Most of us have permission to feel our joy, interest, or surprise,
which are Tomkins's positive emotions. At least we are told these are
"good" emotions. But in fact, when our fear, sadness, and anger are

repressed, our ability to feel excitement, interest, and curiosity is also shut down. Since this is what happened to our parents, they cannot allow us to have these feelings. Kids are shamed for being too excited, curious, or inquisitive.

Harvey Jackins's model of therapy, called Reevaluation Counselling, is similar to original pain work. Jackins suggests that when the emotion accompanying a traumatic experience is blocked, the mind cannot evaluate or integrate the experience. When emotional energy blocks the resolution of trauma, the mind itself becomes diminished in its ability to function. Over the years, the mind is diminished more and more because the blockage of emotional energy is intensified *each time a similar experience occurs*. Every time we have a new experience that is in any way similar to the original trauma, we feel an intensity that is disproportionate to what is actually going on. I referred to this earlier as spontaneous age regression. It's like Pavlov's famous dog, who heard a bell ring each time he was fed. After a period of time, hearing the bell caused the dog to salivate, even when no food was present. Likewise, we might feel intense sadness when we hear a Christmas carol that triggers the memory of an earlier scene involving our drunken father ruining Christmas.

The wounded inner child is filled with unresolved energy resulting from the sadness of childhood trauma. One of the reasons we have sadness is to complete painful events of the past, so that our energy can be available for the present. When we are not allowed to grieve, the energy is frozen.

One of the rules of dysfunctional families is the *no feel* rule. This rule prohibited your inner child from even knowing what he was feeling. Another dysfunctional family rule is the *no talk* rule, which states that the expression of emotions is prohibited. In some cases it may have meant that you could express only *certain* emotions. Different families have variations on their no talk rules.

In my family, all emotions except guilt were prohibited. Emotions were considered weak. I was told over and over again, "Don't be so emotional." My family was no different from the millions of other Western families that carry the by-product of three hundred years of "rationalism." Rationalism is the belief that reason is supreme. Being reasonable is what constitutes being human, while being emotional is *less* than human. Repression and the shaming of emotions has been the rule in most Western families.

## Repressed Emotions

Since emotions are energy, they clamor to be expressed. Children from dysfunctional families often have no allies, no one to whom they can express their emotions. So they express them in the only way they know—by "acting them out" or "acting them in." The earlier the repression takes place, the more destructive the repressed emotions are. These unresolved and unexpressed emotions are what I refer to as "original pain." Original pain work involves reexperiencing these earliest traumas and expressing the repressed emotions. Once this is accomplished, the person no longer has to act in or act out the repressed emotions.

Until recently, there has been little scientific evidence to support original pain work. Freud wrote extensively on repression, dissociation, and displacement as primary ego defenses. He taught that, once formed, these defenses function automatically and unconsciously. However, he could not explain exactly *how* these mechanisms work. For example, what happens in our brain when we stop our painful emotions?

Body therapists have been able to *describe* some of the ways these defensive mechanisms work. We know, for example, that an emotion can be numbed by tensing muscles. People often grind their teeth and tense their jaws when they are angry. Emotions can also be stopped by holding one's breath. Shallow breathing is a common way to avoid emotional pain.

People also stop their emotions by fantasizing. For example, I spent a good part of my early life with an almost phobic fear of anger. My fantasy around expressing anger was one of catastrophic rejection and/or punishment. This fantasy mobilized muscle tension and shallow breathing.

## DISTRESS AND THE BRAIN

Today we're beginning to understand ego defenses on the basis of research into brain chemistry and brain physiology. Letting go of ego defenses connects one with his earliest emotions. Original pain work effects great healing by enabling one simply to feel these unresolved emotions from the past. Why does this heal?

Brain researcher Paul D. MacLean has presented a model of the brain that helps us understand how trauma affects us. MacLean describes the brain as "triune," or three-parted. These three brains within our brain are our evolutionary inheritance. The oldest or most primitive brain within our brain is the reptilian, or visceral, brain. This brain contains our most primitive strategy for safety and survival: *repetition.* A lizard, for example, lives a pretty simple life. His day consists of going to work every morning, hoping to eat a few flies and mosquitoes without getting eaten himself. If he finds a successful path through the grass and rocks, he will *repeat* this pattern till he dies. This repetition has survival value. The visceral brain also maintains our body's automatic physical functions, such as breathing. I like to tell people that our lizards really come out when we first get married and clash with another person's lifelong habits.

The next brain within our brain is the paleomammalian, or *feeling,* brain. This is technically called the limbic system. When warm-blooded mammals came upon the evolutionary scene, emotional energy was born. The limbic system houses our feelings of excitement, pleasure, anger, fear, sadness, joy, shame, disgust, and dissmell.

The most sophisticated brain system within our brain is the neocortex, or *thinking,* brain. It evolved last—over the past two million years or so. It gives us our human abilities to reason, use language, plan ahead, solve complex problems, and so on.

According to MacLean, these three brain systems are independent, but they also work together to maintain the equilibrium of the whole brain. The brain system's equilibrium is governed by the need to keep painful distress at a minimum.

The brain has no trouble with life's occasional distress. It uses the expression of emotion to maintain balance. When our distress reaches a certain peak, we storm with anger, weep with sadness, or perspire and tremble with fear. Scientists have shown that tears actually remove stressful chemicals that build up during emotional upset. The brain will naturally be moved to equilibrium by means of the expression of emotion unless we are taught to inhibit it.

Children growing up in dysfunctional families are taught to inhibit the expression of emotion in three ways: first, by not being responded to or mirrored, literally not being seen; second, by having no healthy models for naming and expressing emotion; and third, by actually being shamed and/or punished for expressing emotion. Children from dysfunctional families commonly hear things like: "I'll give you something to cry about," "Don't you ever raise your voice to me

again or I'll knock your head off." They are often *actually* spanked for
being afraid, mad, or sad.

But when emotions are inhibited, or when stress becomes overwhelming and chronic, the brain has difficulty. When traumatic stress
occurs, the brain system takes extraordinary measures to maintain
balance. These extraordinary measures are the ego defenses.

## The Imprint of Early Trauma

The earlier the emotions are inhibited, the deeper the damage. There
is growing evidence that there is a sequence in brain maturation
which basically follows the evolutionary sequence of brain formation.
Neuroscientists have shown that the visceral brain predominates in
the later stages of pregnancy and in the first postnatal period.

The limbic brain system begins to operate during the first six
months of life. This emotional brain allows for the important early
bonding to take place.

The neocortex is still developing during our early years, and the
thinking brain needs a proper environment and proper stimulation in
order to develop healthily. In his research on children's cognitive
growth, Piaget did not find true logical thinking until approximately
six or seven years of age. (While some of Piaget's findings have been
questioned, seven does seem to mark a turning point.)

When we reflect on the fact that the visceral brain is concerned
with survival issues and is governed by repetition, the idea of *permanent imprint* makes sense. Neuroscientist Robert Isaacson has argued that traumatic memories are difficult to root out because they
are memories of life-saving responses. Since the visceral brain learns
and remembers, but is poor at forgetting, it imprints the trauma with
a permanence that will dominate its future. Whatever a child survives
in the first years of life, a time of intense vulnerability, will be
registered with survival benefits in mind.

## The Compulsion to Repeat

Much of this neurological research supports what every psychothera-
pist from Freud until now knows firsthand: that neurotic people have
a compulsion to repeat.

There is also a neurological explanation for the severe overreactive
responses I mentioned earlier. Brain researchers have suggested that

enlarged neuronal imprints from stressful experience distort how the organism reacts to stimuli as an adult. Ongoing painful experiences actually engrave new circuits in the brain, so that it becomes more and more prepared to recognize as painful stimuli that another person might not notice.

This supports the theory that once the core material is set up in childhood, it acts as an overly sensitive filter shaping subsequent events. The contaminations of the wounded child fall into this category. When an adult with a wounded inner child experiences a current situation which is similar to a prototypic painful event, the original response is triggered as well. Harvey Jackins describes this as a tape recorder whose on button is stuck. Something which is actually trivial or quite innocuous is reacted to with intense emotion. This is a case of responding to what isn't there on the outside because it is still there on the inside.

As I write this, I'm on a cruise ship touring the capitals of Europe. When we reached Le Havre, France, two days ago, my daughter suggested to me that we take the train to Paris rather than go on the tour bus which took two hours longer. My daughter had very little early trauma. She is spontaneous, curious, and loves adventure. I recoiled in obsessive ruminations over her suggestion. I woke up several times in the night catastrophizing: "What if the train is de-railed?" "What if the train is late and the ship leaves without us?" My daughter's simple suggestion touched off a severe overreaction in me. I was traumatically abandoned by my father as a child. Now my obsessive thoughts centered on not making it back to the ship—being *left behind*.

## THE EGO DEFENSES AND THE "GATED BRAIN"

Original pain feeling work rests on the hypothesis that the early emotional pain is numbed out and inhibited. *We act it out, because it has never been worked out*. It can't be worked out because our inhibiting mechanism (ego defenses) keeps us from knowing the emotional pain is there.

"You can't know what you don't know" is a slogan we use in therapy. We act the feelings out; we act them in; or we project them onto others. Since we can't feel them, and since they are unfinished business, they need expression. Acting out, acting in, and projecting these feelings are the only ways our wounded child knows to express them. But acting out, acting in, and projecting are not permanent solutions. My compulsivity (a core wounded child issue) did not end when I quit drinking. I simply changed it to compulsive working.

Until I worked out my wounded child's original pain, I continued to act it out in my insatiable need for excitement and mood alteration. My ego defenses kept the emotions inhibited. It was only ten years ago that I discovered the major patterns of co-dependence, physical and nonphysical incest, and alcoholism, which dominate my multi-generational family history. Until I gave up my delusions and denials about my family and my childhood, I could not do my original pain work.

The brain research work of Ronald Melzack may help to explain how ego defenses work. Melzack discovered an adaptive biological response for inhibiting pain which he calls "neuronal gating." Melzack states that the three separate brain systems within the triune brain have interconnecting fibers that perform both a facilitating and an inhibiting function. Neuronal gating is the way information between the three systems is controlled. What we call repression may take place primarily at the gate between the thinking and feeling brain. To put it

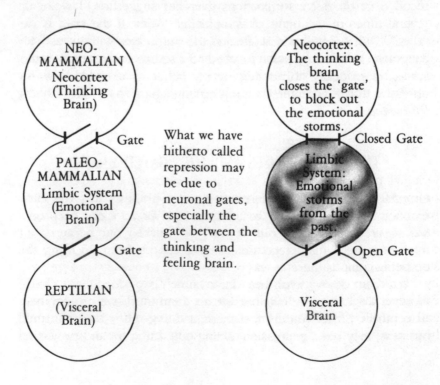

NEO-
MAMMALIAN
Neocortex
(Thinking
Brain)

— Gate

PALEO-
MAMMALIAN
Limbic System
(Emotional
Brain)

— Gate

REPTILIAN
(Visceral
Brain)

What we have
hitherto called
repression may
be due to
neuronal gates,
especially the
gate between the
thinking and
feeling brain.

Neocortex:
The thinking
brain
closes the 'gate'
to block out
the emotional
storms.

— Closed Gate

Limbic
System:
Emotional
storms
from the
past.

— Open Gate

Visceral
Brain

in the simplest way possible, when the emotional pain in the limbic system reaches overwhelm, an automatic mechanism shuts the gate into the neocortex. It's as if there were some loud noise streaming in from another room and you walked over and shut the door.

Freud believed that the primary ego defenses are integrated into more sophisticated secondary defenses as the human being matures. These secondary defenses take on a *thinking* quality: for example, rationalizing, analyzing, explaining away, and minimizing.

Recent work on the limbic system by R. L. Isaacson supports this theory. Isaacson reports that the gating system of the neocortex (the thinking brain) functions "to overcome the habits and memories of the past ... the neocortex is profoundly concerned with suppressing the past." These habits and memories include the deeply grooved imprints (neuronal pathways) created by overwhelming stress and trauma. Our thinking brain can thus function unhindered by the noise and signals generated in our internal world.

But these signals *don't go away*. Instead, researchers theorize that they continue to travel around and around closed circuits of nerve fibers within the limbic system.

So the ego defenses bypass the tension and pain, but the tension and pain remain. They are registered subcortically as an imbalance, an aborted action sequence awaiting release and integration. The energy of the original trauma remains like an electrical storm that reverberates tension throughout the biological system. People with seemingly rational adult lives may continue to live *stormy emotional lives*. Their storms continue because their original pain is unresolved.

## ORIGINAL PAIN WORK

Original pain work involves actually experiencing the original repressed feelings. I call it the uncovery process. It is the only thing that will bring about "second-order change," the kind of deep change that truly resolves feelings. In first-order change, you change one compulsion from another compulsion. In second-order change, you stop being compulsive. This was what I needed to heal my compulsivity. I acted out compulsively because my lonely, wounded inner child had never discharged his original distress. I went to 12 Step programs and controlled my alcoholism, but I kept acting out. I stayed in my head as a professor, theologian, and therapist, but I kept acting out. I read every new book I could get my hands on, and I discussed my problems in therapy, but I kept acting out. I pursued higher consciousness; learned the ways of the ancient shamans; learned energy healing; studied *A Course in Miracles;* meditated and prayed (sometimes for hours); but I kept acting out. I was compulsive even about higher consciousness. What I didn't know was that I needed to embrace my heartbroken little boy's loneliness and unresolved grief about his lost father, his lost family, and his lost childhood. I had to embrace my original pain. This is the legitimate suffering Carl Jung spoke about.

## Original Pain as Grief Work

The good news is that original pain work involves nature's own healing process. *Grief is the healing feeling.* We will heal naturally if we are just allowed to grieve.

Grief involves the whole range of human emotions. The original pain is an accumulation of unresolved conflicts whose energy has snowballed over time. The wounded inner child is frozen because there was no way he could do his grief work. All his emotions are bound by toxic shame. This shame resulted from the rupture of our first "interpersonal bridge." We came to believe that we could not depend on our primary caregiver. In fact, we came to believe that we had no right to *depend* on anyone. Isolation and the fear of depending on anyone are two of the main consequences of toxic shame.

## Restoring the Interpersonal Bridge

In order to heal our toxically shamed emotions we have to come out of hiding and trust someone. In this book, I'm asking you to *believe me* and *trust yourself.* For your wounded inner child to come out of hiding, he must be able to trust that you will be there for him. Your inner child also needs a supportive, nonshaming ally to validate his abandonment, neglect, abuse, and enmeshment. Those are the first essential elements in original pain work.

I hope you will trust yourself to be your inner child's ally in the grief work. The fact is, you can't totally trust me or anyone else. When push comes to shove, I'll probably save my own ass first. But you can trust yourself. Jo Courdet said it beautifully in *Advice from a Failure:* "Of all the people you will ever know, you are the only one you will never leave or lose."

## Validating Your Abuse

Believe me: a lot of what you were told was legitimate parenting was actually abuse. If you're still inclined to minimize and/or rationalize the ways in which you were shamed, ignored, or used to nurture your parents, you need now to accept the fact that these things truly wounded your soul. Some of you were also blatantly victimized through physical, sexual, or emotional battering. Why would such obvious abuse need to be validated? Strangely, the more you were abused, the more you thought you were bad and idealized your parents. That's the result of the fantasy bond I described earlier. All children idealize their parents; this is how they ensure their survival. However, when the abused child idealizes his parents, he must believe that he himself is responsible for the abuse: "They hit me because I'm such a rotten kid; they have sex with me because I'm very bad; scream at me because I'm so disobedient. It's about *me*, not about them—*they're* okay." This idealization of parents is the core ego defense and it must be taken down. Your parents weren't bad, they were just wounded kids themselves. Imagine yourself being parented by a 200-pound 3-year-old who was five times your size, or a

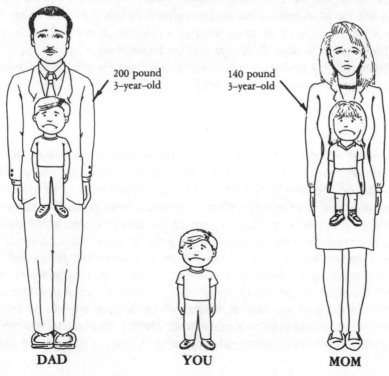

200 pound
3-year-old

140 pound
3-year-old

DAD                    YOU                    MOM

140-pound 3-year-old who was four times your size; your inner child can get the picture. Your parents did the best they knew how to do, but that isn't something a 3-year-old can comprehend.

## Shock and Depression

If all this is shocking to you, that's great, because *shock is the beginning of grief.* After shock comes depression and then denial. Denial kicks our ego defenses back in. It usually comes in the form of bargaining. We say, "Well, it really wasn't *that* bad. I had three squares and a roof over my head."

Please believe me: It *was* really bad. To be spiritually wounded, for your parents not to let you be who you are, is the worst thing that can happen to you. I'll bet when you got angry you were told, "Don't you ever raise your voice to me again!" From this you learned that it wasn't okay to be yourself, and it certainly wasn't okay to be angry. The same with fear, sadness, and joy. It wasn't okay to touch your vagina or penis, even though it felt great. It wasn't okay to dislike the Reverend Herkimer, Rabbi Kradow, or Father Walch. It wasn't okay to think what you were thinking, to want what you wanted, to feel what you felt, or to imagine what you imagined. At times it wasn't okay to see what you saw or to smell what you smelled. It wasn't okay *to be different or to be you.* To accept and understand what I'm saying is to validate and legitimize your spiritual wound, which is what lies at the core of every wounded inner child.

## Anger

The next feeling that usually comes up in grieving is anger. It's a legitimate response to the spiritual wound. While your parents probably did do the best they could, in original pain work your parents' intentions are *never* relevant. What is relevant is *what actually happened.* Imagine that they were backing out of the driveway and accidentally ran over your leg. You've been limping for all these years and you've never known why. Do you have a right to know what happened to you? Do you have a right to be hurt and in pain over it? The answer to both questions is an unequivocal *yes.* It's okay to be angry, even if what was done to you was unintentional. In fact, you *have* to be angry if you want to heal your wounded inner child. I don't mean you need to scream and holler (although you might). It's just okay to be mad about a dirty deal. *I don't even hold my parents responsible for what happened to me.* I know they did the best that two wounded adult children could do. But I'm also aware that I was deeply wounded spiritually and that it has had life-damaging consequences for me. Personally, I hold all of us accountable. What that means is that I hold us all responsible to stop what we're doing to ourselves and to others. I will not tolerate the outright dysfunction and abuse that dominated my family system.

## Hurt and Sadness

After anger come hurt and sadness. If we were victimized, we must grieve that betrayal. We must also grieve what might have been—our dreams and aspirations. We must grieve our unfulfilled developmental needs.

## Remorse

Hurt and sadness are often followed by remorse. We say, "If only things had been different, maybe I could have done something different. Maybe if I had loved my dad more and told him how I needed him, he would not have left me." When I counseled incest and physical-abuse victims, I could hardly believe that *they* felt guilt and remorse about their violation, as if they were in some way responsible for it. When we grieve for someone who has died, remorse is sometimes more relevant; for instance, perhaps we wish we had spent more time with the deceased person. But in grieving childhood abandonment you must help your wounded inner child see that there was *nothing* he could have done differently. His pain is about what happened *to* him; it is not *about* him.

## Toxic Shame and Loneliness

The deepest core feelings of grief are toxic shame and loneliness. We were shamed by their abandoning us. We feel we are *bad,* as if we're contaminated. And that shame leads to our loneliness. Since our inner kid feels flawed and defective, he has to cover up his true self with his adapted false self. He then comes to identify himself by his false self. His true self remains alone and isolated. Staying with this last layer of painful feelings is the hardest part of the grief process.

"The only way out is through," we say in therapy. It's hard to stay at that level of shame and loneliness; but as we embrace these feelings, we come out the other side. We encounter the self that's been in hiding. You see, because we hid it from others, we hid it from ourselves. In embracing our shame and loneliness, we begin to touch our truest self.

## FEELING THE FEELINGS

All these feelings need to be felt. We need to stomp and storm; to sob and cry; to perspire and tremble. All of this takes time. Recovery of feelings is a process, not an event. But it gets better almost immediately. The contact with the inner child, his knowing that someone is there and he will not have to go on alone, is joyous and brings immediate relief. The actual length of time for grieving varies from person to person; no one can say exactly how long the grief process will take. Knowing how to let go of your defenses is the key. Actually, you cannot stay out of your defenses all the time. There are persons and places where it is not safe to do your grief work. And you will need relief from time to time.

So, the sequence or stages of grief go back and forth. You may be in validation one day, then find yourself minimizing three days later. But you can keep moving forward through these cycles. The feeling of the feelings is what is crucial. *You can't heal what you can't feel!* As you experience the old feeling and let yourself be there for your inner child, the healing work naturally takes place. It's important to keep yourself very safe when doing feeling work. It is best done with a partner or a group. Please heed the warning I gave at the start of part 2. Have someone with you so you can talk to them after doing this work. Don't go too fast. It took a long time to get stuck and frozen, and it will take time to heal. If you feel like you're getting overwhelmed, stop immediately. Let what you've done integrate. If the overwhelming feeling persists, seek the help of a trained therapist.

# CHAPTER 4

# RECLAIMING YOUR INFANT SELF

Woman in the person of our mother, is the first being with whom we are in contact.... It all begins with a true fusion of being ... the child is an extension of the mother without clearly perceptible borders. There exists a *participation mystique,* a psychic flow from mother to child and from child to mother.

—KARL STERN

Where the mother is not sufficiently in touch with her body she cannot give the child the bonding necessary to give it confidence in its own instincts. The child cannot relax into her body, nor later its own.

—MARION WOODMAN

INFANT

*(SYMBIOTIC BONDING)*

I AM YOU

| | |
|---|---|
| AGE: | 0–9 MONTHS |
| DEVELOPMENTAL POLARITY: | BASIC TRUST VERSUS MISTRUST |
| EGO STRENGTH: | HOPE |
| POWER: | BEING |
| RELATIONSHIP ISSUE: | HEALTHY NARCISSISM; CO-DEPENDENCE |

## INDEX OF SUSPICION*

Answer yes or no to the following questions. After you read each question, wait and get in touch with what you feel. If you feel a stronger energy for yes, answer yes—for no, answer no. If you answer any question yes, you can suspect that your wonderful, infant inner child has been wounded. There are degrees of woundedness. You are somewhere on a scale from one to a hundred. The more questions you *feel* are to be answered yes, the more your infant self was wounded.

1. Do you have or have you had in the past an *ingestive* addiction (overeating, overdrinking, or overdrugging)? Yes _____ No _____

2. Do you have trouble trusting your ability to get your needs met? Do you believe you must find someone to meet them for you? Yes _____ No _____

---

*I've taken the idea for an "index of suspicion" from the pioneering work of the late Hugh Missildine in his classic book *Your Inner Child of the Past*. Dr. Missildine was my friend and encouraged me greatly to pursue this work.

3. Do you find it hard to trust other people? Do you feel you must be in control at all times? Yes _____ No _____

4. Do you fail to recognize body signals of physical need? For example, do you eat when you're not hungry? Or are you often not aware how tired you are? Yes _____ No _____

5. Do you neglect your physical needs? Do you ignore good nutrition or fail to get enough exercise? Do you go to a doctor or dentist only in an emergency? Yes _____ No _____

6. Do you have deep fears of abandonment? Do you feel, or have you ever felt, *desperate* because a love relationship ended? Yes _____ No _____

7. Have you considered suicide because a love relationship has ended (your lover has left you; your spouse filed for a divorce)? Yes _____ No _____

8. Do you often feel that you don't truly fit in or belong anywhere? Do you feel that people don't really welcome you or want your presence? Yes _____ No _____

9. In social situations, do you try to be invisible so that no one will notice you? Yes _____ No _____

10. Do you try to be so helpful (even indispensable) in your love relationships that the other person (friend, lover, spouse, child, parent) cannot leave you? Yes _____ No _____

11. Is oral sex what you most desire and fantasize about? Yes _____ No _____

12. Do you have great needs to be touched and held? (This is often manifested by your needing to touch or hug others often without asking them.) Yes _____ No _____

13. Do you have a continual and obsessive need to be valued and esteemed? Yes _____ No _____

14. Are you often *biting* and sarcastic to others? Yes _____ No _____

15. Do you isolate yourself and stay alone a lot of the time? Do you often feel it's not worth trying to have a relationship? Yes _____ No _____

16. Are you often gullible? Do you accept others' opinions or "swallow things whole" without thinking them through? Yes _____ No _____


## NORMAL INFANCY

Coming into the world we had very specific needs. In the chart on page 60 I outlined the basic building blocks in developing a reasonably healthy self. These blocks are *guidelines*. Since no two people are exactly alike, we have to be careful not to make absolutes about human development. Nonetheless, we do have commonalities. The great therapist Carl Rogers once said, "Whatever is most personal is most general." What that means to me is that my deepest human needs and my deepest fears and anxieties are more or less shared by everyone. I have been amazed to see that, in sharing my secrets, others can identify with me.


### The Interpersonal Bridge

We will use the basic building blocks I presented as guidelines for each of the dependency needs at our childhood developmental stages. In infancy, we need to be welcomed to the world. We need to be bonded to a nurturing, mothering person who serves as a mirror for us. Infancy is called the symbiotic stage because we are perfectly *co-dependent* on our mother or other nurturing survival figure. We are dependent on them to learn about ourselves and to get our basic physical survival needs met. At this stage we are *undifferentiated*. This means that we are naturally and unconsciously at one with ourself, but that we do not have the capacity to reflect and to consciously know that we have a self. We need the mirroring eyes and the echoing voice of our mothering person in order to discover our I AMness. We were "we" before we became "I." Life begins with a true fusion of being; our destiny depends on the person who happened to be our mother. "The hand that rocks the cradle" does indeed rock the world. If our mother was there for us, we bonded with her. This bond created an "interpersonal bridge," which is the foundation for all future relationships. If the bridge is built on mutual respect and valuing, it forms the blueprint out of which new relationships can be created. If the child is unduly shamed, the bridge will be ruptured and he will come to believe that he has no right to depend on anyone. This will set him up to develop pathological relationships with food, chemicals, sex, and so on.

## Healthy Narcissism

We needed our mothering person to take us seriously; to affirm that every part of us was acceptable; to let us know that someone would be there for us no matter what. These needs comprise what Alice Miller calls our healthy narcissistic supplies. They consist of being loved as the very one you are; being admired and valued; being touched and treated specially; being certain that mother will not leave you; being taken seriously. When we get those needs met in childhood, we don't have to carry them around when we grow up.

## Good Mothering

For a mother to do her job well, she needs to be in touch with her own sense of I AMness. She has to love herself, which means that she accepts every part of herself as okay. She needs especially to accept her body and be relaxed with it. A mother cannot give her child a sense of physical well-being if she herself has no sense of it. Nor can she give her child a sense of confidence in his instincts if she is not relaxed with her own. Erich Fromm has described how an anti-life orientation in a mother will make her child afraid of life, especially the instinctual life of the body.

## Mirroring

Instinctual life is governed by the most primitive part of the brain. It has to do with eating, sleeping, touching, and eliminating, and with sensuality and bodily pleasures and pains. As our chart shows, in the beginning of life, "I am you," "I am another." In other words, you are enmeshed with your mothering person. *You feel what she feels.* You are disgusted when she is disgusted. *You feel about yourself what she feels about you.* In infancy, feeling is primary. It doesn't matter how well Mom is performing the role of a good mother. What matters is how she really feels about her child. If your mother was angry because she had gotten pregnant and believed that she had to get married to have you, you would know it at a deep kinesthetic level.

## Touching

As an infant you needed to be touched and held *when you needed to be touched and held.* You needed to be fed when you were hungry. Schedule feeding was a horror of past generations. Sam Keen points out that Zen masters spend years to reach an enlightenment that every natural child already knows—the total incarnation of sleeping when you're tired and eating when you're hungry. What irony that this state of Zen-like bliss is programmatically and systematically destroyed. As an infant you needed to be bathed and to be kept clean. Your bodily functions were not yet under your muscle control, so you depended on your nurturing person to keep your bottom clean. These were *dependency needs.* You could not fulfill them for yourself.

## Echoing

You needed to hear welcoming, peaceful, warm voices around you. You needed lots of echoing coos! And oohs! And ahs! You needed to hear a safe, sure voice that signaled a high degree of security. Perhaps most of all you needed to experience a person who trusted the world and his or her own sense of being in the world. Erik Erikson posits the first developmental task as the establishment of an inner sense of being, which is characterized by *trusting* the outside world. Carl Rogers has said that one of his most significant learnings is that the "facts are friendly"—that is, that reality can be trusted. Basic trust versus mistrust is the first developmental task. When this polarity is resolved on the side of trust, a basic ego strength accrues. This strength forms the basis of hope. If the world is basically trustworthy, then becoming who "I am" is possible. I can trust that what I need will be there.

Pam Levin sees this first stage as one in which the *power of being* is developed. If all the factors I've enumerated are present, a child can just enjoy *being who he is.* Since the world outside is safe, and since my parents are getting their own needs met through their own resources and through each other's love and support, I can just be. I won't need to please them or fight for survival. I can just please myself and get my needs met.

## PARENTING—THE HARDEST JOB OF ALL

Being a good parent is a tough job. I believe it is *the hardest job any of us will ever do*. To be a good parent, you must be mentally healthy. You need to be getting your own needs met through your own resources, and you need a spouse or significant other to support you in the process. Above all, *you must have healed your own wounded inner child.* If your inner child is still wounded, you will parent your child with this frightened, wounded, and selfish inner child. You will either do a lot of what your parents did to you or you will do just the opposite. Either way, you will be trying to be the perfect parent your wounded inner child dreamed of. However, being just the opposite is equally damaging to your children. Someone once said, "One hundred and eighty degrees from sick is still sick."

Remember, *I am not blaming anyone's parents.* They were wounded adult children trying to do an enormously difficult task. In my case, my parents often did things right in spite of the poisonous pedagogy. My mom tells how painful it was for her to put us through schedule feeding, but she did it because the "experts" recommended it. It was also painful for her when she went against the "experts'" advice and sneaked in to comfort me when I was crying. Those were saving and grace-filled moments. They were motivated by *her* wonder child, who understood basic nurturing!

However, no parent ever was perfect, and no new parent ever will be. What's important is that we try to heal our own wounded inner child so that we don't damage our children.

## GROWTH DISORDER

Fritz Perls described neurosis as "growth disorder." I like that. It's a good way of expressing the problem of your wounded inner child's toxic shame and resulting co-dependence. We would not be co-dependent adult children if our developmental needs had been met.

When these needs are not adequately met in infancy, severe problems result. The Index of Suspicion at the beginning of this chapter describes some of these problems. They can be summed up under the term *narcissistic deprivation*. We did not get the mirroring and echoing we needed. We were not loved unconditionally; as a result, we didn't develop a basic sense of trust. This sets up the insatiable cravings that some people act out with ingestive addictions. It also sets up the need to be continually validated—almost as if we would cease to exist without such validation. Other consequences include insatiable cravings to be touched and hugged; too great a focus of your sexuality on orality; being out of touch with your physical needs (the signals from your body); a tendency to "swallow things whole"—to be the sucker who is born every minute. Most of all, when your infancy needs are not met, it sets you up to feel ashamed of yourself, to feel deep down that something is *wrong with you*.

## Don't Grow Up

Perhaps you learned to stay a child so that you could take care of your parents' narcissistic wounds. If you were a perfectly obedient child, Mom and Dad knew they could count on you always to take them seriously. They could be assured that you would never leave them as their own parents had done. You would be a constant source of value and esteem for them. Thus, you became the one to fill their lost narcissistic needs.

## Emotional Abandonment

Any child from a dysfunctional family system will feel emotional deprivation and abandonment. The natural response to emotional abandonment is a deep-seated toxic shame that engenders both primal rage and a deep-seated sense of hurt. There is no way you could grieve this in infancy. You had no ally who could be there for you and validate your pain, no one to hold you while you cried your eyes out or raged at the injustice of it all. In order to survive, your primary ego defenses kicked in and your emotional energy was left frozen and unresolved. Your unmet needs have been clamoring to be filled ever since your infancy. Just go to the nearest bar and you'll hear the whining voice of an adult infant as he cries, "I thirst, I crave, I want to be loved. I want to matter and be connected."

## DEBRIEFING

The first step in reclaiming your wounded inner infant is a process called *debriefing*. When a person has been through severe trauma, it is important that he take time to talk about it. Debriefing is not original pain work; it is not yet experiencing the original feelings. However, it is the way to begin your original pain work.

I recommend that you get all the information you can about your family system. What was going on when you were born? What kind of families did your mother and father come from? Was your mom and/or dad an adult child? It is a good idea to write out this information as accurately as you can for each stage of development—in this case, infancy. Likely you will feel some pain as you write. Just try to keep the focus on getting as clear as you can about the facts of your childhood.

For example, Qwenella was the reason her parents got married. They were very young, 17 and 18. Her mother was an untreated victim of both physical and emotional incest. Her father was an active alcoholic. Qwenella wrote that she remembers being in her baby bed when her father cursed her for being born. She felt that her mother blamed her (Qwenella) for ruining her life. Both parents came from rigid Catholic families and refused to use any birth control. Her mother engaged in frequent sexual intercourse as a marital duty. By the time Qwenella's mother was 24, she had four children. Imagine a 24-year-old with four children and an irresponsible alcoholic husband! As the child from an unwanted pregnancy, Qwenella was the object of her mother's rage and scorn. Qwenella remembers her mother telling her how ugly she was and that she'd never amount to anything. In family-systems theory, Qwenella carried the role of Lost Child, Mom's Scapegoat, and Victim. These roles enable the members of a dysfunctional family to get their needs met. If the family has no need for another child, or has too many children, the way the unwanted child learns to matter is by *getting lost*. The family says, in effect, "Get lost, child—we didn't really want to have you," or, "We have too many children already!"

Qwenella learned to be the perfect little girl. She was excessively obedient and maddeningly polite and helpful. She wrote that as a crib baby she stayed alone in her room for long hours without crying or making any noise. Later she played in her room for hours by herself,

so as not to bother her mother or anyone else in the family. This is
the classic behavior of the Lost Child. Qwenella grew up and repeated
these patterns in her job and social life. Without therapy, she will
probably carry these patterns to her grave.

## SHARING YOUR INFANCY WITH A FRIEND

Once you've written as much as you know about your infancy, it is
important to talk about it and to read it aloud to someone. If you're in
therapy and your therapist has approved your doing the work in this
book, share your writing with him or her, or with your sponsor if
you're in a 12 Step program. You can share it with anyone you
genuinely trust—perhaps a member of the clergy or a best friend.
What is important is *to have someone hear you and validate your
original pain* as an infant. This person needs to mirror and echo your
reality as an infant. If the person begins to question you, argue with
you, or give advice, *you're not getting what you need.*

It is not advisable to share this with a parent or other family
members unless they are in a personal recovery program. If real
abuse happened to you in infancy, this needs to be validated. *Untreated family members are in the same delusional trance that you've
been in.* They cannot possibly validate and legitimize your pain.

It is possible that your infancy was *not* a painful time for you.
In my workshops many people find that they *were* welcomed into
the world. They were wanted, even though their parents were adult
children. It was not until the next developmental stage that they
were violated. It was there that their parents' narcissistic deprivation
started to kick in.

## FEELING THE FEELINGS

If you're a Lost Child, you've probably already had some feelings
about your infancy. If you have a picture of yourself as an infant, take
a long look at it. If you don't have a picture, find an infant and spend
some time watching him. Either way, notice the infant's life energy.
Here is a perfectly innocent, wonderful child who just wants the
opportunity to live out his own destiny. This child didn't ask to be
born. All he wanted as an infant was some nourishment—food and

love—in order to grow and thrive. Imagine someone bringing this precious infant into the world and not wanting him.

*It would have been more honest to put the unwanted infant in an orphanage. It would have been more loving to put him up for adoption.* At least the adoptive parents would have *wanted* the child.

## WRITING LETTERS

Imagine that you, the wise and gentle old wizard, want to adopt a child. Imagine that the child you want to adopt is *you as an infant.* Further, imagine that you need to write this infant child a letter. Infants can't read, of course, but trust me, it's important to write the letter. (Don't write the letter if you don't really want to reclaim your precious infant. However, I assume that you do, or you wouldn't have bought this book.) The letter need not be long, maybe just a paragraph or two. Tell your wonderful inner infant that you love him and are so glad that he is a boy (or a girl). Tell him that you *want* him and will give him the time he needs to grow and develop. Assure him that you know what he needs from you, that you will give it to him, and that you will work hard to see him as the precious and wonderfully unique person he is. When you've finished your letter, read it aloud very slowly and notice how you're feeling. It's okay to be sad and to cry if you want to.

Following is the letter I wrote.

Dear Little John:

   I'm so glad you were born. I love you and want you to always be with me. I'm very glad you are a boy, and I want to help you grow up.

   I want a chance to show you how much you matter to me.

Love,<br>Big John

### Letter from Your Inner Infant

Now, although you might think it very strange, I want you to write yourself a letter *from* your inner infant. *Write it with your nondominant hand.* If you are right-handed, that means using your left hand. (This technique calls on the nondominant side of your brain, bypassing the

more controlling, logical side. It makes it easier to get in touch with
the feelings of your inner child.) Of course, I know that infants can't
write! But please do the exercise. Remember, if an infant could write,
he probably wouldn't write much—probably just a short paragraph.
Here is how my letter looked.

Dear John:
I want you to come and
get me I want to matter
to someone. I don't want to
be alone. Love,
Little John

## AFFIRMATIONS

If your infancy needs were not met, your wounded inner infant is
still present with all his original energy. He still needs the nurturing
you never got, still needs to hear words that will welcome him into
the world. One way to give yourself what you didn't get is through
affirmations. In her book *Cycles of Power,* Pam Levin presents affirmations for every developmental stage. While an infant can't understand
the actual meaning of words, he can grasp their nonverbal aspect. If
your mother was disappointed that you were a boy or didn't really
want you, she didn't have to tell you so: you knew it. Dad may never
have told you he was disappointed that you were a girl, but you
knew it. More than likely no one ever told you that you weren't
wanted, *but you knew it.*

Some children actually *are* told that they're not wanted. One of my
clients was told that her mother almost died when she was born;
another was told that her father had wanted her mother to have an
abortion. I've heard many other cruel and unbelievable statements of
this kind.

Words are extremely powerful. Kind words can create a whole day of happiness. Critical words can put us in a funk for a week. *Sticks and stones will break your bones, but names will hurt you more.* Saying new, empowering words can touch our original pain and trigger great healing.

Positive affirmations reinforce our beingness and can heal the spiritual wound. Pam Levin has stated that "affirming messages can even produce changes in the cardiac and respiratory rate of patients in a coma."

Repeated positive messages are *emotional nutrients.* Had you heard them, they would have helped your inner infant child grow and develop. Repeating such messages now can produce deep, visceral changes and touch our most primal level of original pain. Using Pam Levin's core model, I've expanded the infancy affirmations to include some other aspects of infants' needs.

Here are the loving words you can say to your inner infant during the meditation. Your inner infant will hear them from you as the gentle and wise old wizard. (Use whichever ones you like best.)

Welcome to the world, I've been waiting for you.

I'm so glad you are here.

I've prepared a special place for you to live.

I like you just the way you are.

I will not leave you, no matter what.

Your needs are okay with me.

I'll give you all the time you need to get your needs met.

I'm so glad you're a boy (or a girl).

I want to take care of you and I'm prepared to do that.

I like feeding you, bathing you, changing you, and spending
     time with you.

In all the world, there has never been another like you.

God smiled when you were born.

## INNER INFANT MEDITATION

You'll need an hour, uninterrupted, for this meditation. I recommend that you have a box of Kleenex or a handkerchief at hand. Sit in a comfortable chair with your arms and legs uncrossed. It's a good idea to tell someone you trust when you are about to do this exercise (unless there's a risk of his shaming you for doing it). You may want to check in with this person when you're finished. Please remember what I told you in the introduction to this section. *Do not do this exercise if:*

- You have been diagnosed as mentally ill or have a history of mental illness.
- You're an untreated victim of physical or sexual violence, including rape.
- You were severely battered emotionally.
- You are a recovering chemical addict without a year of continuous sobriety.
- You do not have your therapist's permission.

If you have religious objections to meditation, you need to know that there is nothing in this exercise that is anti-God. Furthermore, you need to be aware that you go in and out of a trance state several times every day. There is nothing I'll ask you to do that you do not already do or know how to do. Remember that the problem of the wounded inner child results partly from *spontaneous* age regression. In doing a meditation that involves age regression, you are actually taking *control* of this process. Remember also that you can stop at any time if you're feeling overwhelmed. It is perfectly all right to stop in the middle of the meditation if you need to.

The first part of this meditation will be used for all the developmental stages. Record it on your tape recorder, pausing for about fifteen seconds in silence between phrases as indicated.

> **Start by sitting quietly and becoming aware of your surroundings. . . . Locate yourself in space and time. Feel your back and bottom touching the chair you're sitting in. . . . Feel your clothes on your body. . . . Hear as many different sounds as you can hear. . . . Feel the air in the room. . . . Just for now, there's no place you *have* to go and nothing you *have* to do. . . . Just be here now. . . . You can close your eyes if you haven't already done so. . . . You can be aware of your breathing. . . . Feel the air as it comes in and as it goes out. . . . Be aware of how it feels in your nostrils as you breathe in and as you breathe out. . . . If you have interrupting thoughts, that's okay. You can just notice**

them as if they were the sentences going across your TV screen during a program announcing heavy rains or an approaching storm. The important thing is just to notice them. Just allow them to pass by.... As you continue your breathing, you can *hold on* to your consciousness as much as you want.... Or you can *let go* in ways that you know which allow you to relax.... You learned to *hold on* and *let go* as a child.... And you really know just exactly how much to *hold on* and how much to *let go*.... You learned the perfect balance when you learned to breathe as an infant.... You learned to breathe in ... and hold on long enough to oxygenate all your blood cells.... And you learned to *let go* ... and feel the air go out.... As an infant, you learned how to suck your mother's nipple.... You learned to suck your bottle.... And to *let go* as you tasted the warm milk.... You soon learned to *hold on* to your own bottle.... And to let it go when you were finished.... And you learned to hold on to the side of your crib.... And to *let go* when you were ready to lie back down.... So you really *know* exactly how much to hold on and how much to let go.... And you can trust yourself to find just exactly what you need for you....

And now you may be feeling a kind of heaviness in your eyelids.... You can just let them close *tightly*.... You may feel that heaviness in your jaw.... In your arms and hands.... You may feel like you can't move your hands.... And you may feel like there is a heaviness in your legs and feet.... Like you can't move your legs.... Or you may feel just the opposite, like your whole body is floating.... Like your hands and arms are like feathers.... You really know what *you* feel, *heaviness* or *lightness*.... And whatever that is, it is exactly right for *you*....

And now you can begin experiencing some childhood memories.... You can remember your first school days ... and your best friend in those days.... You can remember a kind teacher or neighbor.... And you can remember a house you lived in *before* you went to school.... What color was the house?... Was it an apartment?...A trailer?...Did you live in the city? ...In the country?...Now you can see some of the rooms in that house.... Where did you spend your time in that house? ...Did you have a special room?...Where was the dinner table?... See who is at the dinner table.... What did it *feel* like to be at that table?... What did it *feel* like to live in that house?...

*This is the general introduction for each developmental stage.* The specific *stage-related* instruction is different for each stage.

Now imagine or remember the house your family lived in when you were born.... Imagine the room where you slept after you were born.... See the beautiful infant you were.... Hear your voice as you coo, cry, laugh.... Imagine you could hold your cuddly little self.... You are there as a wise and gentle wizard.... You are viewing your own infancy.... Who else is there?... Your mom?... Your dad?... What does it *feel* like to be born in this house to these people?... Now imagine you are that precious tiny infant looking out at all of this.... Look up at the grown-up you.... See yourself as a magical person, a wizard, or just yourself.... Feel the presence of *someone* who loves you. Now imagine that the grown-up-you picked you up and held you. Hear him tenderly tell you the following affirmations:

Welcome to the world, I've been waiting for you.
I'm so glad you're here.
I've prepared a special place for you to live.
I like you just the way you are.
I will not leave you, no matter what.
Your needs are okay with me.
I'll give you all the time you need to get your needs met.
I'm so glad you're a boy (or a girl).
I want to take care of you, and I'm prepared to do that.
I like feeding you, bathing you, changing you, and spending time with you.
In all the world, there has never been another like you.
God smiled when you were born.

Let yourself feel whatever you feel when you hear these affirmations....

Now, let your grown-up-you put you down.... Hear him assure you that he will never leave you.... And that from now on, he will always be available to you.... Now become your grown-up self again.... Look at your precious little infant self.... Be aware that you have just reclaimed him.... *Feel the sense of that homecoming*.... That little infant is wanted, loved, and will *never* be *alone again*.... Walk out of that room, out of that house, and look back as you walk away.... Stroll forward *up* memory lane.... Walk past your first school.... Walk into your teenage years.... Walk into an early adult memory.... Now walk into where you are *right now*.... Feel your toes.... Wiggle them.... Feel the energy come up through your legs.... Feel energy in your chest as you take a deep breath.... Make a noise as you exhale.... Feel the energy in your arms and fingers.... Wiggle your fingers.... Feel the energy in your shoulders, neck, and jaw.... Stretch your arms.... Feel your face and be fully present.... Be fully restored to your normal waking consciousness.... And open your eyes.

Sit for a while and let yourself reflect on the experience you just had. Feel whatever you feel. Pay attention to the affirmations that touched you the most. Reflect on those words, letting yourself feel the nourishment of them. If you had an angry reaction, let yourself feel the anger. For example, you may have thought, "This is stupid, this is a game, no one really ever wanted me!" Just let yourself feel the anger. Let yourself yell it out! Beat your pillow with a tennis racket or bat if you feel like it. At the end of the reflection, write down your thoughts and impressions if you feel like it. Talk to your spouse, sponsor, or friend if you want to. Be aware that the grown-up adult you can take care of the little you—your infant self.

Some people find that they have trouble visualizing in response to the instructions. We all perceptualize, but not everyone visualizes readily. Each of us has a primary way of mapping the world. If you are primarily visual, you probably say things like, "That looks good to me," or "I can see myself doing that." But if you are primarily auditory, you might say, "That sounds good to me," or "Something tells me to do that." People whose perception is kinesthetic will tend to say, "That feels right to me," or "I'm moved to do it." So don't worry if you have difficulty visualizing—you will perceptualize in your own way.

Sometimes people cannot see, hear, or feel their wounded inner child. I have found that the reason for this is that during the exercise they *are* the child. They are actually in their wounded child state. If that happened to you, just go back and do the meditation again, letting yourself see the grown-up you and hear your grown-up self giving you the affirmations of nourishing love.

Some people feel that the child will be a new burden if they agree to bring him home. If you experienced this, you are probably over-burdened with responsibility already. Just remember that to keep in contact with your inner child takes only a few minutes a day. This is a child you don't have to feed, clothe, or baby-sit. Loving and nurturing your inner child is a way to give time to yourself—which you proba-bly haven't been doing.

Sometimes people feel angry or disgusted when they see the infant child they once were. This indicates a severe level of toxic shame. We shame ourselves the way we've been shamed. If your survival figures rejected you for your vulnerability as an infant, you may reject your-self the same way. If you felt anger, contempt, or disgust when you did this exercise, you have to make a decision about your willingness to accept the weak, vulnerable part of yourself. I assure you that this is a real part of you. It is a part of all of us.

Until you are willing to accept your weakest, most helpless self you cannot be whole and truly powerful. One part of your energy and strength will be involved in rejecting another part of you. It takes a lot of your time, energy, and power to keep this internal warfare going on. Paradoxical as it seems, your strength will only come by accepting your weakness!

Now that you've reclaimed your infant self, spend several days repeating the affirmations to him. Imagine cuddling your infant self and saying out loud: "You belong here! There has never been another you. You are unrepeatable, one of a kind." Add the affirmations that triggered the most emotion—they're the ones you most need to hear. Go sit in a park and look at the grass, flowers, birds, trees, and animals. They all belong to the universe. They are a necessary part of creation. And you also belong. You are just as necessary as the birds and bees and trees and flowers. You belong on this earth. *Welcome!*

## Working With a Partner

If you would like to do these exercises with a partner, that's great. Each of you needs to be there for the other in a special way. Because the inner child needs to know that you're not going to leave suddenly, you have to make a commitment to be present for each other while you're doing this work. You don't need to do anything special, and you certainly don't need to therapize or fix each other. You just need to be as present for your partner as you possibly can. One of you will be the affirmation giver. I advise you to stay with the affirmations as I've worded them. (In a recent workshop a woman got carried away when she gave one of the men in her group affirmations. She told him, "Welcome to the world. You are so wanted. I want to have sex with you." This is *not* what an infant needs to hear from a mothering person!) When one of you has experienced the exercise, switch places.

When you work together it is valuable to hold and caress your partner as you give him the affirmations. This needs to be checked out carefully ahead of time. Most adult children have had their physical boundaries severely violated. Show your partner how you like to be held and caressed. Obviously, if you don't want to be touched, tell him.

When you are ready to do the exercise, read the general introduction of the meditation to your partner. Read it slowly and carefully. You can play some lullaby music in the background. I recommend Steven Halpern's *Lullaby Suite*. After you have read the line "Hear him tenderly tell you the following affirmations," *say the affirmations out loud to your partner*. Then finish reading the exercise. The difference between working the exercise alone and with a partner is that when you have a partner, you say the affirmations out loud while holding and caressing your partner in the physical ways he desires. When you are finished, reverse roles with your partner.

## Working With a Group

In my inner child workshops, most of the reclaiming work is done in groups. I believe that group work is the most powerful form of therapy. At the end of the workshop I tell the participants that they have been the primary resource for one another. I want people to know what they can accomplish by themselves.

However, I always have several trained therapists available during the reclaiming process. They are there in case a person goes into emotional overwhelm. Overwhelm can occur when a person regresses into toxically shamed or enmeshed emotions. These emotions are more disturbing than one's own natural emotions. In fact, one cannot be overwhelmed by one's natural emotions.

The following suggestions are offered to:

- therapists or trained counselors who wish to lead groups through the reclaiming process;
- members of CODA, ACOA, or other recovery groups who are committed to mutual self-help;
- others who are seriously pursuing personal growth and who are willing to conform to the guidelines I provide.

To form a group, you need a minimum of five people and no more than nine. You need *both* sexes in a group—at least two people of the opposite sex. The reason for this is that you were parented by a mom and a dad, and you need to hear male and female voices.

If the group members don't know one another, I suggest you do the following:

A. Spend some time together as a group before you begin the exercises. Have at least three 1½-hour meetings. Spend the first meeting introducing yourselves and sharing safe examples of wounded inner child contamination. Go out and have refreshments together afterward.

  At the next meeting, let each person spend ten minutes sharing about his family of origin and his childhood. (Have a timekeeper.) Let the third meeting be more spontaneous. But be sure to give each person ten minutes to share. You can spend more than 1½ hours if you wish, but I've found that some structure is necessary in order to get maximum benefit. The ten-minute time structure is especially important. Some wounded kids can't stop talking; others are hysterics who use emotional noise (continuous problems) to ensure that they get attention.

B. After everyone has spent time together, each person must *verbally commit to be there for the whole process* (the exercises covering the five developmental stages of childhood from infancy through adolescence). Again, what the wounded inner child needs to know more than anything is that someone will be there for him. Plan your schedules around your group meetings, making sure that each of you can commit to be there.

C. Next, physical boundaries should be clearly set. This involves each person stating very clearly what his physical and sexual boundaries are. If a person in the group makes a sexual joke that disturbs you, you should discuss it. If you are sexually compulsive, make a commitment to yourself not to act out with any member of your group. (If you're not sexually compulsive but feel a sexual attraction to someone in your group, make the same commitment.)

It is crucial for each person to realize that he is there to support and allow the others to *feel the feelings*. The group members' job is to be mirrors and echoes for one another. This involves statements such as, "I see your lips quivering and I hear your sadness as you cry," or, "I felt anger (or fear or sadness) when you were describing your childhood." As a group member, you should *never* therapize, offer advice, or try to "fix" the member who is working. Imagine yourself as a video recorder replaying what you just observed. Analyzing, discussing, and giving advice keep you stuck in your head and out of your feelings. When you discuss and give advice, you take the other person out of his feelings.

Many adult children learned to matter by becoming caretakers. Therefore, they have an *addiction* to fixing and helping. Often they distract the person from his emotions by using statements such as, "Look at the bright side," or "Now let's look at your alternatives," or by asking *why* questions ("Why do you think your father drank?"). The *best* phrases to use are: "How are you feeling now?" or, "What was that like for you?" or, "If your sadness could speak, what would it say?" These encourage people to express their emotions.

Remember, this is *original pain* work. We often try to take people out of their emotions because our own emotions are unresolved. For example, if you begin sobbing, it may touch my unresolved sadness. *If I can stop you, I don't have to feel my own pain.* But my apparent help in stopping your emotions is *no help at all for you.* Actually it's confusing and crazymaking, and it's probably what happened to you when you were a child. Your comforters, who were purportedly helping you, were actually *keeping you from doing what would help you the most—letting you feel your feelings.*

Helpers are *always* helping themselves. Having learned to matter by helping, they overcome their deep sense of powerlessness by helping others.

There *is* a true helping, however. It involves letting other people be *who they are,* letting them have their own feelings and acknowledging those feelings when they are having them. Such acknowledgment can be expressed as: "I see and hear you, and I value you just as you are. I accept and respect your reality."

When you have been brought up in a dysfunctional shame-based family, it is difficult to be there for others in the ways I've described. No one of us will do it perfectly. No group can do it perfectly. When you're aware of being in your own neediness, simply acknowledge that what you're saying to the person is about *you,* not about him.

However, if your partner or a person in your group becomes truly overwhelmed, stop the exercise. Get him or her to look you in the eye and answer short factual questions like, "What color is my shirt? Where do you live? What kind of car do you have? What color is it? How many people are in this room right now? What are their names?" These questions force the person to focus on the sensory-based present. When people feel overwhelmed they are caught in an internal state. They are re-experiencing the accumulated reservoir of old frozen feelings and are caught in the energy of the past. You need to help them get back to the present. The questions will ground them in the now.

When you're ready to do this exercise, first select the person in your group who has the most peaceful voice to put the meditation on tape (p. 94). Record it until it reads, "Now imagine that you are that precious tiny infant looking out at all of this." *Do not record the affirmations;* instead, give each person a copy of the affirmations list. Instruct the group members to touch their left thumbs and one of their left fingers together. Let them hold that touch for about thirty seconds, then instruct them to let their fingers go. Continue recording the meditation with the words "Walk out of the room, out of that house . . ." (p. 97) and so on until the end.

Now play back the recording for the group. When it is finished, everyone will have reexperienced feelings of how it was to be born in their family. And each will have made an *anchor* of this feeling with his left thumb and finger. An anchor is any sensory trigger that is associated with a past experience. (Old songs are good examples of anchors. We hear an old song and we associate it with an old boyfriend or girlfriend or the summer we were fifteen. Facial expressions are anchors. If your dad frowned a certain way before he criticized you, any man who frowns at you in a similar way will fire that old anchor.) Our most automatic anchors are the results of trauma. Chapter 9 has an entire remapping exercise using anchors.

Next, form the group into a circle with one chair in the middle. Group members will take turns working in the center of the circle. When each takes his turn to work, he will *first set his physical boundaries.* For example, tell the group how close to sit to you, and how or if you want to be held, touched, and caressed. The person in the center begins working by touching his left thumb and finger—that is, by touching the sensory anchor they created during the meditation. The purpose of this is to get in *touch* with early infancy memories. Let me note here that you will *always* be more in touch with the memories than you think you are. *Co-dependents will generally think they are not getting the exercise right.* Guard against comparing yourself with others in the group. The toxic shaming that created your co-dependence resulted from your being *compared* with your parents' images of how a child should be.

Be very careful to stay out of your head with self-talk such as, "I know I'm doing this wrong," or, "The person before me started sobbing and I'm not even crying." The only self-talk to give yourself is, "I am doing this *exactly* the way *I* need to do it."

Once you are in the center, having set your physical boundaries and touched your anchor, the process begins.

Each of your group members slowly and affectionately gives you one affirmation he or she has chosen from the list on pages 96–97. There should be an interval of twenty seconds before the next member gives you the affirmation he has chosen. After twenty seconds, the next member gives you an affirmation, until the group has gone around *three* times. (This means that some of the affirmations will probably be repeated.) Be sure you have a box of tissues for the person sitting in the center. When everyone in the support group has given three affirmations, let the person in the middle sit for a couple of minutes. After that time, tap him on the shoulder and let him rejoin the group. *Do not discuss the exercise until every member has had his turn to work.* When everyone is finished, let each person share his experience of being in the center. Remember, each person's experience will be unique.

As you share your experience, try to focus on the following things.

- Which affirmations did you choose to give the person in the center? Was there a pattern? Did you find yourself repeating the same affirmation several times? The affirmations you choose to give are often one(s) *you* most need to hear.

- Was there an affirmation given to you that triggered an immediate release of energy, anger, sadness, or fear? For example, many women sob when they hear the words, "I'm glad you're a girl." Some people cry when they hear, "You'll have all the time you need." Pay attention to *voltage*. Voltage, or emotional intensity, is where the emotional energy is blocked. This high voltage affirmation may be the kind of nourishment you most need in your life.

- Pay attention to the male and female voices. Did a male voice trigger fear, anger, or sadness? Did a female voice trigger a special emotion? This is important information in setting up the championing program in part 3. Knowing the specific kinds of nourishment your inner child needs is vital to your nurturing him or her.

When you've given everyone an opportunity to share, the group process ends.

Here's the way I like to imagine the reclaiming of my infant self.

Now that you've reclaimed your infant self, we can move on to reclaim your toddler.

# CHAPTER 5

# RECLAIMING YOUR TODDLER SELF

Glory be to God for dappled things—
For skies of couple-color as a brinded cow;
For rose-moles all in stipple upon trout that swim;
Fresh-firecoal chestnut falls; finches' wings; . . .
Whatever is fickle, freckled (who knows how?)

—GERARD MANLEY HOPKINS

He who tiptoes cannot stand,
He who strides cannot walk.

—CHINESE PROVERB

TODDLER

*(OPPOSITIONAL BONDING)*

I AM ME

| | |
|---|---|
| AGE: | 9 MONTHS–18 MONTHS |
| | (EXPLORATORY STAGE) |
| | 18 MONTHS–3 YEARS |
| | (SEPARATION STAGE) |
| DEVELOPMENTAL POLARITY: | AUTONOMY VERSUS SHAME AND DOUBT |
| EGO STRENGTH: | WILLPOWER |
| POWER: | SENSING AND DOING |
| RELATIONSHIP ISSUE: | PSYCHOLOGICAL BIRTH; COUNTER-DEPENDENCE |

# INDEX OF SUSPICION

Answer yes or no to the following questions. After you read each question, wait and get in touch with what you feel. If you feel a stronger energy for yes, answer yes; for no, answer no. If you answer any question yes, you can suspect that your wonderful inner child of the past has been wounded. There are degrees of woundedness. You are somewhere on a scale from one to a hundred. The more questions you *feel* are to be answered yes, the more your toddler self was wounded.

1. Do you have trouble knowing what you want? Yes _____ No _____

2. Are you afraid to explore when you go to a new place? Yes _____ No _____

3. Are you afraid to try out *new* experiences? If you do try them, do you always wait till someone else has tried first? Yes _____ No _____

4. Do you have great fears of abandonment? Yes _____ No _____

5. In difficult situations, do you long for someone to tell you what to do? Yes _____ No _____

6. If someone gives you a suggestion, do you feel you ought to follow it? Yes _____ No _____

7. Do you have trouble actually being *in* your experience? For example, when you're on vacation looking at an exciting sight, are you worrying about the tour bus leaving without you? Yes _____ No _____

8. Are you a big worrier? Yes _____ No _____

9. Do you have trouble being spontaneous? For example, would you be embarrassed to sing in front of a group of people just because you were happy? Yes _____ No _____

10. Do you find yourself in frequent conflicts with people in authority? Yes _____ No _____

11. Do you often use words that center on defecation or urination—like asshole, shit, or piss? Does your sense of humor focus on bathroom jokes? Yes _____ No _____

12. Are you obsessed with men's or women's buttocks? Do you prefer to fantasize about or engage in anal sex more than any other kind? Yes _____ No _____

13. Are you often accused of being stingy with money, love, showing emotions, or affection? Yes _____ No _____

14. Do you tend to be obsessive about neatness and cleanliness? Yes _____ No _____

15. Do you fear anger in other people? In yourself? Yes _____ No _____

16. Will you do almost anything to avoid conflict? Yes _____ No _____

17. Do you feel guilty when you say no to someone? Yes _____ No _____

18. Do you avoid saying no directly, but often refuse to do what you've said you would in a variety of indirectly manipulative and passive ways? Yes _____ No _____

19. Do you sometimes "go berserk" and inappropriately let go of all control? Yes _____ No _____

20. Are you often excessively critical of other people? Yes _____ No _____

21. Do you act nice to people when you're with them and then gossip about and criticize them when they go away? Yes _____ No _____

**22. When you achieve success, do you have trouble enjoying or even believing in your accomplishments? Yes _____ No _____**


These questions cover the toddler period. Questions 1 through 9 cover ages 9 months to 18 months. This is the first part of the toddler stage, which involves crawling, touching, tasting, and in general being curious and eager to explore the world around you.

Questions 10 through 22 cover ages 18 months to 3 years. This period is called the *separation* stage. It is a *counter-dependence* stage characterized by *oppositional bonding.* In oppositional bonding, the child will say things such as, "No," "Let me do it," and "I won't," especially in response to parental requests. He disobeys, but always within parental eyesight. The child is still bonded, but must oppose the parents in order to separate and be himself.

This separation process has been referred to as second birth or psychological birth. It marks the true beginning of our I AMness.

Now we begin the journey of exploring our surroundings and discovering who we are by testing our powers. To the 9-month-old, the world is a sensory cornucopia, filled with interesting things to explore. If a basic sense of trust has been established in the first nine months of life, the child will naturally begin exploring his environment. He wants especially to see, to touch, and to taste.

Erik Erikson refers to this as the "incorporation" stage. A child wants to "take everything in" and incorporate it into his life. This basic curiosity, if nurtured, will become the source of all future creative risk taking and adventure.

This is a risky time for children, since they don't know the difference between an interesting-looking dark object and an electric socket. Children in the exploration period require constant care and immense patience. Parents need a fair amount of emotional balance in order to handle this well.

Exploration and separation intensify as the child's muscles begin to develop. He learns to crawl, then to walk. It's all part of the natural plan. Erikson sees muscle development in terms of "holding on" and "letting go." Each of us must learn to balance holding on and letting go. Learning to walk, eat, control elimination, play with toys, swing, swim, and run requires this balance of holding on and letting go. The child learns this balance as he develops muscle power and *willpower.*

The child has good willpower when he can "hold on" appropriately (when you have "to go" and you're at church) and "let go" appropriately (when Mom puts you on the potty).

Holding on and letting go also involve the balance of emotions. The natural life spark moves children to be themselves, to want to do things their own way. At first, children have no emotional balance. Their drive toward autonomy is overreactive. They have not yet tested what they can and cannot do. At this stage they tend to be absolutists and may behave as little "dictators." They throw temper tantrums when they don't get what they want. What they need are firm but patient parents who will set age-appropriate limits and will "child-proof" a room or two. At this age the child needs both parents. Sometimes he's too much for Mom to handle and she needs a rest. Dad needs to support Mom and set healthy limits. Dad is the symbol of individualism; Mom is the symbol of incorporation.

Dad and Mom both need to model the healthy expression of anger and good skills in resolving conflict. Conflict resolution is crucial for the establishment of healthy intimacy. Children need to see their parents resolve their own conflicts. In other words, they need to see an honest relationship in which both parents express their true feelings and resolve their disagreements.

Children need to express their separateness and explore their differences. At first, they want everything that feels good and is plea-surable. As Mom and Dad intervene to set limits, conflict occurs. Children need to learn that *they can be angry at Mom and Dad and Mom and Dad will still be there*. They must be taught how to resolve conflict and that they can't have everything their own way. They need to learn that *no*'s have consequences and that you can't have it both ways. (You can't say "no" you won't go and then when you realize that the family is going swimming, say "yes.") These lessons are learned in the toddler period as the child develops a sense of shame and doubt.

Healthy shame is simply an emotion of *limits*. It gives us permission to be human, to be imperfect. We don't need much shame—just enough to know that we are not God. "Shame safeguards the spirit," Nietzsche said. Doubt keeps us from jumping out of second-story windows and allows us to put up guardrails to secure our safety.

Healthy willpower is the goal of this stage. It allows us to develop the *power of doing*. We cannot do things well without discipline, a balance between holding on and letting go. Someone once said that of all masks of freedom, discipline is the most mysterious. We need discipline to be free.

Without healthy willpower we have no discipline. We don't know how to hold on or to let go appropriately. We either let go inappropriately (act with license) or hold on inappropriately (hoard, overcontrol, become obsessive/compulsive). However, those who do learn to hold on appropriately have a good foundation for fidelity and love; and those who learn to let go appropriately are willing to grieve life's transitions and know when to move on.

One of the major outcomes of healthy autonomy, besides balanced willpower, is the achievement of "object constancy." This means simply that every child by age 3 needs to understand that *nobody's perfect*, neither his parents nor himself. A healthy sense of shame helps to achieve this understanding. "Mom and Dad are human. They will not always do what I want or give me what I want. If they are healthy, they will give me what I *need*. When they set limits, I'll often get angry. But that's the way I learn *balance*." Object constancy allows us to see the world as the *imperfect* phenomenon it actually is. When the child realizes that the *same* parents will sometimes give him pleasure and sometimes take it away, the parents remain *constant*, even though they can be both good and bad from the child's viewpoint. A child also needs to learn that he has polarities. Some days he's happy; some days he's sad. Happy or sad, he is still the same person. Adults who have a wounded inner child who failed to learn this lesson tend to be rigid and absolutist. They think in all-or-nothing extremes.

As children achieve separation, they begin the work of setting boundaries. Knowing what is mine and what is yours is essential for establishing a good relationship. As a toddler, you said "that's mine" a lot. You had to in order to know what was yours and what belonged to someone else.

## GROWTH DISORDER

At this stage it is especially important that parents have good boundaries. It is also important for them to have a strong sense of willpower. As I stated earlier, willpower is an ego strength that forms the substance of good boundaries. In addition, willpower allows you to control your emotions by expressing them when it's appropriate (when someone puts his suitcase on your hat) and suppressing them when it's appropriate (when the policeman stops you for speeding). It also allows you to say *no* to yourself and others. Most important, willpower rests solidly on a good sense of balance.

Parents who are adult children themselves do not have a good sense of balance. They either don't know when to say no or they always say no. Sometimes they say yes and then say no in inconsistent and manipulative ways.

As a toddler, I resolved this issue by learning to hold on excessively. I squelched my sense of autonomy by becoming a perfectly obedient little boy. I was Mom's "little helper" and Grandma's "good boy." I became overadapted. My wonder child went into hiding.

When I tried to express other parts of myself—anger, being messy, laughing loudly, and so on—I was shamed. My potty training must have been a nightmare! For years I have feared going to the bathroom where anyone might know that that's what I was doing. As a child I would go from person to person in the family, telling them not to come into the bathroom, and then I would lock the bathroom door. This is hardly normal, instinctual behavior. I always ran the faucet in the bathroom so that no one would hear me urinating. I wanted to hire a band for #2!

I thought my body was evil, or at least dirty. My religious tradition saw human life as a valley of tears. Life was what you had to endure to get to death. Death was when you had it made! The black habits of priests and nuns and the black box for confessing shame and guilt were the symbols of God in my environment.

My parents too had been spiritually abused by these traditions. My dad had no boundaries; he was shame-based to the core. A toxically shamed person believes that nothing about himself is okay. To be shame-based is to have no limits, which sets you up for addiction. My dad was addicted in all kinds of ways. He couldn't say no. Later, when I was old enough to rebel, I followed his lead.

My mom was *duty-bound.* She was the overadapted good woman, wife, and mother. The problem with duty is that it is rigid, judgmental, and perfectionistic. I thank God for my mother, because I wouldn't have survived without her sense of duty. Holding on is better than letting go when you're raising young children. Nonetheless, perfectionistic duty-bound morality creates shame-based children.

To be duty-bound is to feel that you have no right to joy. The duty-bound mother hates joy because to do what she enjoys produces *guilt.* Duty creates human "doings." As Marion Woodman puts it: "For the perfectionist who has trained herself *to do,* simply *being* sounds like a euphemism for ceasing to exist."

The growth disorder of this period is a loss of balance. Until I recovered my wounded inner child, I either held on excessively or let go excessively. I was either a saint (celibate) studying to be a priest or an out-of-control alcoholic pursuing sexual orgies. I was either good or bad, but never both; and I saw others as either good or bad but never both. What I finally learned in recovery is that I am no "gooder" than I am "bad" (pardon the English). Always being a "good boy" is inhuman, as is always trying to please. I remember well one of my family's rules for expressing oneself: "If you can't say something nice, don't say anything at all." This rule was made famous by Thumper in Walt Disney's *Bambi.* But Thumper was a rabbit!

The wounded child's growth disorder at this stage can be summed up as follows:

*Spiritual wound—denial of I AMness.* It's not okay to be you. The spiritual wound most often starts at this age.

*Toxic shame.* Toxic shame says that nothing about you is okay. What you feel, do, and think are wrong. You are defective as a human being.

*Empowerment for offender behavior.* Lack of discipline creates offender behavior. An offender wants what he wants no matter what the consequences. He takes no responsibility for his irresponsible behavior.

*Compulsive overcontrol.* By overadapting, your inner child became a people-pleasing caretaker. You learned to rule by the letter of the law. You are critical and judgmental of yourself and others.

*Addictions.* Your inner child can't say no. You're an addict. You overdrink, overeat, overspend, or oversex.

*Isolation.* Your inner child is isolated and alone. This is the only way he feels that he has any boundaries. No one can hurt you if you do not interact with anyone.

*Lack of balance—boundary problems.* Because your inner child never learned to balance holding on and letting go, you are (1) stingy either with money, emotions, praise, or love, or you are wild and crazy and totally out of control. You give away everything, including yourself. Your lack of balance leads you to (2) either overcontrol your children (rigid discipline) or refuse to give them any real limits (oversubmission or license); or you may do one and then the other.

There is no consistency or balance in your parenting. Without good counter-dependence skills you have (3) severe relationship problems. You are either enmeshed, entwined, entrapped (can't leave), or isolated and lonely in the relationship.

While the toddler stage was not the time your inner child accepted his family-system roles, a certain propensity for your choice of roles was set up at that time. As my inner child experienced separation and anger as abandonment, I developed a propensity toward people-pleasing and caretaking.

## DEBRIEFING

In getting the facts about your toddler self's history, use the following questions as guidelines.

1. Who was around when you were 2 to 3? Where was your dad? Did he play with you often? Spend time with you? Did Dad and Mom stay married? Where was your mom? Was she patient? Did she spend time with you? Were either or both parents addicts?
2. How did your mom and dad discipline you? If physical—*what exactly was done to you—give details.* If emotional, how were you terrorized? Were you told you would be spanked or punished when your father got home? Were you made to get your own switches, belt, et cetera?
3. Did you have any older brothers or sisters? How did they treat you?
4. Who was there *for* you? Who held you when you were scared or crying? Set firm but kind and gentle limits when you were angry? Who played, laughed, and had fun with you?

Write out as much as you can about your toddler self's history. Pay attention to anything you now know about family *secrets* that you couldn't have known as a child. For example, was Dad a sex addict, having lots of affairs? Is either parent an untreated victim of physical, sexual, or emotional violence? I know a man who found out at age 40 that his mother had been incested both physically and nonphysically. He himself had "acted out" sexually for years; he tended to choose women who were untreated incest victims. He was very bonded to his mom, and my belief is that he carried her unresolved incest and acted it out.

Family *secrets* are always about the family's toxic shame, and you need to understand as much as possible about that. In your writing, focus on all the ways you were shamed—all the ways your feelings, needs, and desires were repressed. Also focus on the *lack* of discipline in your home. Notice *how you were falsely empowered* by not being disciplined. Notice that no one cared enough to give you limits; no one cared enough about you to teach you to give and take. No one taught you to take responsibility for your behavior.

Write about any *traumatic incidents* you remember. Include every concrete detail you can. For example, if you write about the time you were punished for what your brother actually did, write, "My brother and I were playing with two Raggedy Ann dolls. One was tattered and the stuffing was coming out. They were painted red and blue, but the details were fading. My brother grabbed my doll and ripped the arm off of it. He immediately ran to Mom and told her that *I* had ripped *his* doll. He was her favorite! She immediately slapped me twice, one blow hit my back, the other hit my bottom. It hurt and I ran to my room crying. My brother started laughing."

You may not remember all the details, but put down whatever you can remember. There is a therapeutic slogan that says, "You cannot fail with detail." Detail is closer to actual experience and therefore comes closer to touching your actual feelings. For example, it will impact you very little if I tell you that a woman in a recent workshop told me that her father had incested her from ages 1½ to 4. You may be horrified at the *thought* but not have a real emotional response. But now I will tell you that he laid her between his legs every night and made her suck his penis, which he taught her to do by putting a nipple on it. Now you may *feel* some of the horrible betrayal and pain this woman felt.

## SHARING YOUR TODDLERHOOD WITH A FRIEND

As before, it's crucial for you to share the history of your toddlerhood with a nurturing, supportive person. The thing to focus on is that the so-called "terrible twos" behavior is as *natural* as night following day. At 9 months every child will begin to crawl and explore. At 18 months every child will start saying *no* and having tantrums when he doesn't get his way.

Two-year-old behavior has nothing to do with being "bad" or "good." It certainly has nothing to do with anything mythical like *original sin*. I, along with many other children, was taught that I was born stained with the sins of my first parents, Adam and Eve, that I had evil and selfish inclinations, and that discipline and punishment were for my own good (although I was not physically spanked much as a child).

If you watch a toddler at play, you will have to stretch your imagination to conclude that the child is bad and has evil inclinations. The one who wants to spank, punish, and curtail him is his parents' own wounded inner child. The parents' wounded child does this out of an overadapted fear of abandonment or out of the need to get revenge (doing to their children what they wished they could have done to their own parents).

Children are needy and immature, and they are tough to handle in toddlerhood, but they are *not* moral villains! Piaget has shown what the wisdom of the ages has known: The age of reason begins at about age 7. A legitimate sense of morality is not even possible before this.

Share with your support person how your toddler self got violated. Let him be there for you and listen to you read your story. You need an ally to *legitimize* and *validate* the hurt and pain your precious little toddler has gone through.

If you're an offender, you need to have your own abuse legitimized. You had no one to set limits and teach you the discipline of self-responsibility. True, offender behavior is *never* justifiable. But offenders were most often victims first. In part 3 I'll suggest ways you can teach your wounded inner child some discipline. You'll have to work hard on developing your conscience.

Telling your story of violation to your support person is a way of reducing your toxic shame. Toxic shame, you'll recall, creates isolation and fosters silence. The more ashamed a child is, the more he feels he has no right to *depend* on anyone. Because the wounded child never got his *needs* met and was shamed the most when he was the most needy, he may feel that he is bothering people if he asks them to listen to him. In truth, you have *every right* to let others love and nurture you.

Remember, you are doing this for your precious, wounded inner child. *Listen to your toddler self pulling on your heartstrings!*

# FEELING YOUR FEELINGS

If you have a photograph of yourself as a toddler, get it out. See how small and innocent you were. Then, find a child in the toddler stage and spend some time with him. Focus on the normalcy of this developmental stage. It was normal for you to be full of energy, to be rambunctious. Toddlers get into things. You were curious and interested in things. You said *no* in order to begin a life of your own. You were shaky and immature, and your tantrums came from that. You were an innocent and beautiful little person. Focus on what you went through during toddlerhood. Feel whatever feelings come up for you.

# LETTER WRITING

Just as you did for your infant self, write a letter to your toddler self. This letter is from the grown-up you—in my case, a gentle and wise old wizard. One of my letters to my toddler reads as follows:

> Dear Little John:
>     I know you are very lonely. I know you never got to be yourself. You are scared to be angry cause you think there is a terrible fire called hell which will burn if you get angry. You can't be sad or afraid cause that's for sissies. No one really knows the wonderful little boy you are and what you really feel.
>     I'm from your future and I know better than anyone what you've been through! I love you and want you to be with me always. I'll let you be exactly the way you are. I'll teach you some balance and let you be mad, sad, afraid, or glad. Please consider letting me be with you always.
>
>                                                              Love,
>                                                              Big John

When I wrote this, I felt my inner child's loneliness and sadness.

## Letter From Your Toddler

Next write a letter from your wounded inner toddler. Remember to write it with your *nondominant hand*; left hand if you're right-handed and right hand if you're left-handed. Here is what one person in one of my workshops wrote:

Dear Big Richard
Please come and get me
I've been in a closet for
forty years, I'm terrified, I
need you.
          Little Richard

After you've written your letter, sit quietly and let whatever feelings you have come up. If you're with someone, or have a close friend, sponsor, or therapist who knows what you're doing, contract with him to read your letters out loud. Reading them aloud with another face mirroring you can be very powerful.

## AFFIRMATIONS

Once again I'm going to ask you to go back into the past and find your inner toddler and give him the affirmations he needed to hear. These are different from the affirmations you gave your inner infant.

Your toddler self needs to hear the following:

Little _____, it's okay to be curious, to want, to look, to touch and taste things. I'll make it safe for you to explore.

I love you just the way you are, little _____.

I'm here to take care of your needs. You don't have to take care of mine.

It's okay for you to be taken care of, little _____.

It's okay to say no, little _____. I'm glad you want to be you.

It's okay for both of us to be mad. We will work our problems
    out.
It's okay to feel scared when you do things your way.
It's okay to feel sad when things don't work out for you.
I'll not leave you no matter what!
You can be you and still count on my being there for you.
I love watching you learn to walk and talk. I love watching you
    separate and start to grow up.
I love and value you, little _____.

Read over these affirmations slowly and let their meaning sink in.
Now you are ready to reclaim your toddler self.

## TODDLER MEDITATION

You should have your general introduction to all the meditations on
tape. If not, turn to page 94 and record the beginning of the meditation, ending with the line "What did it *feel* like to live in that house?"
(If you are just starting to read here, please read the instructions on
pp. 93–94.)
Now add the following to the general introduction.

Imagine you could walk outside of that house and that you
could see a little toddler playing in a sandbox.... Really look at
him and get a feeling sense of this child.... What color are his
eyes?... What color is his hair?... What is he wearing?... Talk
to this child.... Say whatever you feel like saying.... Now let
yourself float into the sandbox and be the little child.... What
does it feel like to be this small child?... Look up at the
grown-up you....

Hear this grown-up person as a wise and gentle wizard slowly
tell you the following affirmations. Sit in the wizard's lap if that
feels safe.

If you're working with a partner, this is where you give your
partner the affirmations on pages 117–118. (He is looking at his own

grown-up self, but he is hearing your voice.) If you are working alone, you will record the affirmations in your own voice. Allow a twenty-second pause after each affirmation. After you have heard the affirmations, allow two minutes to let your child self feel whatever he feels, then continue:

> If you feel like hugging the grown-up you, please do so. As you hug the grown-up you, feel yourself become the grown-up you again. Hold your little toddler self. Make a commitment to love this carefree, exploring, curious part of yourself. Tell the child: I will never leave you.... I will always be here for you.... Be aware that you have just reclaimed your toddler self....
>
> Feel the sense of that *homecoming*.... Your little toddler is wanted, loved, and will never be left alone again.... Walk away from that house.... Stroll forward *up* memory lane.... Walk past your early school yard. Look at the playground and the swing.... Walk past your favorite old hangout as a young teenager.... Walk past a memory from two years ago.... Feel yourself in the space you're in right *now*.... Feel your toes.... Wiggle them.... Feel the energy come up through your legs.... Feel energy in your chest as you take a deep breath.... Make a noise as you exhale.... Feel the energy in your arms and fingers.... Wiggle your fingers.... Feel the energy in your shoulders, neck, and jaw.... Stretch your arms.... Feel your face and be fully present ... restored to your normal waking consciousness ... and open your eyes.

Sit for a while reflecting on this experience. Let yourself feel whatever it is you feel. If you don't feel anything, that's okay too. Think about what words were most powerful for you. Where did emotions surface for you? How do you feel right now? What are you aware of?

Write down any strong feelings you've had or are having. If you feel like sharing them with your nurturing support person, please do.

## Working With a Partner

If you do this exercise with a partner, spend time legitimizing each other's violations. Be there as a mirror and an echo for your partner, verifying what he says.

You will take turns guiding each other through the meditation. As you see in the text, the only difference for a couple is that your partner says the affirmations out loud. In addition, the partner guide can hold and caress you in whatever way feels safe to both of you. For further information, read the introduction to the partner exercise on page 99.

## Working With a Group

Read the instructions for working with a group on page 99. Once you've recorded the general introduction to the meditation, have your group "voice recorder" add:

> Now imagine that you could walk outside and see a little toddler playing in a sandbox.... Really look at him and get a feeling sense of this child.... What color are his eyes? ... What is he wearing? ... Talk to this child.... Say whatever you feel like saying.... Now let yourself float into the sandbox and be the little child.... What does it feel like to be this small child? ... Look up at the grown-up you.... Hear this grown-up person slowly tell you the affirmations for the toddler stage. Sit in his lap if that feels safe.

*Do not record the affirmations.* Give each person a copy of the affirmations list and follow the instructions on page 102 for making an anchor. Continue reading to the end of the meditation as written *in this chapter.* You will then play back the recording and do your group circle work with the affirmations, as described on pages 102–103.

Be aware that the big adult in you *can take care of the wounded little toddler in you.* Here is the way I think it looks to reclaim my toddler self.

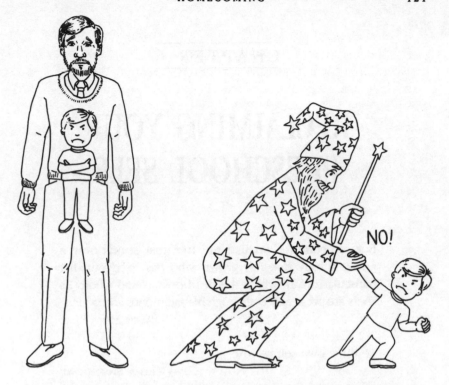

Now it's time to move on and bring your preschool self to the homecoming party you're throwing.

# CHAPTER 6

# RECLAIMING YOUR PRESCHOOL SELF

But sometimes I am like the tree that stands over a grave, a leafy tree full grown who has lived out that particular dream which the dead boy around whom its roots are pressing lost through his sad moods and poems.
—RAINER MARIA RILKE

To thine own self be true.

—WILLIAM SHAKESPEARE

PRESCHOOLER

*(EARLY IDENTITY)*

I AM SOMEONE ⟨ MALE / FEMALE

| | |
|---|---|
| AGE: | 3 YEARS TO 6 YEARS |
| DEVELOPMENT POLARITY: | INITIATIVE VERSUS GUILT |
| EGO STRENGTH: | PURPOSE |
| POWER: | IMAGINING AND FEELING |
| RELATIONSHIP ISSUE: | INDEPENDENCE |

# INDEX OF SUSPICION

Answer yes or no to the following questions. After you read each question, wait and get in touch with what you feel. If you feel a stronger energy for yes, answer yes; for no, answer no. If you answer any question yes, you can suspect that your wonderful inner child of the past has been wounded. There are degrees of woundedness. You are somewhere on a scale from one to a hundred. The more questions you *feel* are to be answered yes, the more your preschool self was wounded.

1. Do you have severe identity problems? Yes _____ No _____
   To aid you in answering this, consider the following questions. Who are you? Does an answer come easily? No matter what your sexual preference, do you feel like you're *really* a man? A woman? Do you overdramatize your sex (try to be macho or sexy)? Yes _____ No _____

2. Even when you have sex in a legitimate context, do you feel guilty? Yes _____ No _____

3. Do you have trouble identifying what you are feeling at any given moment? Yes _____ No _____

4. Do you have communication problems with the people you are close to (spouse, children, boss, friends)? Yes _____ No _____

5. Do you try to control your feelings most of the time? Yes _____ No _____

6. Do you try to control the feelings of those around you? Yes _____ No _____

7. Do you cry when you're angry? Yes _____ No _____

8. Do you rage when you're scared or hurt? Yes _____ No _____

9. Do you have trouble expressing your feelings? Yes _____ No _____

10. Do you believe that you are responsible for other people's behavior or feelings? (For example, do you feel that you can *make* someone sad or angry?) Yes _____ No _____ Also, do you feel guilty for what has happened to your family members? Yes _____ No _____

11. Do you believe that if *you* just behave a certain way, you can change another person? Yes _____ No _____

12. Do you believe that wishing or feeling something can make it come true? Yes _____ No _____

13. Do you often accept confusing messages and inconsistent communication without asking for clarification? Yes _____ No _____

14. Do you act on guesses and unchecked assumptions, treating them as actual information? Yes _____ No _____

15. Do you feel responsible for your parents' marital problems or divorce? Yes _____ No _____

16. Do you strive for success so that your parents can feel good about themselves? Yes _____ No _____

## NORMAL PRESCHOOL

At about age 3 you started asking *why* and lots of other questions. You asked not because you were dumb or a pest, but because it was part of a higher power's biological plan. You asked questions because you had a life energy—a beingness—that pushed you toward ever-expanding life.

To sum up your development so far: you feel welcomed to the world and you know you can trust the world enough to get your needs met; you've also developed enough willpower and internalized discipline to trust yourself. Now you must develop the power of envisioning who you are and imagining how you want to live your life. To know who you are is to have an identity, which involves your sexuality, your beliefs about yourself, and your fantasies. Preschool children ask so many *why* questions because there is so much to figure out. Some of us *still* haven't figured it out.

Because the job of figuring out who you are and what you want to do with your life is so difficult, children are given a special protection to help them. This special protection is called egocentrism. Children are egocentric by nature. They are not selfish. Their egocentrism is a biological fact, not a choice. Prior to age 6 children are truly unable to understand the world from another person's point of view. A preschooler can be emotionally sympathetic but he cannot really stand in another's shoes. The ability to do this will not be fully present until around age 16.

Preschoolers are also very magical. They are busy testing reality in order to separate it from fantasy. This is one way they discover their power. To test is to find out how much power you have.

Preschoolers are very independent. They are busy asking questions, forming beliefs, envisioning the future, and trying to figure out how the world works and what makes things happen. As they develop a more sophisticated sense of cause and effect, they learn how they can influence things. This is their natural, healthy job, and they work at it full-time.

The job of parents is to teach their children and to model for them. While the father models how to be a male, the mother models how to be a female. Mom and Dad must also model a healthy intimate relationship, including healthy sexuality. In addition, Mom and Dad need to model good communication skills, such as clarifying, listening, asking for what you want, and conflict resolution.

Sons need to bond with their fathers. This can happen only if Father spends time with his son. Bonding requires physical touching as well as emotional sharing. It is vital for a girl to have her father, but it is not as crucial as a boy's need for his father. A girl is already bonded with her mother and needs to separate from her. A boy is bonded to his mother, but not in the same way as a girl, because of the incest taboo. A boy must protect himself against carrying his mother's projected sexuality.

As a little boy bonds with his dad, he wants to be like him. He begins to imitate his dad's behavior. He may tell everyone that when he grows up he wants to be like his dad, and he may symbolically act out being his father in make-believe games. Some boys will find heroes to admire and emulate. My heroes were baseball players. I collected baseball cards and dressed in the uniform of my favorite team; a signed baseball was one of my favorite possessions. In the same way, little girls begin to copy their mothers' behavior. They may play make-believe games with baby dolls, pushing them in carriages and fixing them bottles. Little girls may also become delightfully flirtatious as they play dress-up and want to put on makeup.

A biological predisposition to homosexuality may also start to emerge in this period. I want to state strongly that I believe there is growing evidence for homosexuality as an innate tendency, not a pathology or a growth disorder. (In many years of doing therapy, I never counseled a gay person who wasn't fairly clear about his or her sexual orientation early on.) My concern in this book is for the wounded inner child of all people. Most gays carry an excessive amount of shame, as there is particularly strong and widespread shaming of boys who don't display the traditional masculine traits and behaviors. If you are a gay man or woman, your wounded inner preschooler needs to hear that it is perfectly okay to be who you are.

## PRESCHOOL EGO STRENGTH

Erikson speaks of the ego strength of the preschool age as *purpose*. He believes that strength of purpose arises out of a sense of identity. If healthy development has taken place up to the preschool age, a child can say: "I can trust the world, I can trust myself, and I am special and unique. I am a boy/I am a girl. I can start envisioning my future even though I don't have to know exactly what I want to do."

Power comes out of having an identity—the power to initiate and to make choices. The healthy preschooler thinks: "I can be me and all of life is ahead of me. I can play like Mom or play like Dad. I can dream of being a man like Dad or a woman like Mom. I can dream about being adult and creating my own life."

## GROWTH DISORDER

Growth disorder at this stage shows the long-term results of family dysfunction. Children look to their parents to provide healthy models for adult behavior. If Mom and Dad are shame-based co-dependent adult children, it will be impossible for their children to form healthy intimate relationships.

Adult children, having long ago buried their authentic selves and lost their sense of I AMness, cannot give *themselves* to their partners because they don't have a self to give. When adult children marry they choose a person who is a projection of their parents—someone who has both the positive and negative aspects of their parents and who complements their family-system roles. A Hero Caretaker will often marry a Victim, since each can play his role. Each invests enormous amounts of esteem in the other, which is most evident when they try to break up. One or both may become suicidal, claiming that they can't live without the other. Often an adult child who has engulfment issues will marry an adult child who has abandonment issues. As the one with the fear of abandonment comes closer, the one with the fear of engulfment runs away. After a period of separation, the person with engulfment fears becomes lonely enough to allow the partner with abandonment fears to come close for a while. The partner with abandonment fears, remembering the past separation, soon becomes possessive and engulfs the partner, driving him away again. This seesaw dynamic will continue throughout the marriage. Each one creates the other one's response.

Remember our picture of the two adult children who were like a 200-pound 3-year-old and a 140-pound 3-year-old? You and I were the 65-pound 5-year-old. Of course we have to remember that *exactly the same thing happened to our parents*. When the wounded child in Mom or Dad realizes that the other is *not* going to be their longed-for parent, they turn to their children to provide what their parents did not provide.

Consider the Lavender family. Bronco Lavender is a traveling sales-man. He is also a sex addict. He is rarely home, but when he is home, he pretends to have a very intimate relationship with his wife, Glory. Glory was named by her minister father (also a sex addict) in honor of the "glory" of the Lord. Glory is a severe co-dependent who is having an affair with her self-appointed Bible teacher. Bronco and Glory have three children, two boys, 16 and 13, and a girl, 11. The older boy is an enormously talented athlete. He is the star at school and he's Dad's "best buddy." From ages 12 to 14, he frequently violated his sister sexually. The sister is severely obese and is constantly lectured by her mother. I first met the Lavenders when the daughter was brought to me for therapy for her weight problem. The younger son is the apple of his mother's eye. He is artistic, nonathletic, and very religious, which pleases his mom greatly. His dad dislikes him and

teases him by calling him names like sissy and ninny. He is his
father's scapegoat. Here is a diagram of the Lavender family.

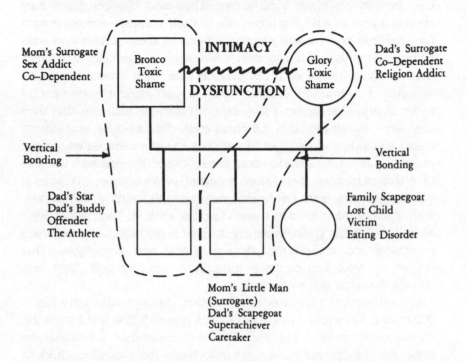

No one in this family has any real identity. Mom and Dad are both
untreated *nonphysical* incest victims. Both were surrogate spouses for
their opposite-sex parents. Bronco's dad was an alcoholic who left him
at age 3. Bronco grew up to be his mom's pride and joy. They did
everything together. Mom frequently dressed in front of Bronco and
used the toilet while he was bathing. "She made me her life," Bronco
told me with tears in his eyes. His mother is now deceased, and Bronco
often bemoans the fact that there "ain't no good women anymore."

Glory was her dad's gift from God. She was put near the pulpit on
Sundays while her father preached. Her mother was a hypochondriac
who was sick a great deal of the time. Glory did the cooking and
washing and was a true blessing to her father. She also slept with him
till she was 11 years old. And while there was no physical sex with
her father, she was clearly his surrogate spouse.

Bronco and Glory were both *used* to fill up the loneliness in their
parents' lives. Think about how it *feels* to be used! Use is abuse, and it

causes lasting anger and pain. Bronco and Glory idealized their parents; put them on a pedestal; felt they deserved sainthood. Bronco and Glory were in delusion and denial. They had no sense of their own I AMness. How could they have? There was no one there for *them* and no way they could be who they were. They had to take care of their parents' neediness and loneliness. This is nonphysical sexual abuse.

Bronco and Glory carried their spiritual wounds into their marriage and continued the same dysfunctional dynamics in their new family. Bronco acted out his sexual abuse by abusing one woman after another (he loved 'em and left 'em). Every time he rejected a woman, he won a symbolic victory over Mom's control. Of course, this was unconscious. He didn't even know he was angry at his mom, because he had been set up to idealize her. Glory was ravaged with shame over her affair. I helped her see that her dad had used her and, it turns out, used other women in the church. Glory used her religiosity to cover up her deep anger and sadness. She was also nonphysically incesting her younger son. He was her "sensitive little man." She could discuss the Bible with him. They took long walks together on Sundays, pondering the glory of God's word. This son was filling the void for Glory's wounded inner child, while the older son was taking care of his dad's shame and pain. Their daughter was eating to fill the void of anger, pain, and loneliness of everyone in the family. She was the one Bronco and Glory worried about—the "family problem," the "identified patient" who was originally brought in to me to be "fixed."

The Lavenders looked good at church on Sunday. No one could really fathom the depth of suffering that was housed there. No one in the family had any identity, since no one had gotten their developmental needs met in the preschool stage.

The Lavender family provides an example of how spiritually wounding the intimacy dysfunction in a marriage can be. When the children fill in the emptiness in their parents' lives, this unhealthy *vertical* or *cross-generational* bonding is particularly devastating to the children's sexual identity. Vertical bonding is quite different from the father/son, mother/daughter bonding I spoke about earlier. Vertical bonding creates a role confusion—the son or daughter inappropriately takes the opposite-sex parent's place in the family system.

Bronco and Glory Lavender failed to create the environment necessary for a child to think, feel, and imagine. Because the children are involved in taking care of their parents' marriage, they are in fact keeping the family together. Their preschool development needs to be independent, to be curious, to test their individuality, to ask questions, and to think about things could not be met. Like all dysfunctional families, the Lavenders were co-dependent. Each person was outerdirected. There was no time for anyone to pay attention to his own internal cues.

In like manner and to varying degrees all dysfunctional families violate their children's sense of I AMness. The dysfunction could be chemical addiction, work addiction, or violence. In each case one parent is involved with his own dysfunction and the other is co-dependently addicted to him. The children are emotionally abandoned. To make matters worse, they become enmeshed in the covert or overt need to maintain the family's precarious and unhealthy balance. In dysfunctional families, *no one gets to be who he is*. All are put in service to the *needs of the system*.

The most common consequence of this is that members of dysfunctional families get fixed in rigid roles. These roles are like scripts for a play; they dictate how each person is to behave and what he *can* and *cannot feel*. The most common role distortions of the preschool years are: Superresponsible One, Overachiever, Rebel, Underachiever, People Pleaser (nice guy/sweetheart), Caretaker, and Offender.

This lack of individual identity is why dysfunctional families are dominated by toxic guilt. Healthy guilt is the guardian of conscience. It develops out of a healthy sense of shame; it is the moral dimension of healthy shame. The toddler's shame is premoral and mostly preverbal. There is no possibility of morality until there is a sense of internalized values. Values result from thinking and feeling. Values presuppose that one has developed some sense of conscience. By the end of the preschool age, children have the beginnings of a true moral sense, a budding conscience.

In dysfunctional families, it is impossible for the children to develop a healthy conscience or a healthy sense of guilt. The lack of individuality prohibits them from feeling that they have the right to a life of their own, so they develop *toxic guilt* instead. This sounds the death knell for the psychological self. Toxic guilt is a way of having power in a powerless situation. It tells you that you are responsible for other people's feelings and behavior; it may even tell you that your behavior made someone else sick, as when a father says, "Look what you kids have done, you've made your mother sick!" This results in your having a grandiose sense of responsibility. Toxic guilt is one of the most damaging ways your preschool inner child was wounded.

## DEBRIEFING

Writing your history becomes easier as you progress through the developmental stages, but most people still don't have many memories prior to ages 7 or 8. Before then, you still thought magically, nonlogically, and egocentrically. Such thinking is like being in an altered state of consciousness. Nevertheless, try to remember whatever you can. Traumatic events usually stand out. They were the most life-threatening and therefore they left the most powerful imprints. Write out whatever you remember about your traumatic violations in this period. Be sure to give specific details.

Also write as much as you can about your family system. What was your dad doing? What was your mom doing? What do you know or guess was going on in their marriage? Pay serious attention to your hunches about the family. Pretend that your hunches are true and see if that gives you a better understanding of your family. If it doesn't, let them go. If it does, live with them for a while.

A client of mine had a hunch that his grandmother was incested by her father. She had grown up on a farm, the only girl among seven brothers. My client had never heard his grandmother talk about her father. She was agoraphobic and quite neurotic. She seemed to hate men and had instilled her hatred in her three daughters, one of whom was my client's mother. My client had all the emotional symptoms of an incest victim. He was acting out sexually, "killing" women with seduction. He would send them poetry and buy them expensive gifts. Just when the woman would fall hook, line, and sinker, my client would leave her, usually in a rage.

Although there was no overt evidence that his grandmother had been incested, he wrote his family history as if she had, and many things fell together and made sense.

As you write your wounded inner preschooler's history, ask yourself who was there for you? Who was the role model you most identified with? Who first taught you how to be a man? A woman? Who taught you about sex, love, and intimacy?

## ABUSIVE BROTHERS AND SISTERS

I have not talked about abuse from older siblings, but this can have an important—though often ignored—effect on your development. Perhaps you had a brother or sister who tormented you. Or perhaps a neighbor child bullied or molested you. Even teasing can be extremely abusive, and chronic teasing can be a nightmare.

Write out as much of your inner preschooler's history as you remember.

## SHARING YOUR PRESCHOOL INNER CHILD WITH A FRIEND

Use the same methods as described in chapters 4 and 5. Focus especially on any incidents of violation that you can remember. Use the following as possible sources for painful feelings:

- Sex play with same-age friends
- Physical or emotional incest
- Being squelched for seeking information
- Poor role models for intimacy
- Being made to feel guilty
- Lack of information about feelings

## FEELING THE FEELINGS

Again, try to find a picture of yourself at this developmental stage. Look at the picture and allow any feelings that you have to emerge. If you have no picture, spend some time with preschool kids. See how wonderful they are. Think of one of them taking on the responsibilities of a marriage partner or being physically incested. Think of their vitality and inquisitiveness being squelched. You may still have an old doll, toy, or teddy bear from this age. See if it still has any energy for you. Let the energy lead you to whatever feelings come.

## LETTER WRITING

For this developmental stage, I'll ask you to write three letters. The first one is from the grown-up you to your wounded inner preschooler. Again, tell him that you *want to be with him* and are willing to give him the attention and direction he needs. Tell him he can ask you all the questions he wants. Above all, tell him you love and value him.

The second and third letters are from your wounded inner pre-schooler. Remember to write them with your nondominant hand. The first letter should be addressed to *your parents*. This letter consists of two paragraphs, one to your mom and one to your dad. Let your wounded inner child tell them what he wanted and needed from them that he never got. This is not a blame letter; it is an expression of loss. One man in a recent workshop wrote:

Dear Mom and Dad,
    Dad, I needed you to protect me. I was scared all the time. I needed you to play with me. I wish we could have gone fishing. I wish you would have taught me things. I wish you weren't drinking all the time.
    Mom, I needed you to praise me. To tell me you loved me. I wish you hadn't made me take care of you. I needed to be taken care of.

Love,
Robbie

*It is very important to read your letter out loud to your support person.*
    The second letter from your wounded inner preschooler is to the grown-up you. It is a response to the letter written from your adult self. This letter may surprise you as you touch your inner child's longing to have an ally. Remember to use your nondominant hand. If you wish, you can share these letters with your support person, your partner, or your group.
    If you're working with a partner, each one should read his letter to the other. After you hear your partner's letter, give him a feeling response. If you felt angry, tell him; if you felt fear, tell him. The feeling may be more about you than about him, but it's an honest response. Also give him feedback concerning the feelings you ob-

served in him. For example, you might say, "I really saw your sadness. There were tears in your eyes and your lips tightened." Try not to say things like, "Boy, you were resentful." Instead of labeling or interpreting, tell him what you *saw* and *heard* that made you conclude that he was resentful. You might also add how awful it must have been to be neglected or abused the way he was. This helps legitimize and validate his pain. When one person has worked, let the other take his turn.

If you're working these exercises as a group, take turns reading your letters, and let each person in the group give his mirroring feedback.

## DYSFUNCTIONAL FAMILY-SYSTEM ROLES

Identify and write down the roles your wounded inner preschooler chose in order to matter in your family. Mine were Star, Superachiever, Caretaker, and Nice Guy. Your roles make up your part in the family drama.

Ask yourself what feelings you had to repress in order to play your roles. Scripts demand that you play your roles in certain ways. Some feelings go with the script and others are prohibited by it. My roles called for me to be up, to smile, and to look happy, and prohibited me from being scared, sad, and angry. I mattered only as long as I was a Star and was achieving. I couldn't be mediocre or need help myself. I had to be strong. If I didn't perform, I felt stripped of the power of doing. Of course, I became addicted to doing.

It's important to feel the life-damaging consequences of your roles. They cost you the loss of your authentic childhood self. As long as you continue to play your roles, you stay in the spiritual wound; you may go to your death never knowing who you are.

In order to reclaim your wounded preschooler, you must give up your rigid family-system roles. Those roles never *really* made you feel that you mattered anyway, and they certainly didn't help anyone else in the family. Think about it; has anyone in your family of origin really been helped by your playing your roles? Just close your eyes and imagine that you couldn't play your major role anymore! How does it *feel* to give up that role?

Try to think of three new behaviors you could use to stop a Caretaking role. For example, you could say *no* when someone asks for your help; you could ask someone to help you do something just for the hell of it; or you could think of a problem you're having right now and ask someone who has expertise in that area to help you. This helps you to change your adapted wounded child role and get in touch with your authentic self. Your authentic self may like to help others. Once you give up the rigid role, you can start helping others because you find it enjoyable rather than because you *have* to in order to feel lovable and valuable.

Go through the rest of your roles, using the format above. Get in touch with the feelings that you had to give up in order to play your roles. By doing so you will be reclaiming the authentic feelings of your wounded inner preschooler.

## EXERCISE

Write down all the ways your family-system enmeshment has had life-damaging consequences. Connect with the feelings of loss your major role has caused. Share this with your support person, your partner, or your group. The roles are very helpful in getting to the original pain. Once you've established your role, you'll see what feelings you had to repress. The repressed feelings *are* your original pain. In role reversal cross-generational bonding, you had to give up your childhood.

## AFFIRMATIONS

The affirmations for the wounded inner preschooler are as follows:

Little _____, I love watching you grow.

I will be here for you to test your boundaries and find out your limits.

It's okay for you to think for yourself. You can think about your feelings and have feelings about what you're thinking.

I like your life energy; I like your curiosity about sex.

It's okay to find out the difference between boys and girls.

I'll set limits for you to help you find out who you are.

I love you just the way you are, little _____.

It's okay for you to be different; to have your own views on things.

It's okay to imagine things without being afraid they'll come true. I'll help you separate fantasy from reality.

I like it that you're a boy/girl.

I like it that you are gay, even though your parents didn't.

It's okay to cry even though you're growing up.

It's good for you to find out the consequences of your behavior.

You can ask for what you want.

You can ask questions if something confuses you.

You are not responsible for your parents' marriage.

You are not responsible for your dad.

You are not responsible for your mom.

You are not responsible for the family problems.

You are not responsible for your parents' divorce.

It's okay to explore who you are.

## PRESCHOOLER MEDITATION

Use the general introduction on pages 94–96. After the sentence "What did it *feel* like to live in that house?" add the following, pausing for twenty seconds at each interval.

Now see your inner child at about age 5.... Imagine he had walked outside the house and you could see him sitting in the backyard. Walk over to him and say hello.... What is he wearing? ... Does he have a doll, teddy bear, shovel, or some toy he is playing with? ... Ask him what his favorite toy is.... Ask him if he has a pet.... Tell him you are from his future and are here to be with him whenever he needs you.... Now let yourself become your inner preschool child.... Look up at the big you (the wise and gentle wizard).... See your kind loving face.... Hear the big you tell the little you to come sit on your lap if you want to.... It's okay if you don't.... Now hear the big you give the affirmations slowly and tenderly....

Record the affirmations on pages 134–135. When you reach the last affirmation, pause for one minute.

**Let the child feel whatever he feels.... Now slowly become the big you again.... Tell your preschool inner child that you are here now and that you will be talking to him a whole lot. Tell him that you are the only person he will never lose, and that you will never leave him.... Say goodbye for now and start walking forward *up* memory lane. Pass by your favorite movie house and ice cream parlor.... Pass by your schoolhouse.... Pass by your high school playground.... Feel yourself coming into the present.... Feel your feet wiggle.... Wiggle your toes.... Feel the energy come up through your body.... Feel your hands.... Wiggle your fingers.... Feel the energy come up through your upper body.... Take a very deep breath.... Make a sound as you exhale.... Feel the energy in your face.... Feel where you are sitting.... Your clothes on your body.... Now slowly open your eyes.... Sit for a few minutes and experience whatever you are experiencing.**

If you feel like it, share this meditation with your support person.

## Working With a Partner

Work with your partner as before (see instructions on p. 99). Each person reads the meditation to the other, saying the affirmations out loud. Do it with as much physical holding or stroking as feels safe.

## Working In a Group

As in the previous group exercises, the affirmations are given in turn by members of the group (see instructions p. 99). The person in the group who has been selected to record the meditation should record the added material in this section up to the passage "Look up at the big you, (the wise and gentle wizard).... See your kind and loving face ..."

Then record the instructions for making an anchor. Finish the meditation starting with the sentence "Say goodbye for now and start walking forward *up* memory lane."

Remember that it's important for everyone in the group to work before you begin talking and sharing about it.

You have now reclaimed your wounded inner preschooler. Be aware that the big you can take care of that preschooler.

If, after you've done any of these exercises, you feel a sense of panic, reassure your wounded inner child that you are here for him. When we first feel old frozen feelings, we feel anxious. They are unfamiliar, sometimes overwhelming and unmanageable. Tell your inner child that you will not leave him and that you are going to discover all kinds of ways to love him and help him get all his needs met. Here is my idea of what my reclaimed preschooler looks like.

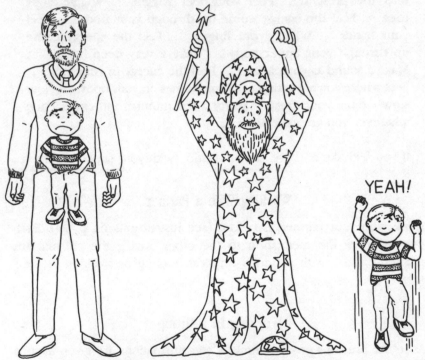

As we get to know one another better, I'm finding out that he's not just a needy kid, but also lots of fun to be around.

# CHAPTER 7

# RECLAIMING YOUR SCHOOL-AGE SELF

Each person's map of the world is as unique as their thumbprint. There are no two people *alike*. No two people who understand the same sentence the same way . . . So in dealing with people you try not to fit them to your concept of what they should be. . . .

—MILTON ERICKSON

I sent my brother away. . . .
I gave him to the dark people passing. . . .
They taught him to wear his hair long,
to glide about naked, drinking water from his hands,
tether horses, follow the faint trail through bent grasses. . . .
I took my brother to the other side of the river,
then swam back, left my brother alone on the shore.
On Sixty-sixth Street I noticed he was gone.
I sat down and wept.

—ROBERT BLY
*A Dream of My Brother*

SCHOOL-AGE

*(LATENCY PERIOD)*

I AM CAPABLE

AGE:  6 YEARS TO PUBERTY
DEVELOPING POLARITY:  INDUSTRY VERSUS INFERIORITY
EGO STRENGTH:  COMPETENCE
POWER:  KNOWING, LEARNING
RELATIONSHIP ISSUE:  INTERDEPENDENCE; COOPERATION

## INDEX OF SUSPICION

Answer yes or no to the following questions. After you read each question, wait and get in touch with what you feel. If you feel a stronger energy for yes, answer yes; for no, answer no. If you answer any question yes, you can suspect that your wonderful school-age inner child of the past has been wounded. There are degrees of woundedness. You are somewhere on a scale from one to a hundred. The more questions you *feel* are to be answered yes, the more your inner school-age child was wounded.

1. Do you often compare yourself to other people and find your-self inferior? Yes _____ No _____

2. Do you wish you had more good friends of both sexes? Yes _____ No _____

3. Do you frequently feel uncomfortable in social situations? Yes _____ No _____

4. Do you feel uncomfortable being part of a group? Yes _____ No _____ Do you feel most comfortable when you are alone? Yes _____ No _____

5. Are you sometimes told that you are excessively competitive? Do you feel like you *must* win? Yes _____ No _____

6. Do you have frequent conflicts with the people you work with? Yes _____ No _____ With the people in your family? Yes _____ No _____

7. In negotiations, do you either (a) give in completely or (b) insist on having things your own way? Yes _____ No _____

8. Do you pride yourself on being strict and literal, following the letter of the law? Yes _____ No _____

9. Do you procrastinate a lot? Yes _____ No _____

10. Do you have trouble finishing things? Yes _____ No _____

11. Do you believe you should know how to do things without instructions? Yes _____ No _____

12. Do you have intense fears about making a mistake? Yes _____ No _____ Do you experience severe humiliation if you are forced to look at your mistakes? Yes _____ No _____

13. Do you frequently feel angry and critical of others? Yes _____ No _____

14. Are you deficient in basic life skills (ability to read, ability to speak and/or write with good grammar, ability to do necessary math calculations)? Yes _____ No _____

15. Do you spend lots of time obsessing on and/or analyzing what someone has said to you? Yes _____ No _____

16. Do you feel ugly and inferior? Yes _____ No _____ If yes, do you try to hide it with clothes, things, money, or make-up? Yes _____ No _____

17. Do you lie to yourself and others a lot of the time? Yes _____ No _____

18. Do you believe that no matter what you do, it is not good enough? Yes _____ No _____

# NORMAL SCHOOL AGE

When you went to school, you left your family system and entered a new stage of socilization and skill building. Having established some sense of power with your reality testing and identity building, you were ready for the world. School would become your major environment for at least the next twelve years. The school age has been called the latency period, in reference to the absence of strong sexual energy. (Sexual energy will begin to surge in puberty.)

During the school age the child's biological rhythm sets the stage for learning the next set of survival skills. Building on the earlier ego strengths of trust and hope, autonomy and willpower, initiative and purpose, the child must now learn everything he can to prepare for adult life. The most important skills he has to learn are those of socialization: cooperation, interdependency, and a healthy sense of competition.

The preparation of one's life work requires academic skills as well: reading, writing, and arithmetic. However, these skills should not have been more important than knowing, loving, and valuing oneself. In fact, a healthy sense of self-worth is essential for good learning.

Skill building in school helped us to think freely and spontaneously about our future. School helped us to *verify* our sense of self. If we fit in, if we learned the material, we felt a new sense of power. We felt *industrious* and *competent*. These were the ego strengths that needed to be developed in school. If we are competent, then we can be industrious and can create a place for ourselves in the world. The achievement of the school-age tasks gives us a sense of new power and hope: "Because I am capable, I can be what I choose to be."

School age should be a time of play as well as work. Children's play is a crucial part of their development. Children learn by imitating and accommodating. *Accommodation* involves symbolic acting. Playing house and playing Mom and Dad are important parts of a child's mental development. For children, play is serious business.

## CONCRETE LOGICAL THINKING

By age 7 or 8 children are able to think logically, but theirs is still a concrete kind of thinking. Not until puberty will they be able to abstract and entertain contrary-to-fact propositions. Only then will a child begin to idealize and idolize. Idealization requires that one make contrary-to-fact hypotheses.

School-age children are concrete-logical. Remember when you learned the Pledge of Allegiance? You said words that you didn't understand. Remember learning your prayers? "Our Father who art in Heaven, *Harold* be thy name. Lead us *snot* into temptation ..." School-age kids are also egocentric in their thinking process. Their egocentrism is expressed in things such as catching parents in mistakes and thinking they are smarter than their parents. This "cognitive conceit" is the core of many interesting phenomena. Children of this age often think they are adopted (the foundling fantasy). If they are smarter than their parents, then they must have come from somewhere else. Schoolchildren's jokes are often about stupid adults. The story of Peter Pan is appealing to children of this age, partly because its characters never have to grow up and be dumb adults.

One important aspect of children's egocentrism is the belief that *adults are benevolent.* Children make this hypothesis and will hold on to it no matter what. I remember being asked to help a group of elementary-school administrators. They were amazed that a teacher whom they had to fire was a rallying point of protest for a sixth-grade class. The strangest thing of all was that the children disliked this teacher immensely. My belief was that this was an example of the children's egocentric assumption that a teacher, being an adult, could not be bad. This helps explain why the wounded inner school-age child will defend his parents, teachers, and abusers. Some children are so traumatized that they finally learn that there *is* something wrong with their adult offenders. But these children are the exception.

Your inner school-age child was a delightful, playful, charming little person, who loved to be connected with his friends and was eager and curious to learn.

## GROWTH DISORDER

If this last point is true, then why do so many kids hate school and find it dull, boring, and coercive? One reason is that education is often a source of spiritual wounding. Children are grouped horizontally by age in most public schools. The assumption is that all ten-year-olds are at the same level of maturity. This is blatantly false. Your inner school-age child could have been wounded simply by being in the wrong grade at the wrong time. Our schools and prisons are the only places in the world where *time is more important than the job to be done*. If you and I head out for Bermuda at the same time and I get there an hour before you, you don't *fail* Bermuda. In our schools, if you did not learn geometry as fast as other kids your age, you failed geometry. To my mind, geometry is not a survival skill anyway—I almost never *geomet*! But the danger here is that your inner child may have been penalized for being immature.

The grading system itself is very shaming and distressing. It puts constant pressure on a child to memorize and achieve. It is clearly perfectionistic. It measures human beings in a spiritually wounding way. As with all perfectionistic systems, *you can never measure up*. This creates toxic shame, which gives one a sense of being defective. After all, if you are you and there is no one else like you, to whom are we comparing you? Actually all perfectionistic systems compare us to a product of someone else's mental projections.

When children fail in school, it cause them great pain; they feel inferior, which creates a *being* wound: "I'm not okay." If children do well in school, that too creates problems. Everything in life becomes a potential A; everything is centered around performance.

Our school system, like our family system, is dysfunctional. It doesn't provide environments that affirm *who we are*. It doesn't treat us as the unique people we truly are. There are no two people alike; as Milton Erickson said, "There are no two people who understand the same sentence the same way." Your inner school-age child was crushed by the burden of conforming to the perfectionistic school system. You either became hopeless about your chance of success and dropped out, or you got taken up into the conformity trance and were soul-murdered in the process. Robert Bly, a profoundly moving American poet, writes of the loss of his brother. In the poem I quoted at the beginning of this chapter, Bly's brother is his spontaneous wonder child—the part that wants to "wear long hair and drink water from his hands." This is the part he lost when he went to school.

Schools reward conformity and memorization rather than creativity and uniqueness.

Many of us who adapted by becoming straight-A students never developed a true sense of competence. I spent a major part of my life trying to heal my being wound by performing and doing. No matter how many straight A's I got, it did nothing to heal the spiritual wound: deep down, my wounded inner child still felt alone and inadequate.

Many of us never learned social skills because we were too busy trying to get all A's. Many of us had very little fun at school because it was a pressure cooker of stressful demands. We were also in a double bind because we knew that academic excellence often kept us from the approval of our peers.

Today the most creative aspects of my life are playful and curious. I'm having fun writing this book. I've had fun lecturing, learning, and creating TV series over the last few years. Most of what I do now is the product of *incidental learning* that is motivated simply by the need or desire to know something. It is centered in excitement and has wonder at its core. Incidental learning is what your wonder child does naturally. You began your incidental learning as a toddler curiously exploring the world. Then you probably got waylaid; most of us did. You were made to conform and forced to learn stuff that bored you.

Unfortunately, the great advances in education reform, which began about twenty years ago and which I saw happening when I was a high school teacher, do not help our wounded inner school-age kids *now*.

While there are many courageous, creative, and nurturing teachers, there are also lots of very angry, abusive teachers. I know: I taught with some of them. These teachers projected their own wounded and angry inner school-age child onto their students. Your inner child may have been victimized in this way. You likely had other kids to legitimize your pain, but they were powerless to change anything.

In some cases your classmates themselves were the offenders. School-age kids can be cruel. Read the *Lord of the Flies*, by William Golding.

I recently connected with a school friend whom I hadn't seen in forty years. He and I spent two wonderful days catching up on each other's lives. I slowly remembered the pieces of his tormented child-

hood. He was an academic genius. He wore glasses and was nonathletic. His early life was an endless torture from the big boys at our
elementary school. Each day was like going into the shame pit. He
often hid in the sacristy of the church, praying to Jesus to help him
understand why they hit him, ridiculed him, and hurt him so much.
Why? When all he wanted to do was to be part of the group! I wept as
I listened to his story. I felt ashamed because I evidently would be his
friend only if *there was no one else around*. The peer group shaming
was so intense that I couldn't risk being associated with him for fear
of their going after me. He cherished my friendship. That was tragic
in itself. I'm happy to report that he survived all this rather brilliantly,
but not without some deep, deep scars to his inner child.

Talking to him triggered my memories of other victims of cruel
peer group shaming. The girls who were too fat; the kids with funny
noses; those who had physical deformities; the guys who didn't play
sports. My counseling files are filled with the histories of men and
women who carried *physical or cultural shame all their lives*. Their
beautiful "beingness" was rejected because they were Mexicans or
other foreigners, or Jews. They were tormented because they stut-
tered or were clumsy or poorly dressed. The children themselves
were carrying the cultural perfectionistic physical measurement stick.

No schoolchild is truly ugly, although some seem awkward and
nerdish. They are simply rough and unfinished, and they deserve our
respect and *help* in developing their strengths.

## DEBRIEFING

By now you have probably become pretty good at personal history
writing. By the way, if you are working on a given stage and suddenly
remember something from a previous stage, that's great. Write it out
and get it validated as soon as you can. Once you've begun this kind
of work, it is very common to have memories pop up from time to
time. The more you get in touch with your wounded inner child, the
more you enter the altered state that was your childhood. As you
reenter that state of consciousness, you start remembering more
things.

Beginning with school age, the memories are usually much more
vivid. Now, write down your inner school-age child's history. Remember, this period covers your life from about age 6 to early puberty,

which generally occurs at about the eighth grade. With puberty a whole new sophisticated mental ability will emerge. (We'll talk about that in the next chapter.) As a guideline, you might take your school age year by year. Use the following headings if they seem appropriate for you.

## Significant Adult Figures

In addition to parents, this includes your teachers, your clergyman or rabbi, and older kids. Write out each person's name and comment on whether he was nurturing or spiritually wounding. Nurturing means that he was truly there for you and valued you for your self. He promoted your I AMness. The people who were spiritually wounding were the ones who toxically shamed you.

## Milestones

Write about the three most important events of each year. For example, I wrote:

6 years old:  1. Started first grade.
2. Peed in my pants one day and was humiliated in front of the class.
3. Daddy was home more than any other time.
7 years old:  1. Passed to second grade.
2. Got a record player for Christmas.
3. Dad lost our car. Had a wreck in grandfather's car.

Continue with this list until about age 13. You'll notice that ages 6 and 7 were not particularly traumatic for me. Let yourself include whatever memories come up, pleasant and unpleasant.

## Traumatic Events

These were the experiences in your life that caused the greatest spiritual wounding. For example, when I was 9 years old, my dad began the first of several physical separations from my mom. These became more and more prolonged as the years went on.

Maybe you've remembered for years some past event that seems rather trivial. You don't quite know why you remember it, but you always have. This may mean that at some level there was violation involved. For example, I have always remembered an incident that took place when I was 5 years old. A teenaged neighbor boy made my sister, who was 6 at the time, touch his penis. Somehow I knew (without really knowing) that I was witnessing something very bad. This was not like my sex play with the two girls next door which happened two years later. We were all the same age, and our play was mostly symbolic. What happened to my sister was true molestation. I now understand why I have been haunted by the memory.

## SHARING YOUR SCHOOL-AGE CHILD'S HISTORY WITH A SUPPORT PERSON

Read your story to a friend, spouse, sponsor, or therapist. Give yourself enough time to get in touch with the violations of this period. Especially focus on the school system itself as spiritually wounding. Be specific about how you were unable to be yourself at school. *Record any abuse you received from teachers or other children.*

## FEELING THE FEELINGS

Get several pictures of yourself as an early school-age child. Ideally, get one for each year. You might have class pictures from your school days. Match your pictures with the various things you've written about that age. For example, I noticed how my facial expressions changed in different pictures. You can often see the hurt and sadness on your face from a certain period of your life. Your pictures may help you connect with your repressed emotional pain, or you may often see your face as emotionless and blank. By 7 or 8 you had started to develop your more sophisticated ego defenses. You had learned how to get into your head and block out your emotions, both past and present.

## WRITING A MYTH OR FAIRY TALE

At this age level I like to introduce a new and very powerful writing exercise—the myth or fairy tale about your childhood. (If the letter writing we've done previously works especially well for you, please continue to use that format, as well. As in the previous chapters, write three letters: one to your school-age child, one to you from your school-age child, and one to your parents and teachers, telling them what you needed from them that you didn't get.)

Your myth or fairy tale can focus on an event or events that occurred during your school years, or on an earlier event that strongly affected you. The good thing about myths and fairy tales is that they get around your rational, thinking brain. Your story can be about animals (a mama bear and papa bear), or about the gods, or about kings and queens.

Your story should have two parts. Part one should begin with "Once upon a time," and describe the events you have chosen, focusing on how they created the spiritual wound. Part two should begin with "And when she/he grew up," and should focus on the later life-damaging effects of the spiritual wound.

Don't be concerned if you can't think of a traumatic event that stands out dramatically in your life. You may have had a chronically depressed or anxious childhood, or you may have been neglected from the word go.

As you may have guessed, the parable of the "Tender Elf" at the end of part one is an adaptation of a myth I wrote about myself. Here is another example from one of my workshop participants.

The facts of this man's life were as follows. His father was wealthy and married his mother because, while on a drunken binge, he got her pregnant. His maternal grandfather threatened a lawsuit if his father did not marry his mother. Six months after they were married, his father divorced his mother. He paid her handsomely and asked her to move to another city as part of the settlement.

The mother, age 17, was in the early stages of drug addiction. She was also a sex addict. She paid an elderly country woman to keep her son. She would leave him for months at a time. She finally married and moved away, totally abandoning her son.

My client was physically, sexually, and emotionally abused by the old country woman. He was a school failure and ran away at 16. From that point on, his life was a soap opera of mediocre jobs and abusive relationships with women.

This is the story he wrote:

Once upon a time there was a powerful king named John. He married a lowly peasant woman named Gretchen. He married her because he got drunk one night and had sex with her and got her pregnant.

Because this was a shameful marriage, Gretchen was kept in hiding. She was finally put in exile on a strange island.

The child of this shameful marriage was also called John. His mother, wanting to keep King John's love, thought he might take her back when he saw the little prince and heard that she had given him the king's name. So she visited the king to show him his son.

King John was furious. He knew that the little prince was of royal blood, but he hated Gretchen, for she reminded him of his shame. The king decreed that Gretchen and little John should be sent to a foreign country across the ocean hundreds of miles away. Gretchen was paid handsomely and was sworn never to tell little John about the secret of his birth.

Gretchen hated little John. He kept her from doing what she wanted. She wanted to drink and carouse with men. She blamed little John for her exile. Finally she paid an old woman in the country to take care of him. The old woman beat him and gave him only the bare minimum to eat.

Although he was truly a prince of royal blood, little John thought he was the bastard son of this old pauper woman. He was laughed at by other country children because of the rags he wore to school. He failed in school because he was terrified to answer the questions the teachers asked. He never had time to study because he was so busy with his chores at home.

When he grew up, he ran away from home. He had no money, and since he had dropped out of school, the only job he could find was to sweep the floors in a merchant's store. He went through one relationship after another. Each time he entered a relationship he was rejected. Each woman he picked was critical and humiliated him.

Once you've written your story, it's very important for you to read it to your support person. This story can help you get in touch with your feelings about your abandonment. It can also help you see the connection between the neglect of your unmet developmental dependency needs and your consequent life history.

We heal our toxic shame when we grasp that our "adult child" issues are about what *happened to us,* and not about *who we really are*! Seeing how we act out our unmet childhood needs helps to reduce our toxic shame. If you're working with a partner, take turns reading to each other. When your partner reads you his story, give him your feeling response. Hold him and nurture him, if appropriate.

If you're working in a group, let each person read his story to the group. When he's finished, have him close his eyes while each person in the group gives him a heartfelt feeling response.

## DYSFUNCTIONAL FAMILY-SYSTEM ROLES

Get in touch with any new roles that you took on during the school-age years and work with them as you did in chapter 6, pp. 134–135. I suggest that you focus mainly on the cross-generational bonding roles because they robbed you of a healthy sex role model. Roles that often come up in this period are: Mom's Little Man, Mom's Surrogate Spouse, Mom's Sorority Sister (Best Friend), Mom's Mom, Dad's Little Princess (Baby Doll), Dad's Surrogate Spouse, Dad's Best Buddy, Dad's Dad. It's important to realize that Surrogate Spouse and Parent's Parent roles are not limited to opposite-sex bonding. A girl can be Mom's Surrogate Spouse; a boy can be Dad's Surrogate Spouse. In all cases, *the child is taking care of the parent.* This is a reversal of the order of nature.

Focus on the *life-damaging consequences of these roles.* I think of Jimmy, for example, whose father was an alcoholic and abandoned the family when Jimmy was 6 years old. His mom was 26 when her husband left her. She was unskilled and had two other children. Jimmy, the middle child and oldest son, worked at whatever odd jobs he could get from age 7 on. He became an enormous help to his mom. He would sit with her for hours at a time, consoling her as she cried about her life. He considered her a saint and could never do enough for her. Jimmy did not notice (no child would) that when *he* cried, his mother either shamed him for it or took him out of his feelings by distracting him. She would tell him what a wonderful grandfather he had and how lucky he was to be living in a house with plenty of food to eat. Children were starving in Latin America!

At age 21, Jimmy joined an order of Zen Buddhists and became a celibate monk. His mom was proud of him and visited him often. After a number of years, Jimmy left the monastery and went through a series of relationships with women. He always found needy women for whom he could be a savior. At 45 he entered a disastrous marriage to an abandoned 26-year-old who had three children. The marriage was a vortex of conflict and withdrawal. Jimmy hated his stepchildren. Early on he had an affair, which led to out-of-control sexual acting out for ten years. Finally, his wife divorced him.

Jimmy's story is typical of many Surrogate Spouse sons. They frequently turn to religion or celibate spirituality. In this way they remain faithful to Mom. Or they are unable to make a commitment to any *one* woman. Since they are already committed to Mom, being committed to another woman would be equivalent to emotional adultery. Such men have been called "Flying Boys," since they fly away from commitment. They are also referred to as "Peter Pans," since they never grow up (never really leave Mom).

Jimmy came to me at 51 years of age, angry and alone. His Surrogate Spouse role had cost him dearly. He felt he mattered only if he took care of needy women like his mother. Deep down, he never felt connected. He had in fact never been loved for who he was. His authentic self (his wounded inner preschool child) had never been acknowledged.

I will present a corrective exercise for breaking these enmeshed roles in chapter 12.

## AFFIRMATIONS

The affirmations for your inner school-age child are as follows:

Little _____, you can be who you are at school. You can stand up for yourself and I'll support you.
It's okay to learn to do things your own way.
It's okay to think about things and try them out before you make them your own.

You can trust your own judgments; you need only take the consequences of your choices.

You can do things your own way and it's okay to disagree.

I love you just the way you are, little _____.

You can trust your feelings. If you're afraid, tell me.

It's okay to be afraid. We can talk about it.

You can choose your own friends.

You can dress the way the other kids dress, or you can dress your own way.

You deserve to have the things you want.

I'm willing to be with you no matter what.

I love you, little _____.

## SCHOOL-AGE MEDITATION

Add the following to your general introduction. Pause 20 seconds at every interval.

What was it like in your house when you first went to school? ... Do you remember your very first day of school? ... Do you remember your first day in any of the different grades? ... Did you have a lunch box? ... A book satchel? ... How did you get to school? ... Were you afraid to go to school? ... Were there any bullies who scared you? ... Who was your favorite teacher? ... Did you have a man or woman teacher? ... Imagine the school playground. ... See your school-age self on the playground. ... What is he doing? ... What is he wearing? ... Walk up to him and imagine you could become him. ... Now you are a young schoolchild looking at the grown-up you. ... You see yourself as a wise and gentle wizard. ... Hear your grown-up voice. ... Hear your grown-up voice saying warm and loving things to you. ...

If alone: *Record* the affirmations for the wounded inner school-age child.

With a partner: *Say* the affirmations to your partner.

**With a group:** Stop here and make an anchor.

**Alone or with a partner:** After you've finished with the affirmations, the meditation continues.

> Let yourself feel whatever you feel. Say goodbye to your gentle wizard, and hug him, if you want to.... Slowly let yourself become your adult self again.... Tell your inner school-age child that you will be here for him from now on.... Tell him that he can count on you....

**For groups:** If you're working in a group, add the following after you've set your anchor. This conclusion is for everyone—working alone, with a partner, or with group. Pause 10 seconds at every interval.

> Start walking forward in time.... See your high school.... What color is it?... See your high school best friend.... Hear a favorite teenage song.... Walk forward in time into your early adult life.... See the house you live in now.... See your room. ... Experience where you are right now.... Wiggle your toes. ... Feel the energy come up through your legs.... Take a deep breath.... Make a sound as you exhale.... Wiggle your fingers. ... Feel yourself fully present, restored in mind and body.... Open your eyes....

If you're alone, reflect on this experience. Write down how you are feeling. If you're with a partner, share how the experience was for you. If you're in a group, take turns sharing how this experience was for you.

You've reclaimed your school-age child! You can take care of him! Here's my picture of my reclaimed inner school-age child.

HI HO!
HI HO!

## CHAPTER 8

# PULLING YOURSELF TOGETHER—A NEW ADOLESCENCE

*What I do is me: for that I came.*
—GERALD MANLEY HOPKINS

I wake and find myself in the woods, far from the castle.
The train hurtles through lonely Louisiana at night. . . .
When I look back, there is a blind spot in the car.
It is some bit of my father I keep not seeing.
I cannot remember years of my childhood.
Some parts of me I cannot find now. . . .
Is there enough left of me now to be honest? . . .
How much I am drawn toward my parents! I walk back
and forth, looking toward the old landing.
Night frogs give out the croak of the planet turning.
—ROBERT BLY
*Night Frogs*

```
ADOLESCENCE

(REGENERATION)

I AM MY UNIQUE SELF

                      AGE:   13–26
DEVELOPMENTAL POLARITY:   IDENTITY VERSUS ROLE CONFUSION
         EGO STRENGTH:   FIDELITY
               POWER:   OF REGENERATION
   RELATIONSHIP ISSUE:   INDEPENDENCE FROM FAMILY
```

# INDEX OF SUSPICION

Answer yes or no to the following questions. After you read each question, wait and get in touch with what you feel. If you feel a stronger energy for yes, answer yes; for no, answer no. If you answer any question yes, you can suspect that your wonderful inner adolescent of the past has been wounded. There are degrees of woundedness. You are somewhere on a scale from one to a hundred. The more questions you *feel* are to be answered yes, the more your adolescent self was wounded.

1. Do you still have trouble with parental authority? Yes _____ No _____

2. Do you continue to experiment with jobs, never feeling like you've found your niche? Yes _____ No _____

3. Are you confused about who you really are? Yes _____ No _____

4. Are you committed to a group or cause? Yes _____ No _____

5. Do you think of yourself as disloyal? Yes _____ No _____

6. Do you feel superior to others because your lifestyle is offbeat and nonconformist? Yes _____ No _____

7. Have you ever arrived at a faith position of your own? Yes _____
   No _____

8. Do you have any real friends of the same sex? Yes _____
   No _____

9. Do you have any friends of the opposite sex? Yes _____
   No _____

10. Are you a dreamer, preferring to read romance novels and
    science fiction, rather than taking action in your life? Yes _____
    No _____

11. Has anyone ever told you to grow up? Yes _____ No _____

12. Are you a rigid conformist? Yes _____ No _____

13. Have you ever questioned the religion of your youth? Yes _____
    No _____

14. Do you rigidly follow some type of guru or hero? Yes _____
    No _____

15. Do you talk a lot about the great things you are going to do, but
    never really do them? Yes _____ No _____

16. Do you believe that no one has ever been through the things
    you've had to go through, or that no one could really under-
    stand your unique pain? Yes _____ No _____

With the advent of puberty, childhood properly comes to an end.
Puberty marks the beginning of our first recycling. As I mentioned
earlier, Pam Levin's book *Cycles of Power* proposes that we evolve
cyclically. Life is a process involving the recurrence of certain themes
and patterns. Each recycling builds upon the preceding stage and
calls for more sophisticated adaptations. Each recycling is a time of
crisis. And each crisis is a time of increased vulnerability and heightened potential. If the critical challenge is surmounted, a regeneration
occurs in which the past is *reformed.*

## NORMAL ADOLESCENCE

A healthy achievement of the critical tasks of adolescence depends on the ego strengths developed in childhood. But the task of adolescence, which is the establishment of a *conscious identity,* is, as Erik Erikson pointed out, "more than the sum of ... childhood identifications." Adolescent identity is a *reformed identity.* To achieve it, we must integrate our genetic abilities and the ego strengths and skills cultivated earlier with the opportunities offered by our culture's social roles. Erikson defines this new ego identity as:

> ... the accrued confidence that the inner sameness and continuity [in my words, your I AMness] prepared in the past are matched by the sameness and continuity of one's meaning for others, as evidenced in the tangible promise of a "career."

What this means to me is that your inner child's sense of I AMness now must be affirmed in two ways. One affirmation will come from the mirroring eyes of a significant other in a love relationship (intimacy). The second affirmation will come from a meaningful career, one that enhances one's *beingness.* The two pillars of adult identity are Freud's famous two marks of maturity: *love* and *work.*

A wounded inner child can be a devastating force of contamination during one's adolescence. Even a person with a healthy inner child will still have to "refight many of the battles of earlier years." For *normal* adolescence is one of the stormiest times in the life cycle.

I like to describe normal adolescence using the letters of the word *adolescence.*

**A**mbivalence
**D**istancing from parents
**O**ccupation
**L**oneliness
**E**go identity
**S**exual exploration
**C**onceptualization
**E**gocentric thinking
**N**arcissism
**C**ommunication frenzy
**E**xperimentation

## Ambivalence

Ambivalence was described beautifully in J. D. Salinger's book *The Catcher in the Rye*. The main character, 16-year-old Holden Caulfield, wants to be an adult. He fantasizes drinking, having women, being a gangster. At the same time, he's terrified of adult life and fantasizes being the protector of his younger sister, Phoebe, and her preteenage friends. Staying with (and protecting) younger children protects him from having to face the adult world. Half of Holden's hair is gray. He is living between two worlds, childhood and adulthood. Ambivalence is the swinging back and forth between these two worlds.

Ambivalence also refers to the emotional upheavals and mood swings that are part of adolescence.

According to Anna Freud, it is normal for an adolescent to abhor his parents' presence one day and desire heart-to-heart talks with them the next day.

## Distancing from Parents

Distancing from parents is a normal part of adolescence. In order to leave home, adolescents have to make their parents unattractive. Yale psychologist Theodore Lidz has underscored the fact that "the conflict of generations is inherent in social living." Eight hundred years before Christ, Hesiod was terribly disturbed with the youth of his day. He wondered what was going to happen to the next generation. I heard a lady in the supermarket make similar statements yesterday!

The peer group is the vehicle by which adolescents achieve distancing. I like to refer to the *peer group parent* inasmuch as the peer group becomes a new parent. The peer group parent is very rigid and rule bound. For example, in my day, "ducktails" was the official hairstyle. My group wore tailor-made trousers with outer seams and pistol pockets. Other teenagers who didn't dress like us were considered "square." We made fun of them!

## Occupation

Several studies have shown that the number-one worry on teenagers' minds is career: What kind of work will I do? Where will I spend my energy? How will I take care of myself? What am I going to be when I grow up?

The life energy itself moves us to consider the kind of work we will spend our lives doing. The choices differ from culture to culture and from generation to generation. In times past, occupational choices were severely limited and pretty well determined in advance. Life was simpler then.

## Loneliness

Adolescence has always been a lonely time. No matter how many peer group buddies a person has, he feels an emptiness inside. The young person does not yet know who he is. He does not know for certain where he is going. Because of a newly emerged ability to think abstractedly, the future (a hypothesis) becomes a problem for the *first time in a person's life*. As a young person contemplates the future, he experiences a sense of absence. If he has a wounded inner child, that experience is intensified.

The adolescent's newly emerging cognitive structure also allows him to reflect on self (become self-conscious). Adolescents can think about thinking. This is why they can ask, "Who am I?" They become painfully aware of themselves. Self-consciousness is enhanced by the emergence of secondary sex characteristics. The newly experienced sexual feelings are powerful; the bodily changes are awkward. One feels embarrassed and strange.

## Ego Identity

I've already given you Erikson's definition of ego identity. The questions of "who am I" and "where am I going" are the results of the adolescent's new mental abilities.

## Sexual Exploration

With the emergence of secondary sex characteristics, a powerful new energy becomes present. This energy is the life spark expanding itself. "Life longs for itself," Nietzsche remarked. Genital sexuality is a species-preserving force. Without the sex drive, the species would die out in a hundred years.

Teenagers will naturally explore their sexuality. The first genital masturbation opens the throttle. Warnings of blindness, warts on the hand, even the penis eventual dropping off, pale into insignificance compared to this feeling. Who needs to see anyway—you can do it in the dark! Other forms of exploration often follow: mutual masturbation, opposite-sex fondling, and, finally, intercourse.

Exploring our genitals is crucial for healthy identity. Sex is who we are, rather than something we have. The first thing we notice about a person is their sex.

## Conceptualization

The ability to think in abstract, logical terms emerges at puberty, moving us beyond the concrete literal thinking of the school-age child. What an adolescent begins to do that a preadolescent cannot do is entertain *contrary to fact* propositions. For example, thinking about the future requires the ability to entertain a proposition that is contrary to fact. Who am I and where am I going? What are my possibilities? In adolescence, identity thinking is possibility thinking. "Suppose I become a doctor ... lawyer ... clergyman ..." and so on. Each of these suppositions involves the creation of a hypothesis that is not restricted by the facts.

Another manifestation of this new cognitive structure is idealization. Adolescents are dreamers. Dreaming and idealizing create models that motivate us. Adolescents also attach themselves to idols. Movie stars and rock stars are the most familiar, but a youth might look to a political or an intellectual idol as the motivator for his own career. Teenagers are naturally religious, and adolescence is the time of greatest religious readiness. A spiritual idol is often the core obsession of adolescence.

Adolescent idealization or idolization can also be directed toward a cult or a cause of some kind. The airport Hare Krishnas, the Chinese Red Guard, Hitler's mobilization of the German adolescents of his day—all attest to the way adolescents can be motivated to take on a cause—positive or negative. This commitment to a cause is the basis of an ego strength that Erikson calls fidelity. This is an important adult strength.

## Egocentric Thinking

Unlike the egocentrism of earlier stages, adolescents are fully capable of grasping another person's point of view. Their egocentrism consists in believing that their parents are as obsessed with them as they are with themselves. Adolescents are naturally paranoid. A casual glance is interpreted as a scathing evaluative judgment. Consider a common scenario. Little Shirley has just been slighted by the boy she idolizes. She arrives home depressed and feeling rejected. Mom says, "Hi honey, how's it going?" Little Shirley runs to her room shrieking, "Can't you ever leave me alone!" David Elkind has coined two phrases to characterize this egocentric quality of adolescent thinking: "the imaginary audience" and "personal fable." Both are grandiose ways of thinking. Shirley *thinks* her mom actually saw the earlier rejection scene and witnessed her humiliation. The acute self-consciousness of adolescence results from the belief that "everyone is looking at me." If the adolescent is shame-based, his self-consciousness is painfully intensified.

The personal fable is the belief that one's life is *utterly unique*. "No one has ever suffered like me," sounds the adolescent self-talk. It continues with "No one understands me," "No one loves me," "No one has ever had to put up with parents like mine." Remember Tom Sawyer's fantasy of dying? Tom sees his aunt and other adults gathered round his deathbed. They are all weeping buckets of tears. Now they finally understand what a unique and extraordinary person he was. This fable usually ends when a person establishes real intimacy. The sharing that takes place in an intimate relationship actually helps people to see how *ordinary* their experience is or was.

## Narcissism

Adolescents are narcissistic. They are obsessed by their own reflection in the mirror, they can spend hours looking at themselves. This flows from their intense self-consciousness. It is also a recycling of their early narcissistic needs.

## Communication Frenzy

In *The Catcher in the Rye*, Holden is always "giving someone a buzz" on the telephone. He has a voracious need to talk. The self-consciousness and aloneness of the developmental stage move adolescents to want to communicate. Talking endlessly to one's friends is a way to feel wanted and connected. I can vividly remember driving with my daughter during her adolescence. She would frantically scream out names of boys and girls as we passed them in the car.

## Experimentation

Adolescents experiment a great deal—with ideas, styles, roles, and behaviors. Often the experiments are in opposition to their parents' lifestyle or values. If Mom believes that "cleanliness is next to godliness," her adolescent daughter can be assured that she has her own identity by becoming a hippie with long hair, taking infrequent baths, and walking barefooted. If Dad's a superachiever work addict, his son can be assured of his identity by dropping out. If the parents are atheists, the son or daughter can have an identity by becoming very religious, or vice versa.

Experimentation is a way to expand one's horizons, to try on other ways of behaving before finalizing one's identity. All in all, adolescence is an integration and reformation of all the previous childhood stages. It is a summing up of all of one's ego strengths. Out of this reformation a new identity begins to emerge.

## GROWTH DISORDER

At best, adolescence is the stormiest time in the life cycle. Anna Freud has said that what is normal in adolescence would be considered highly neurotic at any other time. If this is the case when all the previous childhood stages have been resolved in a healthy way, imagine the problems that result from a severely wounded inner child. Many of us don't have to imagine them, we lived them.

For me, ambivalence turned into manic depressive behavior. Wild and promiscuous acting out opened the door to severe depression. I distanced myself by finding several guys from broken homes to run around with. We rebelled against our rigid Catholic upbringing by whoring and drinking. My own genetic predisposition to alcohol kicked in right away. I was having alcohol blackouts and getting in trouble from age 13 on.

Role diffusion is the danger Erikson points to in adolescence. Experimenting with too many roles, the adolescent loses a context within which to synthesize his ego strengths. As a teenager, I felt terribly confused and terribly alone. I had no father to rebel against or to use as a role model. I chose anti-heroes for role models. This is the dynamic behind what has been called "negative identity." I didn't know who I was, so I identified myself by what I was not. I was different, not like all the "squares" who peopled society. My group ridiculed and made fun of anyone who was not like us, and that comprised almost everyone! People with negative identity drop out and stand on the sidelines of life, making fun of everyone else.

In actuality I was terrified of life. (This has been true of all the negative identities I've known and worked with in therapy.) Having weak to nonexistent ego strengths, there was no way for me *to pull myself together*. Getting drunk was a way for me to feel grown-up and powerful. My inner emptiness drove me to mood alter in any way that I could.

It is in adolescence that we begin to act out our original pain and unmet childhood needs. The juvenile delinquent's violence attests to the undifferentiated rage of his hurt and lonely inner child. Criminality is a way to steal back what was lost in childhood. Drug use dulls the pain of the dysfunctional-family loneliness.

Adolescents often act out their families' unexpressed secrets. Sexual acting out is a natural during this time of emerging sexual energy. Mom's rigid repression of her shamed sexuality may come out in daughter's early promiscuity. Dad's secret sexual affairs may be acted out by his teenage son. The parental intimacy dysfunction, with its loneliness and anger, may be acted out in school failures.

Adolescents are often the scapegoats for family. They become the "identified patients," but they are really the family service bearers. When I ran a drug abuse program in Los Angeles, I never found an adolescent with drug problems whose parents had a healthy marriage. The parents carried multigenerational disease. Their marriages were adult-child marriages and the kids were trying to get them into therapy. When most teenagers act out, it is directly related to the dysfunctional families they belong to.

There is also the question of neglected developmental dependency needs. Adolescence is the time when personal identity begins to be sealed. Kids from dysfunctional families cannot possibly seal their identity, because they have no sense of I AMness when they begin adolescence.

My family was severely enmeshed as a result of my dad's alcoholism and his physically abandoning us. Our enmeshment looked like this.

## FAMILY ENMESHMENT

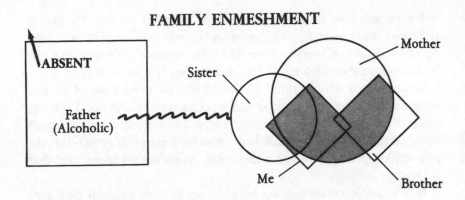

As you can see, none of us had a whole distinct self. Most of each of us was part of the others. When one of us felt something, the others felt it too. If mom was sad, we all felt sad. If she was angry, we all felt it and tried to stop her from being angry. There was very little foundation for me to create my identity.

As role diffusion intensifies, isolation and inner emptiness increase. *The most significant role one has played in the family system up to this point becomes the most available way to have an identity.* By age 21 I was totally confused. I was terrified of my sexuality. I felt empty and insecure. I was frightened and angry. I felt overwhelmed by the prospect of a career. I can remember walking downtown and wondering how all the men I saw had jobs, cars, houses, and so on. Being shame-based to the core, I felt like I'd never be able to make it. So, I fell back on the roles I had been assigned in my family system.

I continued to be a Star. I was senior class president, editor of the school paper, and a high academic achiever. I maintained all of this in addition to my alcoholism and my membership in the "guys without fathers" peer group. But my most significant role was Caretaker. This was the way I truly felt I mattered. When my dad left, I became the Little Man of the House. I was my brother's Little Parent. By caretaking, I mattered. So the way I solved my adolescent identity problem was to become a priest—a celibate priest. Putting on a black cassock and Roman collar gave me an immediate identity. Suddenly I was "Father" John. I was now a *caretaker of souls*. This was the most noble work that anyone could do. This was God's work. Being celibate was the price I had to pay.

By choosing to be a priest, I was doing something that my family, my religion, and my teachers (themselves nuns and priests) lauded. It was a noble sacrifice and a mark of generosity and goodness. It incidentally solved my career fears and maintained my family-system roles. I was a Star and Caretaker, and by marrying Holy Mother Church I would never have to leave my mother. Underneath this false identity, there remained a lonely, confused, and terrified little boy.

## DEBRIEFING

Not knowing who you are is the greatest tragedy of all. The rigid family-system roles sealed during adolescence become the most conscious identity you have. In fact, these roles become addictions. By being in the role, you feel that you matter. To let go of the role would be to touch the deep reservoir of toxic shame that binds your original pain, the core of which is the spiritual wound. When you lost your I AMness, you lost your mattering.

In writing out your adolescent history, focus on how your wounded inner child contaminated your adolescent life. Be sure to detail your traumas: the valentines that never came, the loneliness, the peer group pressure and rejections, the pain about your family.

## SHARE YOUR ADOLESCENT HISTORY WITH YOUR SUPPORT PERSON

Be sure to share your adolescent history with your support person. Your adolescent self is the way your wounded inner child adapted to start his adult life. Remember that your finalized roles are the sealed metaphors of your wounded child's history. You need validation for making the best decision you had available to you.

## FEELING THE FEELINGS

To heal your adolescent, you need to truly leave home. You also need to bring together all your developmental stages. I suggest that you have a big homecoming party with your adolescent as host. I use the following meditation to achieve this.

## HOMECOMING MEDITATION

Record on your tape recorder. Use Daniel Kobialka's tape *Going Home* as background music. Pause for twenty seconds at each interval.

Close your eyes and focus on your breathing.... As you breath in, gently pull your lower stomach in, as you breath out, push your stomach out. Breathe in to the count of four, hold for the count of four, and breathe out to the count of eight.... Do this several times.... Breathe in four, hold four, and breathe out to the count of sixteen.... Then breathe in four, hold four, and breathe out to the count of thirty-two.... Do that three times.... Now resume normal breathing. Focus on the number 3 as you breathe out.... See it, fingerpaint it, or hear "three" in your mind's ear.... Now the number 2.... Now the number 1.... Now see the one become a door.... Now open the door and walk down a long winding hallway with doors on either side. ... On your left see a door that says *Last Year.* ... Open that door and look in. See a pleasant scene from last year.... Close that door and walk to the next door on your right.... Open that door and see your adolescent standing there.... Embrace him. Tell him you know what he's been through.... Tell him it's time to leave home. Tell him that you are there to support him.... Tell him that together you will need to go and get all the other parts of yourself—your infant, toddler, preschooler, and school-age self.... Together with your adolescent, walk to the end of the corridor and open the door.... Look in and see the earliest house you remember living in.... Go into that house and find a room where your infant self resides.... Have your adolescent pick up your infant.... Now walk back into the corridor and open the first door on your left and see your toddler self.... You take him by the hand and walk back into the corridor.... Open the first door on your right and see your preschool self.... Look at him.... What is he wearing? You take him by the hand and walk out of that room. Now find your school-age self.... What is he wearing? ... Ask him to take your adolescent's hand and walk out of the house.... Now you are standing next to your adolescent self.... Who is holding your infant? ... Your school-age self is holding on to your adolescent's arm.... You are holding your toddler's and preschooler's hands.... Now, see your infant become your toddler.... Now see your toddler become your preschooler.... Now see your preschooler become your school-age self.... Now see your school-age self become your adolescent self.... You and your adolescent are standing side by side.... Now see your parents come out of a house you lived in as an adolescent.... You and your adolescent wave goodbye to them.... Tell them all of you is leaving now.... Tell them you know they did the best they could.... See them as the wounded people they actually are (were).... Forgive them for abandoning you.... Tell them you are going to parent yourself now.... Start walking away from that house.... Keep looking over your shoulder.... See them getting smaller and smaller.... Until they are completely out of sight.... Look ahead of you and see a lover/spouse/friend waiting for you.... If you have a therapist, see your therapist there.... If you have a support group, see them there.... If you have a higher power, see your higher power there.... Embrace all of them.... Know that you have support.... That you are not alone.... Know that you have or can create a new family of affiliation.... Now let your adolescent become one with you.... Pick an age from childhood and see the child within you at that age.... Tell him that you will champion him.... That you will be his new loving and nurturing parent.... Tell him that you know better than anyone else what he has gone through, the hurts and pains he has suffered.... Tell him that of all the people he will ever know, you are the only one he will never lose.... Tell him you will take time for him and spend time with him each day.... Tell him you love him with all your heart....

Now look out on the horizon of your mind.... See the number 3.... Feel your toes.... Wiggle them.... See the number 2.... Feel the energy come up through your legs into your upper body.... Feel the energy in your arms.... Wiggle your hands.... Feel the energy going into your head and brain.... Now see the number 1 and very slowly open your eyes and stretch.

Now you've reclaimed your whole inner family system. You've had a homecoming! Here's what mine looks like.

HAIL!, HAIL!,
THE GANG'S ALL HERE!

## FORGIVENESS

The process of reclaiming your wounded inner child is a forgiveness process. Forgiveness allows us to *give as before*. It heals the past and frees our energies for the present.

Forgiveness is not some sentimental or superficial process. Real harm was done to us and it needs to be legitimatized and validated. When we acknowledge the real harm that was done, we demythologize our parents. We see them for the real wounded human beings they actually are (were). We see that they were adult *children* acting out their own contaminations. Sam Keen says it well:

> When I demythologize my past and recognize the ambivalent and tragic character of all human action, I discover a new freedom to change the significance of what has been. . . . Forgiveness alone allows me both to accept my past and to be free from its crippling wounds. . . . Judgment, forgiveness, and gratitude perform the alchemy which transforms the past from fate into

fortune and which changes me from being a victim of causes over which I had no control to being a participant in a past which I continually re-form.

The grief work has to be done. Fritz Perls said: "Nothing changes till it becomes what it is." Only by demythologizing our parents can we grasp the real harm that was done to us. To grasp that real harm was done to us allows us to own our feelings about being violated. To feel the feelings is the original pain work. Once we've connected with and expressed those feelings, we are free to move on. Since we no longer carry unfinished business from the past, we no longer contaminate the present. Our energy is now available for empowering our lives. We can live in the now and create the future.

Forgiveness allows us to leave our parents. Our frozen grief formed the deep resentments that kept us attached to them. Resentments cause us to recycle the same feelings over and over again. Our wounded child's payoff for this is that *we never have to separate from our parents.* As long as we spend our energy secretly hating them, we remain attached to them, and this provides us with a way to avoid growing up. Forgiveness heals our resentments and enables us to divorce our wonder child from the shaming voices of our internalized parental figures. Forgiveness is the way we leave home internally.

Once we've reclaimed our wounded inner child, we must make a decision about our real parents, if they are still alive. What kind of relationship will we have with them? For those whose parents are still *offenders,* the decision should be to *stay away from them. I recommend that you leave them to their fate!* I know of many cases where parents continue to violate their adult children.

If your parents refuse to take any responsibility for their own wounded inner child, you need to remember that *your primary obligation is to your own life. You didn't come into this world to take care of your parents.* I'm not speaking here of infirm or disabled parents. I'm speaking of parents who refuse to take responsibility for their own inner woundedness. Each of you must let your adult decide on your boundaries with your real parents. Remember, your inner child is in your trust now. He expects you to protect him.

For most people, the reclaiming of their wounded child *creates a context for a new and richer relationship with their real parents.* By

becoming a new parent to your inner child, you help him finish
the past and fill the void in his psyche. As the child feels new
hope, autonomy, purpose, initiative, and competence, he can establish
his own identity. Then he can have a healthy relationship with his
parents.

# 3

# CHAMPIONING YOUR WOUNDED INNER CHILD

I want you to imagine what you would do if you had come upon that real child in the original situation.... What's a reasonable, compassionate thing to do for a child that's confused and upset? You sit and talk with the child. You listen to it. You find out what's bothering it, help it understand, comfort it, hold it in your arms; later, you play with it a little, explain things, tell a story. That's therapy in its oldest and best sense: nothing fancy, just kindness and patience.

—RON KURTZ

# INTRODUCTION

Now that you've reclaimed your wounded inner child, you need to champion him. As his champion, you will defend and fight vigilantly for him. Your wounded inner child needs someone with potency and power to protect him. With you as his nurturing and protecting parent, your wounded inner child can begin the process of healing. Championing your inner child is a way to become a new parent to yourself. It also allows your child to do the corrective work that will restore you to your true self. The new permissions and protection you need to give your inner child will form the core of your *corrective experiences*.

Original pain work was necessary for you to connect with your authentic self, your natural wonder child. But even after you've reclaimed him, work remains to be done. Because your wonder child was arrested in early stages of development, he didn't have a chance to learn the things he needed to learn at each developmental stage. Most of the wounded inner child's problems have resulted from these learning deficits. Now these deficits can be repaired.

Corrective experience is a form of reeducation. As your inner child's champion, you will nurture him, which involves good discipline. The Latin root of *discipline* means teaching and learning. The inner child has to be nurtured and taught the things he didn't learn at the proper time and in the proper sequence. Only with such discipline can our wonder child emerge fully.

# CHAPTER 9

# USING YOUR ADULT AS A NEW SOURCE OF POTENCY

Now we can speak ... of the "three P's" of therapy....
These are potency, permission, and protection.
—ERIC BERNE

For you to champion your wounded inner child, he must trust you enough to disobey the parental rules by which he was raised. Healthy permission is allowing the child to be *who he is* and to disobey the old shaming parental rules and beliefs. Such rules and beliefs are powerful: if the child disobeys them, he risks punishment and abandonment. Of course, this is terrifying to your inner child.

Now, as your adult gives your wounded inner child permission to disobey your parents' beliefs and rules, your inner child must believe that you have enough *power* to go against your parents. This power is what Eric Berne called *potency,* the first "P" in therapeutic change. I like to come to my inner child as a wise and gentle wizard because wizards have a lot of potency for kids. When I'm a wise old wizard, my inner child understands my power. I suggested earlier that you think about what it would have been like if the grown-up-you could have been there during the most painful and traumatic times of your childhood. Your inner child would have seen you as godlike and powerful. If you've done the reclaiming work, your wounded inner child already trusts you and believes in your potency. Nevertheless, you need to let your inner child know as much as possible about your power and strength. The following exercise will assist you in this.

## POTENCY LIST

List ten things you now own or are capable of doing that you could
not own or do as a child.
Examples:

1. Own a car
2. Drive a car
3. Have a bank account
4. Have real money in it
5. Buy all the ice cream and candy I want
6. Buy myself interesting toys
7. Have my own apartment, house, etc.
8. Do whatever I want to do
9. Go to movies without asking permission
10. Buy a pet if I want to

Now close your eyes and see your inner child. (Let him appear
at whatever age he appears.) When you see him (hear him, feel
him), tell him about the things on your list. He will be very
impressed!

## ASKING FORGIVENESS

Another way to build trust and establish your potency with your
inner child is to ask his forgiveness for neglecting him over the
years. One way to do this is to write a letter. Mine went like
this:

Dear Little John:
I want to tell you I love you just the way you are. I feel bad for
the way I've neglected you from my teenage years on. I drank
alcohol until we were sick. I drank until we couldn't remember
anything. I risked your precious life over and over again. After all
you went through as a child, this was a terrible thing for me to
do to you. I also stayed up all night partying and didn't give you
proper rest. Later, I worked endless hours and wouldn't let you

play.... All in all, I've been totally insensitive to you. I love you and promise to give you my time and attention. I will be here whenever you need me. I want to be your champion.

Love,
Big John

Next, using your nondominant hand, write a reply from your inner child:

Dear Big John:
I forgive you! Please don't ever leave me.

Love,
Little John

From the moment of reclaiming, it is *imperative* that you always tell your child the truth. The child also needs to hear that you are going to be there for him. Ron Kurtz says:

The child doesn't need to beat on the bed ... to get into pain and scream. The child needs something much simpler. It needs you to be there....

Being there for your child means giving him your time and attention. It's not helpful to be there because you think it's your duty and it makes *you* feel good to care for him. You need to listen to *his needs* and respond to *them*. He needs to know that *he matters* to you.

## TELLING YOUR CHILD ABOUT YOUR HIGHER POWER

Another powerful source of potency for your inner child is for you to tell him about your own Higher Power, if you have recognized one. I like to let my child know that I feel safe and protected in the belief that there is someone greater than myself. I call this someone God.

Most children are natural believers; they have no trouble with the concept of God. I tell my inner child that God showed me what He was like. He came into the world as a man named Jesus. Jesus tells me that God is both my mother and father. Jesus tells me that I can have a friendship with Him. He tells me that God made me the way I am, and wants me to grow and expand my I AMness. He tells me not to judge others and to forgive. Most of all, Jesus modeled His own I AMness. That's why He said, "I am the truth." He was the truth of himself. I like Jesus because I can talk to him and ask him favors. Jesus often gives me the things I ask for without my having to *do* anything to earn them. He loves me just the way I am. My higher power, God, also loves me just the way I am. In fact, my I AMness is like God's I AMness. When I truly *am,* I am most like God. I want my inner child to know that God loves us and will always *protect* us and *be with* us. In fact, Jesus's other name is Emmanuel, which means "God is *with* us." I let my inner child know that there is a power I can call on who is much greater than both of us!

## GIVING YOURSELF A NEW CHILDHOOD

Another powerful way to use your adult potency is a method called "changing your personal history." This method was developed by Richard Bandler and John Grinder and their colleagues as part of a remapping model called Neuro-Linguistic Programming (N.L.P.). I have used this model for the last eight years. It is enormously effective as long as the person has done his original pain work. If the unresolved grief is still there, this method can become just another head trip. Leslie Bandler, another N.L.P. founder, has attested to this in her fine book *The Emotional Hostage,* in which she confesses that she had severe emotional problems in spite of knowing and using very sophisticated N.L.P. techniques.

The technique for changing your personal history is excellent for modifying specific and traumatic scenes from childhood. These often become what Silvan Tomkins calls "shaping or governing scenes," the filters that shape our developmental history. They anchor our pain and unexpressed emotion, and they are recycled throughout our lives.

Changing our personal history will also work with more generalized patterns, such as not feeling wanted as a child. Change history is based on the cybernetic premise that our brain and central nervous system cannot tell the difference between real and imagined experience if the imagined experience is vivid and detailed enough. As Leslie Bandler puts it:

The tremendous effectiveness of change history was discovered by paying attention to how people can distort their internally generated experience and then act on the distortion, forgetting that they created it in the first place.

People often imagine things happening in the future and scare themselves with the pictures they themselves make. As Leslie Bandler points out, jealousy is a prime example:

> ... jealousy is an experience almost always generated as a result of a person making constructed images of a loved one with someone else and feeling bad in response to the picture they have themselves created.

The person feels bad and acts upon that feeling as if it were really a *fact*.

Or consider the power of a sexual fantasy. A person can create an image of a sexual partner or scene and be physiologically aroused by it.

Change history utilizes the same process deliberately. With change history you use the *potency* of your adult experiences to change the internal imprints from the past. Let's look at some examples.

## Infancy

Recall the work you did in part 2. What were your issues in infancy? Did you hear the kinds of affirmations that you needed to hear? Were your stroking needs met? If not, consider the following:

Think of some resources from your potent adult experience that would have helped you in infancy. For example, think of a time when you experienced being welcomed—perhaps when you met a dear old friend. Remember the joyous look on his face when he first saw you. Or you might remember a surprise party that was given for you. You were the center of attention.

In doing change history I close my eyes and go back to 1963, when I was voted "man of the year" at the end of my first year in the seminary. I can feel myself standing there. I can hear the applause and see the brightness of fifty smiling faces as they called out my name. I see Father Mally's face and the face of John Farrell, my best friend. As I feel the feelings, I touch my thumb to a finger on my right hand and hold it for thirty seconds. After thirty seconds I let go and relax my right hand. *I have now made an anchor of the welcoming experience*. Those of you working in groups made the same kind of anchors when you did the reclaiming meditations in part 2. If you are left-handed, make your resource anchor with your left hand.

## ANCHORS

Touching your right thumb and finger together is a kinesthetic anchor or trigger. Our lives are filled with old anchors, the result of neurologically imprinted experience. I've already talked about the brain physiology related to traumatic experience. The more traumatic, the more powerful the imprint. Any time a new experience resembles the earlier traumatic experience, the original emotions are triggered and the *original anchor is fired*.

All of our sensory experience is encoded this way. We have visual anchors. For example, someone might look at you in a way that reminds you of the way your violent father used to look just before he hit you. This could trigger a powerful emotional response—even if you didn't consciously make the connection. Anchors can also be auditory, olfactory, or gustatory. A tone of voice, a certain smell, or a particular food can trigger old memories with their accompanying emotions. Songs are perhaps the most powerful auditory anchors. I'll bet you've experienced riding in your car listening to the radio and suddenly you remembered a person or scene from long ago. Our whole lives are an accumulation of such anchored imprints—pleasant as well as painful.

We can change the painful memories from childhood by putting them together with actual experiences of strength acquired in our adult lives. If you didn't get your infancy needs met, if you were a Lost Child, *you can give yourself a new infancy*. You can do this by anchoring actual experiences relating to the strengths you have now. If you had had these strengths in infancy, you would have fared better. Once we've anchored these strengths, we then anchor the lost feelings of infancy. Then we activate both anchors simultaneously to *actually change your experience* of your infancy. Here are the steps to take.

### STEP ONE

Think of three positive experiences that you have had in adulthood that you needed and missed in infancy. Mine are:

A. The experience of being *welcomed*

B. The experience of *being held and cuddled*

C. The experience of *someone accepting me unconditionally*

## STEP TWO

Close your eyes and remember experience A. You need to actually be there, seeing out of your own eyes, feeling your feelings, etc. When you can feel the joy of being *welcomed,* make a kinesthetic anchor with your thumb and finger. Hold it for thirty seconds and then release it. Open your eyes and focus on something around you. Wait a few minutes, and then close your eyes and do experience B. Anchor it *exactly* as you did experience A.

This is called *stacking* the anchor. Stacking intensifies the power of the resource anchor. It increases the voltage. Open your eyes and spend a few minutes focusing on some object in the room. Then close your eyes and do experience C. Anchor it exactly as you did A and B.

Now you have anchored your positive adult resources. We'll call this anchor Y.

## STEP THREE

Now you need to anchor the feelings of infancy. Go back to the meditation in chapter 4. Follow that meditation until you are the infant in your crib. Anchor the feeling of being alone and unwanted. This is your negative anchor. Put it on your left hand, if you're right-handed, by touching your left thumb to a finger on your left hand. If you're left-handed, put the anchor on your right hand. We'll call this anchor X.

## STEP FOUR

Now you are going to take the strengths you have anchored in Step Two and bring them back into your infancy. You do this by touching both anchors X and Y simultaneously. As you hold them, let yourself feel yourself welcomed to the world. Let yourself feel warm hugging. When you are filled with warmth and strength, let go of both anchors and open your eyes. Let yourself feel the unconditional positive regard.

## STEP FIVE

Sit with this experience for ten minutes and let yourself assimilate it. You have championed your inner infant child. You have mixed your earliest neurological imprints with later, more nurturing ones. From now on, when you enter a new situation and your infancy is triggered, you will experience your new experience XY. The old experience X will also fire, but it will no longer dominate. From now on, when your infancy needs come up, you will have more of a choice.

## STEP SIX

The N.L.P. folks call this step *future pacing*. It consists of imagining a time in the future when you will confront a new situation that triggers your infancy needs: for example, going to a party where you don't know anyone, or starting a new job. You future pace it by firing anchor Y (your positive anchor) and imagining yourself in the new situation. See, hear, and feel yourself handling it well. After you've done that, run through the imaginary scene again without the positive anchor. What future pacing actually amounts to is a *positive* dress rehearsal. Those of us with a wounded inner child tend to do negative dress rehearsals. We create catastrophic images of danger and rejection. Future pacing gives us a way to reshape our inner expectations.

The same basic change-history technique can be used to heal memories from toddlerhood, preschool and school-age. It is important to realize that different traumatic events may call for different resources from your adult. For example, as a preschooler I hit a playmate with a stick. I was goaded into this bullying behavior by some other boys. The father of the boy I hit happened to be a *professional wrestler*! That night he came to our house to reprimand me. I heard him yelling at my father. He was saying that I needed to be whipped with a belt. I remember being terrified and hiding in the basement.

This memory is very different from the preschool memory of being alone in an apartment with my mom on my birthday. I was terribly sad. I didn't know where my dad was and I missed him.

Each of these memories necessitates the anchoring of a different strength.

Here are some examples of changing history at each stage of my childhood.

## Toddlerhood

I cannot remember any specific traumatic events during these years, but when I look at the Index of Suspicion for the toddler stage, I know my toddler needs were not met. So, I like to work on the entire developmental stage.

1. I think of a time during adulthood when:

   A. I respectfully said I would not do something.
   B. I wanted something and went after it.
   C. I expressed anger respectfully.

2. Using each of these experiences, I create a stacked anchor.

3. I create an anchor of an imagined scene in which I was spanked for being curious and exploring the exciting things in the living room. When told to stop, I said, "No, I won't." That's when I got the spanking.

4. Firing the two anchors simultaneously, I redo the imagined scene. I say I won't, express my anger, and go exploring and touching everything I want.

5. I reflect on my issues around toddler independence and consider how these needs impact my present life.

6. I imagine myself in the future looking through a sporting goods store. I touch anything that strikes my fancy and say no every time a salesperson tries to help me.

## Preschool

In this period I work on the scene with the boy I hit and my fear of his wrestler father.

1. I think of strengths that my potent adult *now* has that, had I possessed them then, would have enabled me to handle that situation less stressfully. For example, I could:

   A. Call the police
   B. Call on my higher power for protection
   C. Take responsibility for bullying the child and apologize

**2.** I stack an anchor composed of A, B, and C as a positive resource.

**3.** I anchor the scene of hiding in the basement in terror when the boy's father came to reprimand me.

**4.** I fire the two anchors and redo the scene till it feels better.

**5.** I reflect on the impact of that scene in my life. (I have an abnormal fear of brawling-type men.)

**6.** I future pace to a scene where I successfully confront a "brawler" male.

## School-Age

During my school years my family was slowly disintegrating. There are many traumatic events that I could work on, but I'll select Christmas Eve when I was 11 years old. My dad had come home drunk. I had been looking forward to the whole family spending time together. My dad was supposed to be home by 1:00 P.M. We had planned to get a Christmas tree in the afternoon and the whole family was to decorate it together that night before going to Midnight Mass. My dad didn't arrive home till 8:30 P.M. He was so drunk he was staggering. I had grown more and more angry as the day went on. I was also very scared when he was drinking. He was not violent, but he was unpredictable. I isolated myself in my room, got into bed, pulled the covers over my head, and refused to speak to anyone.

**1.** I think of the strengths my adult now has that could have helped me handle the scene differently. For example, I can now express anger firmly in a way that is still respectful to the other person. I'm physically stronger and independent; I can leave a painful situation that is out of my control. I am now articulate and can say the things I need to say. To do the change-history exercise, I think of a time when:

   A. I expressed anger in a straightforward and valuing way.
   B. I left a painful situation.
   C. I was speaking to an authority figure in a coherent and articulate manner.

**2.** I make a stacked anchor involving these three experiences.

**3.** I anchor the original scene—my withdrawal from my drunken father on Christmas Eve.

**4.** I fire the two anchors simultaneously and redo the early scene. I walk out of my bedroom and confront my father. I say, "Daddy, I'm sorry you have an illness; I know you must be lonely and filled with shame. But I will not let you continue to ruin my holidays and my childhood. I'm not going to stay here and be in pain. I'm going to my friend's house for Christmas. I will not let you shame me any longer."

Notice that I do not imagine my father's response. When you redo such a scene, you should focus only on *your* behavior and your internal state. You cannot change another person.

**5.** I reflect on how that scene has governed portions of my later interpersonal behavior. I realize how many times I've been moved to an anger/isolation sequence by this old anchor. I'm happy to change this old memory.

**6.** I think of a situation in the future where the expression of anger will be called for. I rehearse the scene with my positive anchor. I then rehearse it without the anchor. It feels good to assert myself and hang in there.

Several questions usually come up when I teach the change-history method.

*What if I don't really feel a change after I work on a scene?*
You may need to work on the same scene a number of times. I've done the Christmas Eve scene a half-dozen times and I've done some others a dozen times. Remember that the original anchors are very powerful. To counteract them, you need very well-formed new anchors.

*How can I form better resource anchors?*
The resource anchors are the key to doing effective work. Achieving well-formed resource anchors requires time and practice. The conditions for well-formed anchors are:

1. *High intensity access.* This means that the best resource anchors are made when you're experiencing the positive resource most intensely. Internal memories are experienced in two ways: asso-

ciated and dissociated. Associated memories occur when you're *actually experiencing* the old memory. Dissociated memories occur when you're observing the old memory. Try this experiment: Close your eyes and see yourself standing in the middle of a jungle. See a large tiger charging out of the underbrush coming toward you. See a huge boa constrictor on your left about to strike you.... Now float into your body and actually be there. Look down at your hiking boots and your khaki pants. Look up and see the tiger coming at you. Hear his shrieking, growling roar. As you start to run, you see a huge boa constrictor on your left about to strike at you.... Now open your eyes.

Compare what you felt in both exercises. The first was a *dissociated* internal experience. The feeling intensity is usually very low. The second was an *associated* internal experience. The feeling intensity is usually much more powerful.

Now make the well-formed anchors you need to work with *associated* memories. You want high-voltage energy to combat the old anchor.

2. *Well-timed application.* The resource anchor needs to be set when the energy is at its highest voltage. To do this well takes practice. I like to hold my anchors for thirty seconds to a minute in order to anchor the highest voltage possible.

3. *Duplication.* Fortunately, you can test your anchors. If you've made a good anchor, it can be fired anytime. When you touch your thumb and finger you can feel the resource energy start circulating. I always wait five minutes and check my resource anchors. If they are not of high voltage, I redo them. In fact, I make it a rule *always* to check my resource anchors to be sure they're well formed.

*What happens to the resource anchor once I've used it to collapse the old anchor?* The resource anchor is still there in a diluted form, but it needs to be set again if you want to use it for some other event. You can make touch anchors in a variety of ways anywhere on your body. I use my fingers because they are handy.

A final exercise will help you determine how well you've changed that past piece of your personal history (i.e., collapsed that old anchor). This exercise involves testing the negative anchor X. Close your eyes and spend a couple of minutes focusing on your breathing. Then slowly fire your left-hand anchor. Pay close attention to what you feel and experience. If you've done your change-history exercise well, the negative experience should feel different. It usually *does not feel dramatically different.* Usually it just feels less intense. That's what I realistically expect from the change-history technique—a lessening of intensity. All of our human experiences are *useful in some context.* It's prudent to suppress anger and withdraw when a violent drunk or a physical offender is raging at you. The job of championing is not to take anything away from your inner child's experience, but to give him some more flexible *choices.* Change history does that. It allows your adult to protect your inner child while he experiences another choice. This softens the rigidity of the original experience.

## MAKING A SECURITY ANCHOR

Another way you can use your adult's potency to champion your inner child is to make a security anchor. This involves thinking of the two or three experiences in your life where you felt the most secure. If you have trouble thinking of these, you can simply imagine a scene of absolute security. The three experiences I used to make my security anchor were:

A. A time in the monastery when I felt completely one with God
B. A memory of being held in a love embrace by someone who loved me unconditionally at that moment
C. A memory of being wrapped in my soft comforter, waking up after ten hours of sleep and having no obligations or responsibilities (There was nothing I had to *do* and nowhere I had to *go.*)

Make a stacked anchor of your three security experiences. You can use more experiences if you want to. I consider this anchor a *permanent* one. I worked for thirty minutes every day for one entire week to make mine. It is very powerful. Whenever my inner child gets scared, I fire the anchor. It's wonderful! It takes me out of any fearful state. The fearful feelings try to come back, but the anchor interrupts an "awfulizing spiral." It gives me some moments of safety and relief. Sometimes it relieves my child's fears completely.

## LETTING YOUR ADULT FIND NEW FATHERS AND MOTHERS FOR YOUR INNER CHILD

Another way to champion your inner child is to let your adult find new sources of nurturing for him. I call these sources new mothers and fathers. The crucial issue here is to let *your adult* find them, not your inner child. When your wounded inner child does the choosing, it sets you up to reexperience your earlier abandonment. The wounded inner child wants his real parents to love him unconditionally. To him, the logical thing is to find adults who have the positive and negative traits of his abandoning parent(s). Of course, this leads to great disappointment. The inner child projects onto his adult parent substitute a godlike esteem that cannot be lived up to. As a limited human being, the adult parent substitute cannot meet the child's fantasy expectation. The wounded inner child then feels let down and abandoned. Your inner child needs to know that *childhood is over* and that you can *never go back and really have new parents*. You have to grieve the loss of your real childhood and your real parents. Your child needs to know that *you as an adult* will do the necessary reparenting. However, the adult in you can find people who can nurture and stimulate your growth. For example, the poet Robert Bly is one of my new fathers. He is inspiring and insightful. He touches my wonder child and stimulates me to think and feel. He is sensitive and kind. And even though I don't know him personally, I love him and embrace him as a father. A priest named David is another of my fathers. He gave me unconditional positive regard during my last days at the seminary. I wanted to leave, but I felt I'd be a failure if I did. I was terribly confused and inundated with shame. Father David was my spiritual counselor. No matter how much I beat up on myself, he gently focused on my strengths and my value as a person. An Episcopal clergyman, Father Charles Wyatt Brown, is yet another of my fathers. He accepted me unconditionally when I was just getting started as a lecturer.

I also have intellectual fathers such as Saint Augustine, Saint Thomas Aquinas, the French philosopher Jacques Maritain, Dostoevski, Kierkegaard, Nietzsche, and Kafka. (To tell the truth, my kid only tolerates our intellectual fathers. He trusts me that they are nurturing fathers for us, but he thinks they are extremely boring!)

I have found several mothers for my inner child and me. Virginia Satir, the wonderful family-systems thinker and therapist, is one of them. So is Sister Mary Huberta, who took a special interest in me in elementary school. I knew that I mattered to her. We still write to each other. I have an old girlfriend who will always be one of my mothers. In my spiritual quest, Saint Teresa, the Little Flower, modeled maternal nurturing for me. I've had powerful nurturing from Mary, the mother of Jesus. She is truly my heavenly mother.

God is my main father. Jesus is both my father and my brother. Jesus shows me how God, my father, loves me unconditionally. I have had great healing reading the biblical stories of the Prodigal Son and the shepherd who goes after the lost sheep. In that story the shepherd leaves his whole flock to go and look for one lost sheep. No *sane* shepherd would do this. His flock represents his worldly wealth. To risk losing all his sheep in order to find one lost sheep would be frivolous and irresponsible. The point of the story is that God's love for us goes to this extreme. My inner child feels like the lost sheep sometimes, and he rejoices when I show him that our Heavenly Father loves and protects us.

Currently, I have four very close male friends. They are my brothers in the truest sense of the word. Often they are also my fathers. On many occasions, George, Johnny, Michael, and Kip have nurtured my scared and shame-based little boy. They have called me to my potency by loving me unconditionally. My kid and I know that they will be there for me. Recently I've added Pat to the list. He and I are both on the workshop circuit and we both have best-selling books. He understands certain issues that others cannot share. In many ways, the adult can take what he gets from other adults and let it be parenting for the inner child.

Unless we reclaim and champion our inner child, his neediness will become all-consuming. Children need their parents all the time. A child's needs are insatiable. If we let our inner child run the show, we will drive our friends and loved ones crazy with our neediness. Once we've done our original pain work, we can learn to trust our adult to get the nurturing we need from other adults.

For a number of reasons, my last birthday was an especially lonely time. My friend Johnny was sensitive to my inner state. Johnny also knows I'm a passionate golfer. So he had a putter custom-made for me. Normally my friends and I do not exchange birthday presents. Johnny's gift was very special and precious. My adult accepted it as an act of fathering. With that gift, Johnny was fathering me.

# CHAPTER 10

# GIVING YOUR INNER CHILD NEW PERMISSIONS

> When we think about the well-being of our children, we plan to provide for them what was lacking for us.... Then, when the first child arrives we come face to face with the reality that parenting is much more than a loving dream.... Some days we find ourselves doing the very things we vowed we would never do.... Or we give in.... We need to learn skills, often many skills, that we did not learn in our families of origin.
>
> —JEAN ILLSLEY CLARKE AND CONNIE DAWSON

> Our own inner child has to be disciplined in order to release its tremendous spiritual power.
>
> —MARION WOODMAN

Once you start to champion your wounded inner child, you come face to face with another dilemma. Since most of us are from dysfunctional families, we really *do not know how* to be nurturing parents to our inner child. Our wounded inner child is childish. He was either overdisciplined or underdisciplined. We must become good nurturing disciplinarians if we want our wounded inner child to heal. Your inner child needs to internalize new rules that will allow him to grow and flourish. Your adult needs to gather new information about what constitutes good discipline and to learn new skills for interacting with your inner child. You'll use your adult potency to give your inner child new permissions. He needs permission, to *break* his old parenting rules, permission to be his authentic self, and permission to play.

## NURTURING DISCIPLINE

Someone once said that "of all the masks of freedom, discipline is the most impenetrable." I like that. Without discipline our inner child cannot truly be free. M. Scott Peck has important things to say on this point. Peck sees discipline as a set of techniques geared to ease life's inevitable pain. That's a far cry from what I learned as a child. Deep in my subconscious, discipline means punishment and pain. For Peck, good discipline is a set of teachings about how to live our lives more gracefully. Good discipline involves rules that allow a person to be who he is. Such rules enhance our being and protect our I AMness. Here is a set of nurturing rules for you to teach your wonderful inner child.

1. It's okay to feel what you feel. Feelings are not right or wrong. They just are. There is no one who can tell you what you *should* feel. It's good and it's necessary to talk about feelings.

2. It's okay to want what you want. There's nothing you should or should not want. If you're in touch with your life energy, you will want to expand and grow. It's okay and it's necessary to get your needs met. It's good to ask for what you want.

3. It's okay to see and hear what you see and hear. Whatever you saw and heard *is* what you saw and heard.

4. It's okay and it's necessary to have lots of fun and play. It's okay to enjoy sexual play.

5. It's essential to tell the truth at all times. This will reduce life's pain. Lying distorts reality. All forms of distorted thinking must be corrected.

6. It's important to know your limits and to *delay* gratification some of the time. This will reduce life's pain.

7. It's crucial to develop a balanced sense of responsibility. This means accepting the consequences for what you do and refusing to accept the consequences for what someone else does.

8. It's okay to make mistakes. Mistakes are our teachers—they help us to learn.

9. Other people's feelings, needs, and wants are to be respected and valued. Violating other people leads to guilt and to accepting the consequences.

10. It's okay to have problems. They need to be resolved. It's okay to have conflict. It needs to be resolved.

Let me comment briefly on each of the new rules.

## New Rule One

It is very scary for your wounded inner child to break the old family *no-talk* rules, or the rule that says feelings are weak and should not be expressed. You must be careful to give your child some guidance in this area. By all means give him permission to feel what he feels and teach him that feelings are not right or wrong. But you need to get some clear guidelines on expressed feelings. There are some situations in which it is not safe or appropriate to express feelings. For example, don't encourage your inner child to express his feelings to the policeman when he gives you a ticket. Rarely is it appropriate to express your abandonment feelings to your parents. You need to express these feelings in the ways I described in part 2.

Your inner child also needs to learn the difference between *expressing* a feeling and *acting* on a feeling. For example, anger is a perfectly valid feeling. It signals that a violation of our basic needs or rights has occurred or is about to occur. Expressing anger is valid in this situation, but it is not valid to hit, curse, scream, or destroy property.

You need to provide a safe, nonshaming environment where your child can express his feelings freely. This may necessitate your joining a support group in which the participants are working on similar issues.

In addition, you need to teach your inner child that your feelings

are a part of your personal power. They are the psychic fuel that
moves you to get your needs met. They signal you when there is
danger, when you are being violated, and when you have lost something of value.

## New Rule Two

This rule counteracts the toxic shaming your wounded inner child
feels about needs and wants. Remember the drawing of our 180-pound
3-year-old parents? As adult children they never got their needs or
wants met, so when you were needy or wanting, it made them angry
and they shamed you.

Your toxically shamed inner child doesn't believe he has the right
to *want* anything. You can champion him by listening carefully to
what he needs and wants. You may not always be able to give him
what he wants, but you can listen and give him permission to want it.
Without desire and wanting, our life energy gets crushed.

## New Rule Three

Rule three counteracts the delusion and lying that occur in dysfunctional families. Little Judy comes home from school and *sees* mother
crying. She asks, "What's the matter, Mom?" Her mom answers, "Nothing. Go outside and play!" Little Farquhar sees his dad lying next to
the car in the garage early one morning. Curious and confused, he
asks his mom why Dad is sleeping in the garage. She answers that Dad
needs to sleep on the cement floor in the garage because "he has a bad
back"! Little Billy *hears* his mom and dad fighting. He is awakened
out of a deep sleep. He goes to their room and asks what's the matter.
They say, "Nothing. Go back to sleep. You must be dreaming!"

Children who get these kinds of messages quit trusting their own
senses. Without sensory data it's hard to live in reality. Children are
sensory experts. We need our inner child's sensory expertise. To get
it, we must give our inner child permission to look, listen, touch, and
explore the world.

## New Rule Four

Rule four is about playing and having fun. Playing is a way of just
*being*. I've learned to schedule blocks of time for playing. During

those times I may play golf or go fishing or *do nothing*. I like to go places and just wander around. Wandering around and having nothing to do are adult forms of play. We get our *being* needs met when we allow our inner child to play.

Another wonderful form of play for adults is sexual play. The best form of sexual play is when our adults usher our parents out of the room, guard the door, and let our natural inner kids have at it. The inner child loves to touch, taste, smell, see, and talk during sex play. He loves to spend time exploring, especially if he was taught that sex was shameful and looking was prohibited. It is very important to let your inner child romp and play sexually. Your adult needs to set the moral limits you believe in. But within those limits, it's good to have lots of sex play in your life.

## New Rule Five

Rule five may be the most important of all. Early on, your natural inner child learned to adapt in order to survive. In dysfunctional families there is a lot of lying. The delusion and denial that surrounds the family is a lie. The false roles family members play are lies. Hiding the unpleasant aspects of family life necessitates lying. Lying becomes a way of life in dysfunctional families, and your inner child will find that it takes real effort to unlearn.

Your wounded inner child also has ways of thinking that violate reality and distort the truth. All children think magically and in absolutist ways, and this must be confronted.

Your wounded inner child is also shame-based. His shame-based thinking must be corrected. Following are some of the common thinking distortions to watch out for when you are dialoguing with your inner child:

*Polarized thinking.* The wounded inner child perceives everything in extremes. It is either/or; there is no in between. People or things are either good or bad. The wounded inner child thinks that if someone doesn't want to be with him every minute of every day, then the person doesn't really love him. This is absolutist thinking. It results from the poor resolution of object constancy in the toddler stage. Absolutizing leads to hopelessness. You must teach your inner child the truth that everyone is both good and bad, and that there are no absolutes.

*Catastrophizing.* Your wounded inner child was taught to awfulize and catastrophize by the wounded inner child in your parents. The burden of raising you was often too much for your adult child parents to bear. They fretted, worried, and hypnotized you with their endless stream of anxious reminders. Just when you needed the security to experiment and explore, you were terrorized with wails of "watch out," "be careful," "stop," "don't," and "hurry up." It's no wonder that your inner child is hypervigilant—he was taught that the world is a frightful and dangerous place. You can champion your inner child now by giving him permission to venture out and try things, assuring him that it is okay, that you are there to watch over him.

*Universalizing.* Your wounded inner child tends to make sweeping generalizations out of single incidents. If your boyfriend says he'd like to stay home tonight and read, your inner child sounds the death knell on the relationship. If someone turns you down for a date, your wounded inner child concludes, "I'll *never* get another date. No one will *ever* want to go out with me." If you're learning to water ski and you fail to get up on the skis the first time out, your inner child concludes that you'll *never* learn to ski.

You can champion your child by confronting and correcting his universalizing. One way to do this is to exaggerate words like *all, never, no one, always, ever,* etc. When the child says things like, "*No one ever* pays attention to me," you answer, "You mean that not one single person in the whole world has *ever, ever, ever* looked at you or talked to you?" Teach him to use words like *often, maybe,* and *sometimes* instead.

Words anchor our experiences. We literally hypnotize ourselves with words. Our wounded inner child scares himself with distorted words. But words used accurately are our vehicle for being truthful and honest. Our inner kid needs to learn now to be honest.

*Mind-reading.* Mind-reading is a form of magic. Children are naturally magical, and when parents say things like, "I know what you're thinking," they reinforce the child's magic. Children whose senses are shamed rely more and more on magic. Your inner child might say things to you like, "I know my boss is getting ready to fire me. I can tell by the way he looked at me."

Mind-reading also flows from your wounded inner child's projections. Let's say your inner child doesn't like someone, but your parents used to scold you for not liking everyone. So your child's sense of dislike is now hidden and shame-bound. This is demonstrated when the child says, "I think so-and-so really dislikes *me*." In reality, your inner child really dislikes *him*.

It is very important to confront your inner child's mind-reading. The world has enough real threats in it without our fabricating more. Teach your inner child to check things out. Give him permission to ask lots of questions.

Honesty and truthfulness create trust, and trust engenders love and intimacy. Each time your inner child tries to lie or exaggerates or distorts reality with absolutizing and magic, you must correct him. Nurturing love and discipline reduce the pain that comes from lying and distortion.

## New Rule Six

Rule six involves the voracious neediness of the inner child. All children want what they want *when* they want it. They have a low tolerance for frustration and delay. Part of growing up is learning to delay gratification, which helps reduce life's pain and difficulties. For example, overeating causes stomachaches and discomfort; spending all your money at once leaves you without any reserves.

When a child is deprived and neglected, he has a much harder time delaying gratification. Our wounded inner child believes that there is a severe scarcity of love, food, strokes, and enjoyment. Therefore, whenever the opportunity arises to have these things, our inner kid goes overboard.

For years I found myself putting more food on my plate than I could eat. However, I always ate it all. I also found myself buying many things that I didn't need just because I had the money. I'd pile them up in my room until I was surrounded by my stuff. I also found myself feeling jealous of any other therapist or speaker who was popular. As if there were not enough recovering people to go around; or as if there were a limited amount of love and admiration and, if another person got it, I would be left out. All of this was the out-pouring of my wounded inner child. He believed that I would never get my share of things so I'd better get as much as I could while I had the chance. His indulgences have caused me much pain over the years.

I now champion my wounded inner child by taking very good care of him. I promise him wonderful things and *I always keep my promises to him*. You must always follow through with your promises if you want to win your inner child's trust. By giving my child lots of good things, I'm teaching him. He still takes over from time to time, but it's so much better than it used to be. I'm proving to him that we can have *more* pleasure if we delay gratification.

For example, I recently did an experiment with him. He loves candy, pie, sundaes, and so on. I let him eat all the sweets he wanted for a week. We evaluated how we felt at the end of that time. We felt terrible—five extra pounds, my gut hanging over my uncomfortably tight size-38 pants. I then refused to let him eat any sweets for the first six days of the following week. We exercised as often as possible. On Sunday I let him eat sweets. We then evaluated how we felt. Much, much better. Actually, we didn't eat a lot of sweets on Sunday.

This diet may not get the endorsement of the AMA or the nutritionists, but I proved to Little John that there is *more pleasure* in delaying gratification than in pigging out.

## New Rule Seven

Rule seven is a key to happiness. So much human suffering comes from the wounded inner child's taking on too much responsibility or refusing to accept enough responsibility.

You need to face squarely the consequences of your behavior. By reclaiming your wounded inner child you've begun the work of being *responsible*. Most of the inner child's responses are not true responses; rather, they are anchored reactions and overreactions. A true response results from one's true feelings and conscious decision. In order to give a true response, one must be in touch with his feelings, needs, and wants. Adults with a wounded inner child are to some degree out of touch with all of these.

To champion your inner child is to teach him to act rather than react. To take action you have to be *able to respond. Response ability* comes when you are in control of your inner child's life rather than the other way around.

The best illustration I know of the importance of taking this responsibility is an intimate relationship. Intimacy can take place because we all have a wonderful, vulnerable inner child. Two people "in love" reenact the symbiosis of the earliest mother/child bonding. In essence, they fuse into each other. They feel an omnipotent sense of oneness and power. Each shares his deepest, *most vulnerable self* with the other.

This very vulnerability causes people to fear intimate relationships and ultimately can destroy intimacy. The destruction of intimacy in a relationship occurs when either or both partners refuse to take responsibility for their own vulnerable inner child.

Let's see what happens when two adult children fall in love. Their wounded inner kids are elated. Each sees in the partner the positive and negative qualities of his or her original parents. Each believes that, this time, their child's unmet needs will finally be taken care of. Each overinvests power and esteem in the other. Each wounded child sees the other as his or her original parent. Shortly after they are married, they will begin to make demands on each other. These demands mask primarily *unconscious* expectations that flow from the longing and emptiness in each partner's wounded inner child. Nature abhors a vacuum, and the life spark pushes the wounded inner child to finish what is unfinished. He looks for the parental nurturing he never got but still longs for. A partner may even *provoke* the other to act like his or her original parent. At times one may *distort* what his partner does so that the partner looks like his original parent. All in all, it is not a pretty picture! It is equivalent to two 4-year-olds getting married and trying to assume adult responsibilities.

If you've reclaimed your inner child, you have a chance. By championing your inner child, *you take responsibility for his vulnerability*. When you commit to reparent your inner child, you safeguard yourself from bonding with someone with the expectation that he will be your lost parent. *Intimacy works if each partner takes responsibility for his or her own vulnerable inner child*. It will not work if you try to set up your partner to give you what your parents failed to give.

## New Rule Eight

Rule eight is a way to teach your inner child a healthy sense of shame. Toxic shame forces us to be more than human (perfect) or less than human (a slob). Healthy shame allows you to make mistakes, which are an integral part of being human. Mistakes serve as warnings from which we can learn life-long lessons. Having permission to make mistakes allows our inner child to be more spontaneous. To live in dread of making a mistake causes you to walk on eggs and live a guarded, shallow existence. If your inner child believes he must watch every word so that he never says the wrong thing, he may never say the right thing. He may never ask for help or say that he hurts or that he loves you.

## New Rule Nine

Rule nine is the Golden Rule. It asks you to teach your inner child to love, value, and respect other people as you love, value, and respect yourself. It also lets your inner child know that when he violates this rule, he will have to accept the consequences. Our wounded inner kids need to learn accountability and healthy guilt. Healthy guilt is moral shame. It tells us that we have violated our own and others' values and that we must pay the price for doing so. Healthy guilt is the basis of a healthy conscience, which our inner child needs. The offender behavior I discussed earlier occurs mainly because the wounded inner child has never developed his own conscience. In the case of an abused child identifying with his offender, the child has his offender's distorted value system. In the case of empowerment through indulgence and submission, the child believes that the standard rules for average people don't apply to him: his "specialness" gives him permission to be above the rules.

## New Rule Ten

Rule ten lets your inner child know that life is fraught with problems. So often the inner child is outraged over problems and troubles. "It isn't fair," he moans. "I can't believe this has happened to me," is a statement I often heard as a therapist. As if problems and trouble were a dirty trick spawned by some sadistic cosmic spirit! Problems and troubles are part of every person's life. As M. Scott Peck said, "The way to handle life's problem is by solving them." In fact, the way we handle our problems and troubles determines the quality of our lives. I heard Terry Gorski, a therapist in Chicago, once say that "growth is moving from one set of problems to a better set of problems." I like that. It has been absolutely true in my life. Each new success brings brand-new problems.

We need to teach our inner child that problems are normal and that he must accept them.

We also need to teach our inner child that conflict is inevitable in human relationships. In fact, intimacy is impossible without a relationship that has the capacity for conflict. We need to help our inner child learn how to fight fair and resolve conflict. I will say more on that in chapter 12.

Learning these new rules gives your inner child permission to break the old rules. Once the new rules are internalized, they are second nature to the inner child and will foster self-love and a healing of the spiritual wound.

## PERMISSION TO BE YOU

Your inner child needs your unconditional permission to be himself. The nurturing discipline I just described will go a long way toward facilitating this self-restoration. Another way to help is to give your inner child permission to give up the ridid role(s) he took on in order to balance the family system and to feel that he mattered. I've said enough about the roles and how they get set up in dysfunctional family systems. You started giving your inner child permission to give up these rigid roles when you reclaimed your toddler self and your preschool self. Let those sections serve as a general model for all your false-self roles.

### Giving Up False-Self Roles

#### STEP ONE

First you need to get a clearer picture of your family-system roles. How did you learn to matter as a child? What did you do to keep your family together and to take care of its needs? Some common roles are: Hero, Star, Superachiever, Mom's Little Man, Mom's or Dad's Surrogate Spouse, Dad's Little Princess, Dad's Buddy, Mom's Sorority Sister, Mom's or Dad's Enabler or Caretaker, Mom's Mom, Dad's Dad, Peacemaker, Mediator, Family Sacrifice, Scapegoat, or Rebel, Underachiever, Problem Child, Lost Child, Victim, and so on. The roles are inexhaustible, but each has the same function: to keep the family system in balance, frozen and protected from the possibility of change. Each role also gives the person playing it a way to cover up his toxic shame. A role provides structure and definition; it prescribes a set of behaviors and emotions. As we play out our roles, our authentic self becomes more and more unconscious. As I said earlier, over the years we become *addicted* to our roles.

To champion our inner child is to give him permission to choose whatever part of the roles he wants to keep and to let go of the rest. It's important to tell your wounded inner child clearly that the roles *have not really worked.* I asked my inner child, "Has your being a Star, Superachiever, and Caretaker really saved anyone in your family?" The answer was an immediate no. I then asked him, "Has your being a Star, Superachiever, and Caretaker given you an abiding sense of inner peace?" Again, my inner child's answer was no; he still feels empty, lonely, and depressed a lot of the time. Next I asked my inner child, "What emotions have you had to repress in order to be a Star, Superachiever, and Caretaker?" The answer was that I couldn't be scared or angry. I always had to be strong, cheerful, and positive. Underneath my superhuman roles was a frightened, shame-based, lonely little boy.

## STEP TWO

Now you're ready to let your inner child feel the feelings that the roles prohibited. Tell him it's okay to be sad, afraid, lonely, or angry. You've already done a lot of this work in part 2, but as your inner child's new champion, you need to let him know that he has permission to feel the specific feelings that his rigid roles have prohibited. This gives him permission to be himself.

It's especially important that you protect him during this step, as feelings are scary when they start to come up. Your inner child can easily get overwhelmed. You have to go slowly and give him lots of gentle encouragement. Whenever we change old family-of-origin patterns, it feels *unfamiliar* (literally, "unfamily"). We do not feel "at home" with new behavior. Experiencing new emotions will feel strange, maybe even crazy, to your inner child. Be patient with him. He will not risk experiencing these new feelings unless he feels absolutely *safe*.

## STEP THREE

To explore your new freedom, you need to find new behaviors that allow you to experience your self in another context. For example, I asked the creative part of my adult, What are three things I can do that will take me out of my Star and Superachiever roles? Ask your creative adult to decide on three *specific behaviors*. My creative adult came up with the following:

1. I can go to a seminar or workshop where no one knows me and concentrate on just being a participating member of the group. I did this when I took my Neuro-Linguistic Programming training.

2. I can do a mediocre job on some task. I did this with an article I was writing for a newspaper.

3. I can support someone else in being the center of attention. I did this by sharing the podium with a colleague in L.A. The limelight was focused on him.

These were good new experiences for me. I learned what it felt like to be part of a group rather than the Star. I let myself choose not to perfect. I enjoyed playing a supporting role for someone else. My inner child liked doing these things. He was so tired of always having to be the Star and Superachiever.

Taking this step with my Caretaker role was even more important, because that was my most significant way of mattering. Modifying this role was also more frightening. The first time I worked on it, I came up with these new behaviors:

1. I cut my counseling hours from fifty to forty hours a week.

2. I changed my private phone number (which I had been giving to my clients) to an unlisted number. I installed an answering service for counseling emergencies.

3. I refused to spend my free time at social events answering people's questions concerning their personal problems.

At first I felt guilty each time one of these behaviors was tested. I felt I was being selfish. Gradually my inner child came to see that people still valued and respected me. Learning that I was valuable and lovable *without* doing things for others was an important step in my personal growth.

## STEP FOUR

Finally, you need to help your inner child decide what parts of his roles he wants to keep. For example, I love to speak to hundreds of people in lectures and seminars. My inner child loves to crack jokes and hear people laugh. He also loves the applause at the end of a talk or workshop. So, he and I decided we would continue doing this work.

My inner child let me know that I was killing him with my roles of People-Pleaser, Caretaker, and being a Star. For example, at my workshops and seminars, I would never take time out. I'd talk to people, answer their questions, try to do therapy in three minutes, and sign books at every break. I would also stay for an hour and a half after the lecture or workshop was over. This would sometimes amount to twelve hours at a stretch. Flying home from Los Angeles one night, my inner child just started crying. I couldn't believe what was happening, but I got the message. While my inner child wanted us to be a Star, the Caretaker had to go. So I chose some things that my inner kid likes. For the last few years, we always fly first class. We are frequently picked up in limousines. We have several people assigned to take care of us at every break during workshops. We use the break to rest and eat some fresh fruit or other light food. Now my inner child and I are giving quality care to others. But we are also taking quality care of ourselves. And we are letting others take care of us. We have chosen to be a Star, but not at the expense of our beingness. We have chosen to give care, but we are not obsessed with it. Nor do we believe that we will not matter if we don't give care to others. I give care to my inner child. I champion him and tell him I love him just the way he is. My child no longer believes that he must give up his authentic self in order to be loved. We both know that the most crucial relationship in our life is the one we have with each other. I've given him permission to be who he is, and that's made all the difference.

# CHAPTER 11

# PROTECTING YOUR WOUNDED INNER CHILD

Children who are not loved in their very beingness do not know how to love themselves. As adults, they have to learn to nourish, to mother their own lost child.
—MARION WOODMAN

The child wants simple things. It wants to be listened to. It wants to be loved.... It may not even know the words, but *it wants its rights protected* and its self-respect unviolated. It needs you to be there.
—RON KURTZ

The third "P" in therapy is protection. The wounded inner child needs protection because he is immature and somewhat raw. He still feels ambivalent about you as his new parent: some days he trusts you absolutely; other days, he feels scared and confused. After all, you've gone many years without paying any attention to your inner child. As in any healthy relationship, your inner child's trust will have to be built up over time.

## GIVING TIME AND ATTENTION

As I stated earlier, children know intuitively that what you give time to is what you love. It is vitally important to learn when your inner child needs your attention. I'm still working on this myself, so I can tell you only what I've learned so far. My inner child usually needs my attention when:

I am *bored.* My kid sometimes gets bored in *my own* lectures and workshops. He gets bored when I'm in long intellectual conversations. He begins to fidget and wiggle. He asks me to look at my work over and over again to see how much longer he has to endure.

I am *frightened.* My inner child was programmatically terrified as a little child. He will come up when the slightest threat appears.

I am *witnessing a loving and warm father-son scenario.* It never fails. Pat Cash ran up in the stands and hugged his father when he won Wimbledon and my inner child started bawling. The same thing happened when Jack Nicklaus won his fifth Masters Championship and his son was hugging him as they walked to the 18th green. It happened again when Dustin Hoffman won the Academy Award. He called to his father watching in the hospital and my inner child started crying. My inner child is deeply hurt over my father's abandoning him. Even though I've done a lot of work on this issue (I actually held my father on his deathbed and have no unfinished business with him), I still feel a deep wound over my early loss of him.

I am *tired.* I get whiney and irritable when I'm tired. I have to be careful to take care of my child or else he will lash out at the closest person around.

I am *playing a competitive game.* My inner child is a poor loser. He fakes it pretty well, but he really hates to lose. I can get extremely emotional on the golf course. As I've monitored my behavior, I've been appalled at the age level I regress to. When I missed an easy putt recently, I heard myself say, "I don't know why I do anything at all!" A fairly wide-sweeping statement for a missed putt that I forgot about two hours later.

I am *overreacting.* Overreactions are spontaneous age regressions. I know my inner child is present when I hear my voice getting louder and more and more defensive.

I feel *slighted or rejected.* My child picks up the most minute signal of rejection or disinterest. I have to be extremely careful, because he will sometimes pick it up when it's not really there.

I am *unexpectedly exposed.* This doesn't happen often, because as a shame-based person I've learned to be very guarded. But any sudden rupture of my expectations will cause my inner child some embarrassment.

I am *hungry.* My inner child gets very irritable when I'm hungry.

I am *with my best friends*. This is a joyous time for my inner child. He loves to be with my best friends. He feels safe and joyous. He loves to tell jokes, laugh, and have fun.

I am *lonely*. For a long time I didn't recognize the feelings of being lonely. Now I know I'm feeling lonely when I seem to feel numb and I want to eat sweets. I also know I'm feeling lonely when I want to make a lot of phone calls.

Whenever my inner child is present, I acknowledge him. When he's happy and having fun, a simple recognition is enough. When he's tired, hungry, disheartened, sad, or lonely, I need to talk to him. I have found two methods to be very useful for communicating with my inner child.

## COMMUNICATING WITH YOUR INNER CHILD

You've already learned the first technique—writing letters. This method can be used for your daily communications with your inner child. Remember to use your dominant hand when you are in your adult and your nondominant hand when you're in your inner child. Here's the way I do it. When I get up in the morning, I choose the time that I will give that day to my inner child. Sometimes when the child emerges in times of distress, loneliness, or boredom, I do the communicating then and there. But usually I pick a twenty-minute time in advance. Today it was 8:30 P.M. I needed a break from writing this book and my child was getting bored. Here is what I wrote today:

BIG JOHN:     Hi Little John! How old are you right now?
LITTLE JOHN:  I'm six.
BIG JOHN:     Little John, how's it going for you right now?
LITTLE JOHN:  I'm tired of writing. I want to play and I have a knot in my shoulder.
BIG JOHN:     I'm sorry, I didn't know I was pushing so hard. What would you like to do now?
LITTLE JOHN:  I want to eat the ice cream Katie brought.
BIG JOHN:     I'd forgotten all about that. Let's go down and get some now.

Following this short written conversation, I went down and fixed a bowl of home-made ice cream my niece, Katie, had brought me earlier that day. I had actually forgotten about it, but Little John remembered. After we ate the bowl of ice cream and rested for a while, I went back to writing.

I don't always spend twenty minutes with Little John, but I allot that time to him. He has a short attention span. I've found that as I've given Little John more and more recognition, he needs less time. He knows I'm there for him and he trusts me. I've been doing the written dialogue work for a couple of years now. It is a simple form of communication, but some people complain that it takes too much time. I agree. It certainly involves a commitment of time and effort in the beginning. But your inner child is worth it!

The second way to communicate is through visualization. Many people have used this method to do their inner child work. It's my favorite way.

Close your eyes and visualize a room with two comfortable chairs placed face to face. One chair is larger than the other. It is on the right-hand side of your image. The other chair is for a child, but it is high enough so that the child's face is level with the adult's. Here I have drawn my adult self (the wise and gentle wizard) in one chair and my inner child in the other chair. Look and listen carefully as your adult and your inner child converse.

Always begin by asking your child how old he is. Next, ask how he is feeling. Be sure to clarify his wants by asking for specific behavioral details. For example, a member of my male support group realized recently that his child was angry at him. When my friend asked his inner child what he wanted, the child answered that he wanted to go to Astroworld (a Houston amusement park) and ride several rides. He named the roller-coaster, the Ferris wheel, and the wild rapids ride. My friend is in his fifties, but he reluctantly honored his inner child's request. He got together several other couples and they went to Astroworld. My friend rode all the rides his child had suggested, plus a few others. He had a terrific time!

When he came to our next share meeting, I could see some visible changes. This man is a very busy banker, an expert in complicated and detailed financial planning and investing. His inner kid was sick of it, so he let him know what he needed to do to break out of the work rut he was in. Three days after that share group, my friend invited me to go with him to Astroworld!

Your inner child needs you to give him your time and attention. By doing this, you will let him know that he has a real champion.

## FINDING A NEW FAMILY

Championing your inner child involves getting him a new family of choice. A new family is necessary in order to give your child protection while he is forming new boundaries and doing his corrective learning. If your family of origin is not in recovery, it is almost impossible to get support from them while you're in your own recovery process. Often they think that what you're doing is stupid and they shame you for it. Often they are threatened by your doing this work, because as you give up your old family roles, you disrupt the frozen equilibrium of the family system. You were never allowed to be yourself before. Why would they suddenly start allowing that now? If your family of origin was dysfunctional, it is the least likely place to get your nurturing needs met. So, I advise you to keep a safe distance and work on finding a new, nonshaming, supportive family. This could be a support group of friends, it could be the group you joined to work on your inner child, or it could be any one of the myriad 12 Step groups now available all over the country. It could also be a church synagogue, or therapy group. Whatever your choice, I urge your adult to find a group for both of you. You are the champion for your inner child and he needs the support and protection of a new family of affiliation.

Consider the case of Sibonetta, who grew up with a violent father

and emotionally abusive and shaming mother. Sibonetta's father is
dead now and her mother has remarried, but her mother still calls
her frequently. Sibonetta has been making splendid progress in therapy, yet I can always tell when her mother has called. Sibonetta goes
into a setback for several days every time. I contracted with Sibonetta
to join a Coda group (Co-dependents Anonymous). She did so reluctantly. I was her champion and she did not want to entrust her secrets
to anyone else. I knew that this was not healthy, so I insisted that she
join a group and go to thirty meetings in thirty days. I hoped that such
a saturation would entrench her in the group. The strategy worked.
She began to feel at home in the group, and after the thirty days were
up, she continued to go to four meetings a week. I noticed that her
energy level was higher and that her mother's phone calls seemed
less upsetting. She would talk about the phone calls in group and
they would suggest things for her to say. They also supported her in
getting an answering machine so that she could screen her mother's
calls and call back when she was ready. The group gave her much
more varied support than I could give her, and their feedback was
more powerful than my solitary voice. Sibonetta now has a new
family of affiliation to support her in her struggle to end her mother's
tyranny.

## THE POWER AND PROTECTION OF PRAYER

Your inner child needs to see that your adult has a source of protection beyond your finite human self. And even though you are magical
and godlike to your inner child, it is very important for him to know
that you have a Higher Power available to you. Even if your adult
doesn't believe in God, your inner child believes in something greater
than himself. Children are natural believers in a Higher Power.

Prayer is a powerful source of protection for your wounded inner
child, and he will like it when you pray with him. I like to close my
eyes and see my inner child at whatever age he appears. I either sit
him on my lap or we kneel side by side and pray. I say an adult
prayer while Little John says a childhood prayer. He likes "Now I lay
me down to sleep" when we pray at night; sometimes we say this
prayer together. The Memorare is a prayer I learned in Catholic
elementary school. It is a prayer to Mary, the mother of Jesus. I like
feminine power in my spirituality. I think of God as mothering and

gentle. She holds me and rocks me. Little John likes this too. The Memorare says:

> Remember, O most Blessed Virgin Mary that never was it known that anyone who fled to your protection, implored your help, or sought your intercession, was left unaided. Inspired by this confidence, I fly unto thee, O Virgin of Virgins, my mother. To thee do I come, before thee I stand, sinful and sorrowful. Despise not my petitions but in thy mercy hear and answer me. Amen.

My adult doesn't like all the references to virginity because I don't believe Mary was a virgin. But I have gotten some powerful protection from that prayer. I've told Little John all about it and he's very impressed. You will have to find prayers that work for you and your inner child. But I wholeheartedly recommend that you give your wounded inner child the powerful protection that comes from prayer.

## STROKING YOUR INNER CHILD

We know that children can die if they are not physically held and stroked. Infants need to be touched and stimulated in order to live and grow. If they are not, they become sick with a disease called *marasmus* (literally "wasting away"), just as if they were starving. A child suffering from marasmus regresses to the fetal state. It's like a reversal in growth. Without strokes, a baby withers and wastes away. As the child grows, lots of verbal encouragement needs to be added to stroking. This is a form of protection.

Since children can't live without strokes, they get them by hook or by crook. If they can't get good strokes, they'll go for bad ones. You will drink polluted water if there is no other water available.

Your wounded inner child probably settled for lots of polluted water. That's why the affirmations we used for each developmental stage are so important. You need to keep using them. They are the emotional strokes your child needs for nourishment. Go back now and look at the affirmations for each stage. Recall which affirmations were the most powerful for you. Use these for your special strokes. Your inner child needs to hear them every day when you are first learning to champion him. Mine are as follows:

## INFANCY

Welcome to the world.... I'm glad you're a boy.... You will have all the time you need to get your needs met.

## TODDLERHOOD

It's okay to say no.... It's okay to be angry.... You can be angry and I'll still be here.... It's okay to be curious, to want to look and touch and taste things.... I'll make it safe for you to explore.

## PRESCHOOL

It's okay to be sexual.... It's okay for you to think for yourself.... It's okay to be different.... You can ask for what you want.... You can ask questions if something confuses you.

## SCHOOL-AGE

It's okay to make mistakes.... You can do some things in a mediocre manner.... You don't have to be perfect and always make straight A's.... I love you just the way you are.

These affirmations are tailored especially for me and my needs. You can do the same with your affirmations.

I also recommend that you write your affirmations. Work on one affirmation at a time, writing it fifteen to twenty times a day. Carry the affirmation around with you. Look at it often and say it out loud.

Put all the affirmations on 5-by-7 cards and put them in conspicuous places in your house or apartment. Get friends to read you these affirmations. Record them on a tape recorder and play them back to yourself.

## Exercise for Installing Soothing Strokes into Old Traumatic Memories

When your parents were the most upset (yelling, raging, threatening, labeling and judging), your wounded inner child internalized their words the most dramatically. It was at such times that your survival was threatened the most. You imprinted their words and remembered them.

You need to go back into those scenes and let your championing adult give your wounded inner child some new words that are nurturing and soothing. Without some new and soothing auditory imprints, your wounded inner child will continue to talk to himself with the old shaming words. The following exercise will help you remap the old shaming scene and install a new voice. It is preferable to select a traumatic memory on which you have already done some original pain work. If you select a scene you have not worked on, *be very careful, as you can easily get overwhelmed. Follow the instructions exactly.* I recommend that you either record this exercise on your tape recorder or have a therapist, trusted friend, or support person take you through the steps.

### STEP ONE

Imagine that the grown-up you is sitting in a movie theater looking at a blank screen. Now look around and notice the details on the walls of the theater. What do you see? Look up at the ceiling. See it inlaid with beautiful carvings. Now look at the screen again and see the title of a film. Read the words "Old Traumatic Scene." Now imagine that you are floating out of your body and sitting ten rows in back of yourself. You can see the back of your own head and you can see yourself looking at the screen. Make an anchor with your left thumb and one of your fingers.

### STEP TWO

Holding your anchor, see yourself looking at a black and white movie of the old traumatic scene. See yourself watching it from start to finish. When it is finished, see yourself looking at a still shot of the last frame which contains a picture of your wounded inner child exactly as he appeared in the traumatic scene. He is sitting all alone.

### STEP THREE

Let go of your anchor and float back into the self who viewed the movie. You are now in your body. Imagine yourself walking into the picture on the screen. Now you are there with your wounded inner child. Ask your child if you can hold him. If he says yes, pick him up and gently stroke him as you tell him the soothing things he needed to hear when he experienced the trauma. If he doesn't want to be held, just tell him the soothing words.

For example, I have a traumatic memory in which I was shamed by my grandmother because I was sobbing hysterically over my dad's leaving the house vowing to get "stinking drunk." He and my mom had just had a noisy fight. I remember being terrified. In working on that scene, I gently hold my ten-year-old wounded inner child and say, "It's okay, John. It *is* very scary to think of your dad getting drunk again. It is perfectly normal for you to be frightened, to be afraid your dad will never come back or that he will hurt your mom. You can cry as long as you want. I'm here to protect you now."

**STEP FOUR**
**When you have finished nurturing your child, imagine the entire traumatic scene being played backward this time in full color. Imagine that you and your wounded inner child are standing inside the movie as if time had reversed direction.**

Wait about ten minutes and then reflect on the old traumatic scene. Notice whether it feels any different to you. Notice whether you can hear the sounds of your new championing voice. If you can't, you need to work on it some more. A scene can be worked on many times.

## Asking for Strokes

Learn to *ask for strokes when you need them*. Most of us were toxically shamed when we expressed a need for strokes. We never learned how to nourish ourselves emotionally. Now you need to give your inner child permission to do that. When someone shames you, it's very healthy to call a friend and ask him for a stroke. You can call and say, "Tell me I'm a good and valuable person," or, "Tell me how much you love and value me," or, "Tell me some of the things you like about me." Think of what you would do if you were starving. You'd find some food or you'd ask a friend for it. Your inner child doesn't realize that you can do the same when you are *emotionally* hungry.

*It is perfectly healthy to ask for the specific kind of strokes you need.* You already know what some of them are. Beautiful women are often overloaded with strokes about their physical beauty. If you are an attractive woman, you need to ask for different kinds of strokes. For example, if a man tells you how beautiful or sexy you look, tell him, "I *know* that; what else do you like about me?" I get a plethora of strokes for my mind. I'm told things like, "You're a genius. I don't know how you do it." What I want are *body* strokes. So, I'm teaching my inner child to say, "I know I'm smart; how do you like my body?" This is not easy. Because most of our parents were adult children who themselves were "stroke deprived," they were pretty stingy about giving strokes.

Besides stroking your child often and in the specific ways he needs, teach him the following:

- Give all the strokes you can to others.
- It's okay to give yourself strokes.
- It's okay to ask for strokes.
- It's okay to ask for the kind of strokes you need.

Your inner child needs this continuous stimulation and protection.

As your inner child's champion, you can give him the three "P's" of therapy that Eric Berne described. These three "P's"—potency, permission, and protection—are also the elements of healthy parenting. I like to add a fourth "P." Championing is an ongoing process that involves corrective learning. This demands effort and *practice*. Let's look at that fourth "P" now.

# CHAPTER 12

# PUTTING CORRECTIVE EXERCISES INTO PRACTICE

We sit as many risks as we run.
—HENRY DAVID THOREAU

It will work, if you will work.
—THERAPEUTIC SLOGAN

The best news is that since the child was wounded through neglect and learning deficits, we can *learn* to get the child's needs met as an adult. We can develop skills in all areas of human interaction. It's not a question of unlearning; it's a question of learning things for the first time.
—KIP FLOCK

You have already grieved the loss of your unmet developmental dependency needs. Now you can learn a variety of exercises that will give you corrective experiences. Corrective work is the most hopeful aspect of inner child work. Our woundedness is partly the result of learning deficits, and we can correct those deficits with new learning. We do some of this new learning incidentally as we respond to the social demands of growing up. But for most of us with a wounded inner kid, there are still large areas where the lack of these developmental skills causes great pain and discomfort. Many adult children do not know that their abortive behavior is due to learning deficits.

They relentlessly shame and blame themselves for their failures and character defects. Doing corrective exercises helps your wounded inner child to understand that your *defects* are actually *deficits*. The behavioral contaminations from your wounded inner child are actually ways he learned to survive. Psychiatrist Timmen Cermak compares these survival behaviors to the characteristics of post-traumatic stress disorder. Soldiers in battle, and other people going through traumatic events, must use all their resources to survive. They do not have time to express their feelings, which is necessary to integrate the trauma. Later on, the unresolved grief manifests itself in traits such as anxiety attacks, overcontrol, memory lapses, depression, age regressions, and hypervigilance. These are the traits associated with post-traumatic stress disorder (PTSD). If I gave you the entire list of PTSD traits, you'd see how closely they resemble the wounded inner child's contaminations I described in chapter 1.

The following exercises will correct your learning deficits from the past. More than anything, they will enhance your inner child's ability to just *be* and to be more loving and intimate.

Several other writers have offered rich corrective resources for each developmental stage. I've mentioned Pam Levin's book *Cycles of Power*. I would also like to cite *Recovery from Co-Dependency,* by Laurie and Jonathan Weiss; *Windows to Our Children,* by Violet Oaklander; *Adult Children of Abusive Parents,* by Steven Farmer; *Breaking Free of the Co-Dependency Trap,* by Barry and Janae Weinhold; and *Therapeutic Metaphors for Children and the Children Within,* by Joyce Mills and Richard Crowley. In what follows I've drawn heavily from these sources.

These exercises work best if you apply them to the areas where you were most neglected. By now you should have a pretty good idea about the developmental stages where your inner child got stuck. I recommend that you work especially on those stages.

## EXERCISES FOR GETTING YOUR INFANCY NEEDS MET

In infancy we needed to be secure enough to *just be*. Most of our wounded inner kids were taught that it was not okay to just *be*—that we could matter and have significance only if we were *doing* something. This led to the loss of our sense of I AMness. Now we need to learn how to do nothing and just *be*.

The following exercises will aid you in just being who you are at any given moment. Choose the ones that appeal most to you.

- Get into a hot tub and spend time focusing on your bodily sensations. Take time just being there.
- Treat yourself to regular massages.
- Let someone give you a manicure and fix your hair.
- Have a friend feed you—either cook for you or take you out to dinner.
- Sit quietly wrapped up in a comforter or blanket. In winter, wrap up by a warm fire and roast marshmallows.
- Spend lots of time in sensual touching with your lover.
- Have your lover gently bathe you.
- Give yourself a bubble bath or lounge in a tub of warm water and bath oils.
- Block out periods of time for doing nothing; make no plans, have no commitments.
- Spend thirty minutes to an hour floating in a swimming pool on a warm summer day.
- Hang in a hammock for a long time.
- Listen to soft lullaby music. (Try Steven Halpern's *Lullaby Suite* or *Lullabies and Sweet Dreams*.)
- When you're working, have liquids available for frequent sipping.
- Suck on mints or Life Savers while you start a new job or when you start to do something for the first time.
- Change your eating habits. Instead of "three squares," eat a number of small nutritious meals throughout the day.
- Have some special support persons (ideally of both sexes) who will hug you and hold you for clearly contracted periods of time.
- Take as many naps as you can on days when you have plenty of time.
- Get plenty of rest before doing anything new.
- Practice "trust walks" with a friend. Have him blindfold you and lead you around for a contracted period of time.
- Risk trusting a friend whom you have good feelings about. Let him make plans and control what you do together.
- Get a partner and gaze at each other for nine minutes. Laugh, giggle, do whatever you need to do. Just hang in there; do not talk. Just *look* at each other.

• Meditate on nothingness. When we mediate on nothingness, we are meditating on being itself. Infancy is the time when we were grounded in the power of being. There are many approaches to meditating on pure being or no*thing*ness. Such meditations aim at creating a state of mindlessness, sometimes referred to as creating "the silence." To learn to be mindless as an adult connects the inner child with the adult in a most profound way.

## MEDITATION TO TOUCH THE POWER OF BEING
What follows is a very simple form of mindless meditation. Great spiritual masters spend years mastering this. It's worth practicing. I recommend you put this meditation on a tape recorder. Use your favorite meditation music in the background.

Start by focusing on your breathing.... Just become *aware* of breathing.... Notice what happens in your body when you breathe in and out.... Notice the air as it comes into your nostrils and as it goes out.... What is the difference?... Allow yourself to breathe into your forehead and breathe out any tension you discover there.... Then breathe in around your eyes.... And breathe out any tension you find there.... Then around your mouth.... Then down into your neck and shoulders.... Then down your arms and out through your hands.... Breathe into your upper chest and breathe out any tension. Breathe into your abdomen.... Breathe into your buttocks and breathe out any tension you find there.... Breathe into your calves, and breathe out any tension you find there.... Now let your whole body relax.... Imagine you are hollow on the inside.... Imagine that a warm golden sunlight is passing through you.... Let yourself begin to feel either a heaviness or a lightness.... You decide what it is you are feeling.... Your eyelids are very heavy.... Your arms are heavy.... Your legs and feet are heavy.... *Or* you may feel very light.... Like your whole body is floating.... Imagine that the horizon of your mind is getting darker and darker until you are gazing into pure darkness.... In the center of that darkness, you begin to see a pinpoint of light.... The light begins to slowly grow larger and larger.... Until the whole horizon is illuminated with light.... Now gaze into the light.... The pure light.... Be aware of the

nothingness you are experiencing. . . . There is no thing there. . . .
Just pure beingness. . . . Now slowly see the number three
appear in the center of your horizon. . . . Be aware of your
breathing again. . . . Let your consciousness scan your whole
body beginning at your toes and coming up your legs, hips,
stomach, upper chest, arms, hands, neck and shoulders, face,
and brain. . . . Be aware of your own I AMness. . . . You are
vividly in touch with you. . . . With your own I AMness. . . . Now
see the number two. . . . And wiggle your toes. . . . Wiggle your
hands. . . . Feel your body touching your chair and your feet
touching the floor. . . . Hear as many sounds as you can hear
around you. . . . Now see the number one and very slowly open
your eyes. . . .

Sit quietly for a few moments of reverie when you are finished. . . . Let
yourself just be.

All these exercises are very useful for taking care of your infancy
needs. They can be particularly effective when:

- You're in the beginning of a new cycle of your development.
- You have to start something new.
- You have suffered a loss.
- You have a brand-new infant.

These exercises need to be done slowly and then mulled over. *Being*
experiences are like healthy eating—they need to be chewed thor-
oughly, not gobbled down. If you gobble your food, it is hard to
digest. Undigested, the food's energy isn't available to you. The same
is true of your "being" experiences.

## EXERCISES FOR GETTING YOUR TODDLER NEEDS MET

### Crawling and Sensory Exploration Stage

Fritz Perls often said that we need to "lose our minds and come to
our senses." Our inner child had his senses blocked out at an early
age. We need to get back in contact with the sensory world around
us. Here are some things you can do to restimulate your early toddler
exploratory needs.

- Go to a flea market or a large department store. Go from item to item, looking, touching, and examining whatever strikes your fancy.
- Go to a cafeteria or restaurant that has a buffet. Choose lots of different foods. Try out foods you've never tasted before.
- Go to the grocery store and buy foods that you wouldn't normally eat with your hands. Take them home and eat with your hands. Be as messy as you want.
- Spend some time chewing or gnawing on something that is crunchy.
- Spend time in the produce section of your grocery store, smelling the different fruits and vegetables.
- Go somewhere you've *never been before*. Pay attention to as many details of the new environment as you can.
- Go to a playground and just hang out with the kids. Swing on the swings; go down the slide; climb on the jungle gym.
- Go to the beach and spend several hours playing in the sand and water. Build something out of the sand.
- Get some clay and play with it. Experiment with shapes and forms.
- Get some finger paints and spend an afternoon finger painting. Use as many colors as you possibly can.
- Go to a Montessori classroom and let yourself be guided by the environment. Try out whatever strikes your fancy.
- Dress up in the brightest-color clothes you can find and go somewhere.
- Make noises with things around the house just to see what they sound like. Don't forget the pots and pans and silverware.
- Go to an amusement park and spend hours looking around and riding on the rides.
- Walk through a beautiful park or garden and smell as many smells as you can. Let yourself skip from one smell to another.
- Go to a museum of fine arts and look at the brilliant colors in the various paintings.
- Get your friend or lover to go for a long walk with you. Hold hands and let your senses take you in whatever direction you feel like going.
- Go to a park with a friend and practice Zen seeing. Take turns closing your eyes and holding your friend's hand. Take your friend to a leaf, a tree trunk, a wild flower. When you squeeze his hand, let him open his eyes as if his eyes were the shutter of a camera. Open and close your eyes when your partner squeezes your hand and *see* the pure essence of the sight they've prepared for you.

- Walk barefoot through a field or around the house. Feel the different textures of things: grass, dirt, fur, cardboard, newspapers, rugs, pillows, towels, wood, metal, tile, and so on.
- Have a conversation with your partner without talking—just through gestures and touching.
- Write out a list of sensation words and then see what comes to mind when you say each one aloud. Some words might be *bumpy, prickly, tingly, feathery, slippery, hard, soft, thin, fat, dark, bright,* and so on.
- Reown your eyes by staring at things. For example, walk past a bus stop and see the people there as if you were a camera taking a picture. Sit down and describe in writing what you saw in detail.
- Sit in front of a flower, a tree, or an apple in a kind of meditative state. Allow yourself to become one with the object. *See* the object in all its wonder. Allow your hand to follow what your eyes see and draw what you see.
- Have a conversation in gibberish with a friend. See if you can figure out what the other is saying.
- Play a "mystery" sound game with a friend. Turn your back or cover your eyes while your friend makes a sound by pouring water, beating a drum, tapping a pencil, scratching his head, and so on. Then change places.
- Get a gang of people together to sing songs. Try open-ended songs like "I wish I were an apple on a tree" and make up new verses. Have the whole gang listen to children's songs, especially folk music.

## Reconnecting with Desires

Perhaps the most important exercise in this section is to help your inner child reconnect with his desires. The most damaged part of our wounded inner child is his will. The will is desire raised to the level of action. Desire flows from a connection with our needs. As a child in a dysfunctional family, there was no way our inner child could pay attention to his own internal signals because he was so busy dealing with family distress. Early on he lost contact with his own needs and desires. I knew what my mom and dad wanted before they knew what they wanted. By becoming expert at knowing what *they* wanted, I lost connection with what *I* wanted. I literally learned to ignore what I wanted, and after a while I stopped wanting altogether. Your adult must help your inner child recognize his own desires and protect him while he risks attaining what he wants.

One of the simplest ways to identify your desires is to make a list of your substitute behaviors. Then confront yourself with the question, What am I really needing or desiring when I behave this way? Here is a list of common substitute behaviors:

- Telling lies
- Eating when you're not hungry
- Reaching for a cigarette
- Pouting
- Insulting someone you care about

When I am aware that I am doing one of these behaviors, I sit down, close my eyes, and pay exquisite attention to the signals inside of me. I often hear my inner child asking for something he wants. Here are some examples of the desires underlying the substitute behaviors listed above.

- I want to express anger.
- I'm frightened and/or lonely and I want to be with someone.
- I don't smoke anymore, but when I did, I usually was in the pain of my chronic depression.
- I want someone to know that I really matter.
- I want your attention.
- I need physical strokes.

There are many other substitute behaviors that people use when they are unaware of what they desire. Some are fairly general, some are quite idiosyncratic. Each of us must help his inner child by paying attention to substitute behaviors.

Jon and Laurie Weiss have their clients create an "I want" or "I wish" list. They ask them to carry a paper and pencil with them at all times. Every time they notice something they want, they are to write it down. Each client agrees that he will actually get some items on his want list and report to his therapist (could be a support partner or sponsor) what he's done. This is an excellent exercise and I encourage you to do it.

## EXERCISES FOR THE SEPARATION STAGE OF TODDLERHOOD

As children learn to *stand on their own two feet,* they begin separating. There are several exercises you can practice if you've discovered that your wounded inner toddler did not get his separation needs met.

*Practice saying "no" and "I won't."* This is usually pretty scary if you've been punished and/or abandoned for saying "no." Jon and Laurie Weiss suggest a three-step method for practicing saying no. I will summarize it:

1. The first step is to say no in private. You need to say it often (twenty times a day) and out loud. Say no to the things you do not want to do. This helps you feel the natural rebelliousness you felt as a 2-year-old.

2. The next step is to say no in a semipublic context. In their therapy groups, the Weisses have a client who is working on this issue say *no* or *I don't want to* loudly and at random, and not necessarily in response to anything that is going on in the group. Obviously, this behavior would be rude in any other context. I recommend that you contract to practice this with a partner or a group you are in. You can contract with a close friend to say no to everything he asks you to do. Do this for a specified period. Always say no first and then discover whether you really want to do it. The Weisses encourage their clients to say no and then discuss whether they really do or do not want to do something.

3. This is the real thing! You are to say no to someone and mean it. Your no should respect the other person's feelings, but *do not take responsibility for their feelings.* I like to tell a person my honest feelings or opinion about what he's asked even when I don't agree. For example, my friend Mike asked me to go bowling recently. I told him, "I think bowling is fun. And no, I've got too much to do today. Maybe some other time." I like to stroke the idea if I really like it. I also like to use the word *and* rather than *but* if at all possible. Sometimes I say, "Thanks for asking me! And no, I'm already committed."

Some no's are much harder than others. It's hard to say no when I really want to do something or when it touches a vulnerable area of my unfulfilled needs. A person who is starving to be touched and held may experience great difficulty in turning down a sexual come-on.

The more you help your inner child identify his needs and teach him to take care of them, the easier it will be to say no.

Another good way to strengthen your inner toddler's independence is to take an assertiveness training course. Such courses offer your inner child group safety and carefully planned structured exercises for learning to say no. There are also several good books on assertiveness training. Two of my favorites are *Your Perfect Right,* by Robert Alberti and Michael Emmons, and *When I Say No I Feel Guilty,* by Manuel Smith.

If you are a rebel, you probably say no *too much*. You may say no when you want to say yes. Dialogue with your inner toddler. Tell him that you will protect his rights. Tell him that he can stop spending all his energy to ensure his rights. Tell him that rather than waiting to find out what others want in order to resist them, he can now determine what *he* wants and needs and ask for it directly.

## Establishing Your Own Separate Domain

Have a discussion with those you live with concerning the importance of each person's having his own separate possessions and his own time and space. Agree to draw up a personal set of rules governing your own separate domain. A set of rules might look like this:

- Some of my time is my own. I may or may not share it with you.
- No one may use anything that belongs to me without my permission.
- If I give you permission to use something that is mine, I expect you to put it back where you found it.
- My room (or whatever space I have) is sacred to me. If you find my door closed, please knock and ask my permission before entering. Sometimes I may lock my door to ensure my privacy.
- For a given period of time, I want to negotiate my own special place to work, my own special place at the dinner table, and my own special chair. I am willing to renegotiate these spaces at an agreed upon time in the future.

Another useful practice in changing an enmeshed or co-dependent relationship is to *make a list of what belongs to you*. Get some white stickers and write your name on them. Go around your home and stick them on everything that is yours. You may also want to *make a time chart* and post it outside your door. Indicate which times belong to you for privacy and solitude and which times you are willing to share with others.

## Practice Expressing Current Anger

Our anger is part of our personal power. It is the energy we use to protect our basic needs. Without our anger we become doormats and people pleasers. In childhood you were most likely severely shamed and punished when you expressed anger. Your inner child learned to stop himself from feeling his anger. Over the years he became so numb that he didn't know he was angry any longer.

Your inner child may also have learned to use "feeling rackets" to cover his anger. A feeling racket is a feeling used to manipulate someone else and to replace the feeling one is actually having. Your inner child may have learned that if he acted hurt or started weeping when he was punished for his anger, he could not get a nurturing response from his caretaker. He thus learned a feeling racket—to be hurt or sad when he feels angry.

A guilt racket is formed differently. A child expressing anger is often *made to feel that* he is bad. He is taught that any expression of anger is disrespectful and disobedient. Such behavior violates the Fourth Commandment and is morally wrong. When a child experiences anger toward his parents, he immediately feels guilty. He has done something wrong. Much of the guilt people have about their parents is actually disguised anger at them. Most of us confuse healthy anger with the volatile build-up and explosion that results from repressing our anger until we can't hold it any longer.

Anger doesn't have to be volatile. On a scale of one to a hundred, temper tantrums are at the top of the scale. Most of us don't understand that anger begins with *mild* distress or upset. If it is expressed immediately, it is comfortably and smoothly discharged. The reason why most people think of anger as volatile is that they were never taught skillful ways to express their anger.

Because your inner child believes that anger is volatile, he fears it. Most adult children are manipulated by anger. They will give up their own reality to stop another person from being angry.

By helping your inner child to get in touch with his own anger and teaching him how to express it, you will reduce his fear of it. He can learn that he does have control over his anger. He can learn to see others' anger as belonging to *them,* and he can refuse to take responsibility for it.

If taking an assertive training course is not practical for you, I recommend that you *practice* expressing anger in the following ways:

1. When you are *first* practicing expressing anger, withdraw when you feel angry. Sit down and *think* about it. Be clear about what you're mad at. Write it out if necessary. Be clear about what you want the other person to do or not to do. For example, I recently had a situation that angered me. I asked an employee to call me and he agreed. When 2:00 P.M. came, he didn't call. I waited for thirty minutes. I had several other things I needed to do. By 2:30 I was furious. I waited till the voltage subsided, then worked on expressing my anger.

2. Practice what you are going to say. Do it out loud. If it's possible to practice expressing your anger to a friend who is not involved, do that. I rehearsed, "I'm angry at you. I asked you to call me at 2:00 P.M. on Tuesday. You said, 'That's just fine.' And you did not call."

3. As soon as you feel ready, contact the person you are angry at. Tell him you are upset and want to talk to him. Contract for a specific time.

4. Express your anger to the person who offended you. I like to preface my expressions of anger with the statement, "My anger most likely has elements of my own history in it; and I'm probably not fully aware of that, but I am angry at you ..."

Sometimes I am aware of my own historical issues. When that's the case, I tell the person. For example, I might say, "My dad used to tell me he'd call me and he never did. I'm angry at you. I asked you to call me at 2:00 P.M. ..." You might not get the response you want from the person you are angry at, but the important thing is to express your anger.

Anger needs to be discharged as soon as possible. Once you've learned a healthy way to express your anger, do it as close to the actual moment as you can. The only reason why I suggest you wait at all is that it is usually very frightening when you first begin learning to express anger. Because of the terror around anger, it is usually overreactive and comes out as rage.

## Practice Expressing Past Anger

Once your inner child knows that he has you to protect him, anger from the past usually starts surfacing. Your inner child may still be angry about things that happened in your childhood. As you champion your child, you want to finish the past. Going *directly* to people who hurt you in the past is usually not useful. Old anger can be symbolically worked out. Just close your eyes and see your inner child. Ask him how old he is. Then imagine yourself floating into his body. Now you are a child. Look at your adult self and *take your adult's hand. Make an anchor with your right fist.* Now let the person you are angry at appear. Really look at him. What is he wearing? Now tell him what you're angry at. Keep your fist clenched the entire time. When you've said everything you need to say, take a deep breath and relax your fist (i.e., let your anchor go). Become your adult self again. Pick your inner child up and take him out of the room you are in. Slowly open your eyes.

Assure your inner child that it's okay to feel and to express anger. Assure him that you will be there to protect him. Assure him that he can be angry at you and that you will not leave him.

There are other ways to work on anger and resentment. Some are best done in a therapeutic context. If you have any doubts, be sure to talk to a qualified therapist.

## Danger: A Note About Rage

Working on rage should never be attempted without expert help. Rage is anger that has been shame bound. Shame-bound anger grows in intensity over the years. It's like a ravenous wolf held captive in the basement. As the years go on, the energy intensifies and the wolf craves to get out. When we begin letting out rage, it is primitive and unfocused. We may scream and holler; we may hit and swing our arms in all directions.

Rage contains elements of terror. This is why we often scream when we rage. The characteristic that most often leads to rage is being overwhelmed, feeling out of control. Our lips quiver, our voice cracks, and we say things that are irrelevant or exaggerated. We want to hurt the other person. There is an absolutist quality to rage. Being angry all the time and overreacting to little things may be a sign that there is a deeper rage that needs to be worked on.

It's prudent to fear rage—our own and other people's. Everyone present, including yourself, needs to be protected while you are doing rage work. Consult a trained counselor for this work.

## Practice Confrontation

If someone is violating your boundaries, you need to help your inner child protect him- or herself. I like to use an "awareness model" to practice confrontation. The awareness model focuses on the four powers each of us possesses in order to interact with the world. These powers are our senses, our minds, our emotions, and our wills (our desires and wants). I use "I" messages to convey the truth of my awareness. "I" messages are self-responsible statements. The whole model looks like this:

> I see, hear, etc. . . . . . . . . .  (senses)
> I interpret . . . . . . . . . . . . .  (mind, thinking)
> I feel . . . . . . . . . . . . . . . .  (emotions)
> I want . . . . . . . . . . . . . . . .  (desires)

Example: Joe and Susie have been to their square-dancing group. Susie's inner child is upset because Joe chose a very pretty woman as a partner for one of the figures that Susie had not yet learned. That night Susie tells Joe, "*I saw* you choose Sarah Low to dance with. *I heard* you giggling with her. *I interpreted* this to mean you were attracted to her. *I felt* scared and abandoned. And *I want* you to talk about that with me."

Joe told her he did think Sarah Low was cute and he liked the way she danced. He also told Susie that he loved *her* (Susie) and would much rather be with her. He said he wanted to teach Susie the new step so that they could dance together more.

Susie's inner child didn't like it that Joe thought Sarah Low was cute. But she felt a lot safer. Susie's inner child has to learn that being normal involves *both/and*. Joe can love her *and* still think Sarah Low is cute.

Joe is quite centered and responds to Susie in a loving way. This will not always be the case in your relationships. You might get anything from defensiveness to rage when you confront someone. Unless you are confronting a violent offender, it is very important to confront when you feel upset with a significant person in your life.

Confronting is honest and creates trust; therefore, it is an act of love. When I confront, I value myself and set a boundary. I also trust and value you enough to tell you what's going on in me.

## Practice Polarity Thinking

Polarity thinking is synthetic thinking. It is the opposite of the polarized thinking I spoke of earlier. You need to help your inner child learn polarity thinking. No person or situation is all good or all bad. Polarity thinking allows you to see the "both/and" of life. In New Rule Five, I urged you to confront your inner child's absolutizing. Thinking in extremes is devastating to adult relationships. It is the birthright of a child to expect unconditional love from his parents, but no adult partner will be able to give us unconditional love. *Even the healthiest grown-up love is conditional.* As adults, there are conditions we must meet if we expect another to share love with us. No partner will be perfect; no partner will always be nurturing or always be there for us. Most of us will have roving eyes occasionally. Learning to see that reality is *"both/and"* is the beginning of wisdom. Practice looking at people's assets *and* liabilities. Tell yourself that every created thing is both plus and minus. Remember, there is no light without darkness; no sound without silence; no joy without sorrow; no holding on without letting go.

Our inner child loves to make people into gods. He does this for protection. We have to tell our inner child that there are no fairy godmothers. Anytime we make someone into a guru, we diminish ourselves. Tell your inner child that you will be their guru. I am Little John's wise and gentle wizard.

## Practice Fight-Fair Rules

The ones I like are:

1. Stay in the now. Fight about what just happened, not about something twenty-five years ago.

2. Avoid scorekeeping. Our inner kid likes to save things up and later dump them on people.

3. Stay with concrete, specific behavioral detail. The inner child does better with stuff he can see, hear, and touch. Saying to someone, "You make me sick," accomplishes nothing.

4. Be rigorously honest. Go for accuracy rather than argument.

5. Avoid blame and judgment. These are cover-ups for *your* shame. Stay with "I" messages and use the awareness model.

6. Use the listening rule, which has you repeat to the other person what you heard him say (to *his* satisfaction) before you get to answer him. The wounded inner child was rarely listened to. He is shame-based and defensive. The listening rule will work miracles if two people will commit to practice it.

7. Avoid arguing about details: "You're fifteen minutes late." "No I'm nine minutes late." The concrete literal school-age inner child loves to argue about details.

8. Hang in there unless your inner child is being abused. *Always* withdraw or find protection if you're being abused.

9. I teach my inner child the following boundary concerning conflict: "I did not come into the world to be measured by your fantasies, beliefs, or expectations. I will not be measured or controlled by them. If we have conflict, I will hang in there and fight fair. I ask you to do the same. If you become abusive in *any way,* I will leave."

## Practice Setting Physical Boundaries

I teach my inner child the following physical-boundary statement: "I have the right to determine who can touch me. I will tell others when and how they may touch me. I can withdraw from physical contact anytime it feels unsafe to me. I can do so without explanation. I will never let anyone violate my body unless my life is in danger."

## Practice Being Ornery or Stubborn

Do this especially when you want something very badly.

## Practice Changing Your Mind

Do this five or six times a day while you're practicing your toddler needs.

# PRE-SCHOOL PRACTICE EXERCISES

Your preschool inner child had several important tasks to accomplish. He needed to establish the scope of his power by defining himself. As your inner child's mind and imagination developed, he began thinking about his experiences, asking a lot of questions, and coming to some conclusions about his sexual identity. He used his imagination to create some images about grown-up life. He imagined what it was like to be Mom or Dad, what it was like to work and have sex.

He needed to bond with the same-sex parent in order to love himself as a male (or female).

Both male and female preschoolers think about a lot of things and begin to formulate a primitive conscience. The formation of conscience leads to the recognition that some things are right and some are wrong. This led to the experience of guilt. Guilt is the emotion that safeguards our conscience.

## Practice Asking Lots of Questions

The wounded inner child operates out of the family trance. He takes people's word without asking for clarification. He puzzles, guesses, analyzes, and fantasizes his way through life. Sometimes he acts as if he knows everything because he was shamed whenever he made the slightest mistake. Learn to recognize that your inner child is confused. Here are a few examples of my inner child's signals of confusion: I feel sad and happy about the same things; I can think of two opposite behaviors and they both have lots of merit; I'm not sure what another person wants from me; I'm not sure what another person is feeling; I'm asked about what I want and I don't know.

When your inner child is confused, write out what you're confused about. For example, I feel happy because a relationship has ended. I also feel sad because it ended. I ask myself, "What's the source of my happiness?" The answer is that I'm free to start a new relationship. It feels good to be out of a rut. I feel sad because I remember the good times with that person. I also can remember some very bad times with that person. There is nothing wrong with feeling both happy and sad; we often feel two different feelings toward the same person. Writing out questions helps me clarify my sense of confusion.

If you're confused about someone's feelings or needs, ask him questions until you feel less confused. He too may be confused about what's going on inside of him.

Learn to ask lots of questions. Teach your inner child that it's not easy to understand others. No one of us understands the same sentence the same way. Asking questions is an important permission to give our inner child.

## Practice Clarifying Communications

In one of your significant relationships contract with your partner to spend time clarifying your communications. Practice two kinds of listening: tape-recorder listening and active listening. Tape-recorder listening is simply retelling a person exactly what you heard him say. I use the simple formula: "What I heard you saying was bluppidy blup. Is that right?"

Active listening is listening with your eyes! You listen to the words but you look for the person's affect (signs of feeling). Affect is manifested in eye movements, facial expression, muscle tension, variations in lip size, breathing patterns, and other physical signals such as posture.

With active listening you pick up on the person's *process* as well as the *content* of his communication. Actually your inner child is quite adept at picking up on other people's processes. But the inner child does this unconsciously.

By practicing active listening you can become more *conscious* of the other person's process. Listening also helps us check out what the other person is saying. Few of us saw this kind of careful communication modeled in our family systems. I have often interacted with someone relying on guesses and unchecked assumptions. When such fantasies are treated as facts, serious relationship problems develop.

## Practice Being Aware of Your Feelings

Remember that feelings are our primary biological motivators. What you feel at any given moment is the core of your authentic reality at that moment. Your inner child has had his feelings so bound with toxic shame that to feel *anything* is to feel toxic shame. Here are some suggestions to encourage your inner child *to feel and express his feelings in safety*.

For twenty-one days, spend thirty minutes a day just noticing what you're feeling. To help Little John feel his feelings, I use the gestalt therapy technique of exaggeration. If I notice that I'm feeling sad, I let my face droop with sadness and may even pretend to cry. If I notice that I'm angry, I exaggerate the anger in my body: I clench my fist or, if my jaw is clenched, I clench it even harder. I make growling sounds. Sometimes I hit a pillow with my fist.

I also give my feelings words. I ask my feeling what it wants to say. Then I say it out loud. I let Little John express the emotion as strongly as possible.

Don't fail to do this exercise with feelings of happiness and joy also. If you're happy and smiling, smile even bigger. Shout with joy. Jump and dance. Use this technique anytime you're aware of a feeling and in an appropriate setting to express it. (Not in the middle of a sales meeting!)

Listening to music or watching a movie or TV show may trigger strong emotions. Some of these may take you by surprise, because at first they seem unrelated to or out of proportion to the trigger. Instead of pushing down the feeling, take a deep breath and really let yourself have it. Exaggerate it physically as fully as you can. Express it verbally as fully as you can. When you're finished, think about it. It's important to be conscious that you are thinking about your feelings. Your inner child often confuses thoughts with emotions. Name the emotion for your inner child. Affirm and support the emotion, and assure your inner child that it's okay to have it.

## Practice Setting Emotional Boundaries

I like to teach my inner child that he has the right to set his own emotional boundaries. My emotional boundary statement is:

"Emotions are not right or wrong. They simply are. What you feel about me is about your emotional history; what I feel about you is about my emotional history. I will respect and value your emotions and I ask you to do the same for me. I will not be manipulated by your anger, sadness, fear, or joy."

## Practice Setting Sexual Boundaries

Sexual identity is one of preschoolers' core interests although they are not very sophisticated about sexual matters. Life energy is sexual energy and it moves the preschooler to find the limits of his power by establishing a self-definition, an identity. Sexual identity is the core of our true identity. Sex is not something we have, it is who we are. Your inner child's beliefs about sexuality are forged in the matrix of: the degree of functional intimacy in your parents' marriage; bonding with the parent of the same sex; and your parents' beliefs about sex. If you have not truly explored your own sexuality, it's important that you do so. Your inner child is loaded with parental injunctions about sexual matters. He needs you to make your own sexual boundaries and keep them clearly in mind. I think it's useful to write them out, as writing helps clarify things. To arrive at a written position, make a list of all your beliefs about sex. Include things like frequency of sex; the right time for sex; the range of permissible sexual behaviors; sex talk; perverted sexual behavior; foreplay; male sexual response; female sexual response. Next to each item, write out where your belief came from. For example, if under the column for perverted sexual behavior, you listed oral sex, ask yourself who told you that oral sex was perverted. If your answer is anything other than your own experience or your own actual chosen preference, you might want to seriously consider experimenting with such a behavior. We need to help our inner child establish our own sexual beliefs by developing an informed conscience. This involves using our adult experience and reasoning as well as prudently considering the cultural and spiritual traditions we have inherited. It seems obvious to me that a minimal standard would forbid the exploitation and/or violation of another person. This allows a wide range of sexual experiences that are perfectly okay between adults. Each person needs to make his own choices about his own sexual boundaries.

An example of a written statement for your sexual boundary is: "I will determine with whom I will be sexual. I have the right to determine how, when, and where I will be sexual with another person. My only guideline is respect for my own and my partner's dignity. In view of that, I would never do anything that would exploit or violate myself or my partner.

## Practice Freeing Your Imagination

Often the inner child feels hopeless. Such hopelessness resulted from having his imagination squelched at an early age. Your inner child may have been called a dreamer, or he may have been shamed for imagining. Give yourself regular periods of time to sit for thirty minutes and envision new possibilities for yourself and your life. Go on a fantasy trip. Let yourself be whatever you want to be. Start your fantasy with "What if ..." Write out your fantasies when you're finished. Over time you may find a certain vision recurring. Take it seriously! A written statement for your imagination boundary might be: "I can and will envision my own future no matter how outlandish my vision may appear to you."

## Confront Your Magical Expectations

Magic is different from fantasy. Fantasy is an act of the imagination. Magic is the belief that certain behaviors, thoughts, or feelings can actually make things happen in the world when there's no true cause-and-effect relationship. "Say the magic word" is a common parental injunction and the wounded inner child is often filled with magic. She thinks that if she's a perfect cook and sexual partner, her husband will stop working obsessively or drinking or gambling. He thinks that if he works obsessively and makes a lot of money, she will automatically be happy.

"Trying" is another magical behavior. Lots of wounded inner kids learned that *if you try hard, you don't have to do it*. In therapy, "Trying is dying." So often after I've given a person a homework assignment in a therapy session and heard their meek little inner child answer, "I'll try," I know that this means *they won't do it*. Sometimes I illustrate this by saying, "Try to get out of your chair." When they start to get up, I say, "No, sit down and *try* to get out of your chair." After several times they get the picture. You either get up out of a chair or you don't. But you don't try to.

Marriage is often a magical event for the inner child. She thinks, "If I can just get married, all my problems will go away. If I can just get married, I'll be happy." Getting a degree, owning a home, having a child, having a swimming pool, falling in love, and making a six-figure income are other forms of magic.

In championing your inner child you must challenge each and every magical childhood belief. Life is difficult; there is no Santa Claus; there is no one to kiss the boo-boo! *It is not fair a lot of the time*.

## Learn to Love Yourself as a Man

It is important for a man to feel like a man. This is true no matter what your sexual orientation is. I believe that to feel like a man our inner little boy needed to be loved by a man. So many of us lost our fathers. They deserted us physically or emotionally. They died young in wars or from accidents or disease. They died psychologically under the burden of a dehumanizing workload. Our wounded inner boy had no father to *bond with,* and, therefore he never broke the bond with his mother. Without father-bonding your inner boy never felt a man's love of a man. So how could he love himself as a man? Consequently, he either runs to mothering women to get fixed when he is hurting or continues to try to fix needy women, or a little of both. The loss of Father is the male wound. It cannot be healed by a woman.

You can work on correcting this loss by finding other men to share with. This kind of male sharing needs to be very different from the male camaraderie many of us have known that consisted of competition and bragging rites about female conquests. The new sharing necessitates breaking the pattern of our cultural male script. It demands that we be vulnerable with each other—sharing fears and disappointments. This sharing of vulnerability creates a true bond of love and intimacy. In that bond one can feel the accepting and mirroring eyes of a man. And as that reflected love and valuing is internalized, one begins to love oneself as a man.

I have some men in my life now who truly love me. I feel bonded with them. I can be vulnerable with them. I tell them of my fears; I cry in front of them; I share my successes with them. They tell me that they love me. They hug me. Their love and sharing has made a huge impact on Little John. He feels more like a real little man. I feel like a man.

## Learn to Love Yourself as a Woman

To love herself as a woman, your inner little girl needed to be loved by a woman. This has nothing to do with sexual orientation. It has to do with your very beingness. Much has been written about the failure in mothering many people have experienced. This failure has special impact on daughters. The failure in mothering is due mainly to the failure in marital intimacy. Because of this failure, Mom is frustrated and lonely. She may turn to her son and make him her Little Man, thus rejecting her daughter. Or she may turn to her daughter and use her to fill her emptiness. The daughter cannot be loved for herself in such an enmeshed situation. She has no mirroring that would allow her to develop a sense of self. She takes on the lonely, shame-based self of her mother, who is longing for her husband's love.

When a little girl does not have the healthy love of her mother, she grows up missing crucial aspects of her sexual identity. This is why so many women magically believe that they are adequate as women only *if a man loves them*. If their male relationship ends, they panic. They then rush into another male relationship in order to feel okay. If this sounds like you, you need to let your wounded inner child experience the love of a woman. Find two or three women who are willing to commit to being vulnerable with you. Don't try to do therapy with one another or fix one another. Be there to support one another in seeking self-actualization. Women already bond together on the basis of vulnerability. Too often the bond is common victimization. Your inner little girl needs to know that she has you to champion her in becoming undependent. She needs to know that she can make it with you and your support group, that she does not *need* a man to be happy. She may *want* a man in her life as a part of her natural female drive for sexual love and male bonding. But she can achieve that best when she is self-sufficient and undependent. Your women's support group can be there for you as you pursue this goal.

## Confront Your Toxic Guilt

As I've pointed out, we need healthy guilt to form a conscience and set limits on our behavior. Without it, we would be sociopathic. But the wounded inner child carries a lot of unhealthy toxic guilt. Toxic guilt denies you the right to be your unique self. It enhances your spiritual wound.

Toxic guilt is twofold. One form of it results from living in a dysfunctional family system. Each person in such a system is thrust into a rigid role in order to keep the system in balance. If a person tries to give up his role, the family will rise up and spew guilt on that person. If a person tries to *leave* the family and have a life of his own, he will be guilted. The best way to confront such guilt is to help your wounded child give up his rigid family system role(s). Practice the methods I described earlier (chapter 10, pp. 202–203).

The second form of guilt results from anger turned against oneself ("retroflected anger"). Your wounded inner child was often angry at your parents, but he was unable to express that anger. Consider the following scenario:

Three-year-old Farquhar has been told that it is time for bed. He is absorbed in play and having a great time. He tells his mother, "No, I'm not going." His mother picks him up and takes him to bed. He screams and tantrums and yells, "I hate you!" When his father hears this, he jumps to his feet and grabs little Farquhar. He sternly tells him he has violated God's Fourth Commandment, "Honor thy father and thy mother." Little Farquhar feels terrible. He has violated God's own rule! Now he feels angry and guilty at the same time. Over the years, in order to alleviate his painful guilt, he will do what he thinks others want him to do—but he will feel resentful all the while.

To work on this guilt you need to express the underlying anger directly. Use the imagery technique I described on p. 227 to clear out the old anger. Divorcing the guilting parent by doing the original pain and grief work will also help.

You can reinforce this work by becoming conscious of how your toxic guilt was formed in specific incidents. Make a list of childhood events about which you were made to feel guilty. Compare your behavior to the normal behaviors for the specific age levels I described in part 2. In most cases you will find that you acted in an *age-appropriate* manner—your *healthy* behavior was condemned as bad. Redo these events in your imagination and assert your rights. Little Farquhar might say, "Hey, I'm just a normal little three-year-old who loves to play. I'm trying to set my boundaries. I'm angry at you for spoiling my fun."

Finally, you may want to pay special attention to feelings of guilt that resulted from violation and abuse. Your egocentric inner child more often than not personalized the abuse he received. This is dramatically true for those of you as children were incested and physically battered.

Also take a look at ways you may have been guilted in relation to the needs of your family system. A male client of mine was set up by his father's abandonment to be his mother's caretaker. His inner child feels guilty anytime his mother is in need, which is most of the time. He told me that whenever he is in a particularly difficult or stressful situation, he wonders what would happen to his mother if she had to face such a situation. His inner child feels comfortable only when he knows his mother is happy. Since it is rare that she is happy, he feels guilty a lot of the time.

Another client of mine kept her parents' marriage together. She had a severe eating disorder that began shortly after her mother had an an affair and her father threatened divorce. As her anorexia worsened, the mother and father began to bond together in their common concern over her physical condition. In talking to her I found that she felt very guilty about everything in her life. But she was especially guilty over the possibility of her parents' divorce. She felt responsible for keeping their marriage together.

In both cases it's crucial to do the original pain work described in part 2. You need to continually instruct your inner child that he is not responsible for his parents' dysfunctionality.

## EXERCISES FOR YOUR SCHOOL-AGE INNER CHILD

When your inner child went to school, he left the rather limited confines of the family and moved on to the larger family of society. He had two major tasks to accomplish in order to make this a healthy adaption. The first task centered on the development of social skills: interacting and cooperating with his peers, and being competitive in a balanced way so that he could enjoy winning and accept losing.

His second task was to acquire the kinds of learning necessary for developing a career that would ensure later economic survival.

Your inner child also had to learn that the people outside his family are often very different. They belong to different ethnic, religious, political, and socioeconomic groups. Your inner child needed to find his own unique identity in reference to all the differences he experienced in his interactions with the larger society.

If you felt that your school-age inner child was wounded, here are some exercises you can do.

### Make a Life Skills Inventory

List the skills you already have. Next, make a list of life skills that you do not have—skills that would make your life easier. In my case, I wish I had studied my English grammar. I got through it because I had a great memory and would cram for exams. If you read my first book, you'd see how I've struggled with grammar. I also lack mechanical skills. (I can put in light bulbs and that's about it!)

Pick one area that would help you the most and either (a) take a course in it, or (b) get someone to teach you that skill.

It is also important to tell your wounded inner child over and over again that much of life is based on learned skills. He often thinks that people have succeeded because of some "magical power." We need to tell our wounded inner child that often people are ahead of us because they had better models and got to practice more when they were young. Keep telling him that he lacks certain skills because no one has taught them to him. With you as his champion, he can learn them now. I know one woman whose inner child was liberated when her adult confronted her shaming inner voice that said, "I guess I'm just not attractive to men," with, "You just never learned to flirt or show interest in a man." This new approach gave her child the confidence to ask an experienced woman friend for advice. She had one absolutely hilarious evening and got lots of tips that paid off.

## Make a Social Skills Inventory

Make a list of social skills you need to learn. These are skills that make it easier to go to social gatherings; to get along at the office; to meet people; to be more politic; to be a better "small talker," and so on.

Take the skills one at a time and find a model who does that skill rather well. Watch him to see what he does. Take notes.

Pay attention to every detail. After you've gathered some data on what that person does, sit down for periods of fifteen to thirty minutes and in fantasy see him doing the things you want to do. Chunk it down to a small frame of behavior. Watch him do that behavior and anchor it. Then, while holding your anchor, see yourself doing the same behavior. Take the next chunk and repeat the procedure. Do this for about a week. Then see yourself doing the entire sequence. Practice that for a few days. Then try it out. You can use this method for learning any new social skill. This is a variation of the N.L.P. exercise you did earlier.

## Practice Values Clarification

Your values are your intellectual boundaries. Your inner child often doesn't know what he believes, because he was coerced and brainwashed in secular and church school.

The book *Values Clarification* by Sidney Simon, Leland Howe, and Howard Kirschenbaum is a classic in the field. These authors posit that a value is not a value unless it has seven elements. They are:

1. It must be chosen.
2. There must be alternatives.
3. You must know the consequences of your choice.
4. Once chosen you prize and cherish it.
5. You are willing to publicly proclaim it.
6. You act on this value.
7. You act on it consistently and repeatedly.

Make a list of your own most cherished beliefs—your Ten Commandments. Then evaluate them according to this list and see how many of your beliefs meet these value criteria.

The first time I did this exercise I was shocked and mildly depressed. Very little of what I professed to believe was in actuality a value.

Using these criteria, you can start working on your own values formation. You can keep what you've got and start changing what you don't want. It can be exciting for both you and your inner child to form your own values.

## Practice Setting Intellectual Boundaries

It's important to teach your inner child to say the following:

> I have the right to believe whatever it is that I believe. I need only take the consequences for my beliefs. All beliefs are partial. Each of us sees things from our own limited point of view.

## Evaluating Your Competitive Spirit

It is important to be a winner; it is also important to be a gracious loser. I remember an evening of playing cards with my family. We were playing for money, and as the game got more expensive, my mother-in-law began to regress. When she lost the largest pot of the evening (about two dollars), she threw her cards down and quit. She was only 77! Obviously the game had triggered a spontaneous age regression. In a culture where winning is exaggerated out of all proportion, we take losing hard. I remember wanting to quit playing a game with my children. I was getting angrier and angrier as I lost. I was only 42!

It's good to get a group together and play games where all can win (making a crossword puzzle together). This is also useful in working on team building in business.

The business world is often a place of cutthroat competition. If the competition is too cutthroat, your inner child may be tempted to throw in the towel. You need to be careful not to let your inner child go into a fit of depression when there is favoritism at the office. You can count on the fact that there will be the equivalent of sibling rivalries and teacher's-pet situations in business. You need to be a strong champion for your child. What helps the most is to keep your work goals clear. Decide what you want and what you are willing to do, and then go for it. Remember to protect your child every step of the way.

Win/win is the only way that works for all. Practice setting up win/win situations in your life. Your inner kid will really like it.

## Practice Negotiating

Your wounded inner child often wants what he wants when he wants it. He thinks his way is the only right way. Your adult must teach him that compromise and cooperation are the keys to interdependent living and happy adult relationships. Children will cooperate if given the chance to experience the *fruits of compromise*. Most of our wounded inner kids have never seen a conflict resolved in a healthy way. The rule of *incompletion* dominates dysfunctional, shame-based families. Incompletion means that the same fights go on for years.

You can learn to use disagreement as the fuel for new and expanding ideas. Debate and argument are tools for finding out what path each person needs and wants. It's good to have rules to guide the debate, and it's *essential* to have a referee. Get a threesome together and practice having debates over things you disagree on.

Use the listening rule and stay with self-responsible "I" messages. Go for negotiated compromise. Always have a renegotiation clause in your agreement. That means that either party can reopen the discussion in a reasonable period of time if he feels uncomfortable with the issue as negotiated. Again, always go for the win/win solution.

Successful negotiation gives your inner child good experience with handling conflict. He sees that conflict isn't a horrible, traumatic event; in fact, it is crucial for the establishment of healthy intimacy. Each of us has a wonderful, unique, precious, unrepeatable inner child. It is inevitable that two unrepeatables will come to cross purposes. This is to be expected. Resolving our conflicts makes life an exciting adventure.

In this section we've looked at homecoming as the four dynamic elements of any good therapy. We champion our wonder child by offering him our adult *potency*. This potency gives the child *permission* to break free of the old poisonous rules and to experience the new corrective ones. The new rules comprise the essence of nurturing discipline. Such discipline is necessary to curb the inner child's egocentric childishness and call out his spiritual childlikeness. Such childlikeness needs to be *protected* so that as we *practice* these new corrective experiences, our full creative power can emerge. Our creative power is rooted in our wonderful child. Let us turn to that child now.

## EXERCISE FOR BREAKING YOUR PRIMARY PARENTAL ENMESHMENT

This is the exercise I use in relation to the enmeshed dysfunctional family system roles I discussed in chapter 7. These roles involve cross-generational bonding. They often involve nonphysical sexual abuse.

The exercise is adapted from the work of Connirae and Steve Andreas and can be found in its original form in their book *Heart of the Mind*.

I recommend that you either record this exercise on your tape recorder or have a therapist, trusted friend, or support person take you through the steps. Give yourself thirty minutes to do the entire process. Find a quiet space where you will not be distracted and go through this process *standing up*. Allow for pauses of 30 seconds when you see the dots.

### STEP ONE: The Enmeshed Parent

Close your eyes and focus your attention on memories of the parent you feel the most enmeshed with. Really see, feel, or hear that person in your internal experience. Let them be present to you in their *most attractive behavior.* Your unconscious will know exactly what that behavior is. . . .

Trust the first thing that comes to your mind. If you cannot visualize your parent, just sense or pretend that he or she is there.

### STEP TWO: Feeling the Enmeshment

Now see your wounded school age inner child standing next to that parent. . . . Notice what the child is wearing. . . . Hear your child talking to the parent. . . . Now float into your inner child's body and look out of his eyes at your parent. . . . Look at your parent from different angles. . . . Notice how your parent sounds. . . . How your parent smells. . . . Now walk over and embrace your parent. . . . What does it feel like to be in physical contact with that parent? . . . In what ways do you feel over-connected to your parent? *How* do you experience yourself as being connected? How do you experience that parent as attached to you? Is it a physical attachment? Is it an attachment to some part of your body? (Many people experience this connection in the groin, stomach, or chest area.) Is there a cord or some other means of attachment between you? Is there a rubber band around you? Get a full experience of the quality of this connection.

### STEP THREE: Temporarily Breaking the Enmeshment

Now sever this connection for a moment. . . . Just allow yourself to notice what it would be like. If you are attached by a cord, imagine cutting it with scissors. . . . If you are attached to your

parent's body, imagine a laser beam of miraculous golden light
that severs you and heals the wound simultaneously.... You
will feel discomfort separating at this point.... This is a signal
that this connection serves an important purpose in your life.
Remember that you are not disconnecting. You are only experiencing what it feels like to separate temporarily.

STEP FOUR: Discovering the Positive Purpose of the Enmeshment
Now ask yourself, "What do I really get from this parent that
satisfies my basic needs?" ... "What do I really want from that
parent?" ... Wait until you get an answer that touches you to
the core—such as safety, security, protection from death, feeling that you matter, that you are lovable and worthwhile....
Now reconnect the attachment to your parent.

STEP FIVE: Using Your Adult Potency
Now turn to the right or left and see yourself as a wise and
gentle wizard (or as fully self-actualized as your most powerful
self). Become aware that this older you is capable of giving you
what you want and believe you are getting from your enmeshed
parental relationship. Really look at your resourceful adult self....
Notice how this part of you looks, moves, and sounds. Go over
and embrace your grown-up self.... Feel the power and potency
of your adult.... Realize that the worst thing you've always feared
has already happened to you.... You were violated and abandoned by being enmeshed,... and your adult part has made
it,... your adult has survived and functioned in spite of it.

STEP SIX: Transforming the Connection with Your Parent
into a Connection with Yourself
Turn again to your enmeshed parent.... See and feel the connection.... Sever the connection and immediately reconnect with
your adult self in the same way you were connected to your
parent.... Enjoy feeling interdependent with someone you can
completely count on: yourself. Thank your adult for being there
for you. Enjoy receiving from your adult what you wanted from
your parent. Your adult is the person that you can never lose.

### STEP SEVEN: Respecting Your Enmeshed Parent

Now look at your enmeshed parent and notice that he has a choice. He can reconnect the cord to his adult self. Remember that your parent has the same options for reclaiming and wholeness that you have. In fact, notice that your enmeshed parent has no chance for true wholeness if he stays attached to you. . . . You are loving him by giving him a chance for wholeness. Also notice that you now have an opportunity for a true relationship with him for the very first time.

### STEP EIGHT: Relationship with Self

Now float back into your adult self. . . . Feel the interconnection with your wounded inner school-age child. Realize that you can now love and cherish this child and give him what he needed from his parent.

## FINISHING YOUR MYTH OR FAIRY TALE

As a final exercise, finish the myth or fairy tale you wrote when you were working on reclaiming your school-age child (p. 149). Start with the words *And then.* . . .

Here's how my story ended:

And then Farquhar heard Joni's voice. It so moved him that he committed to create a quiet time each day when he could listen to Joni. The first thing Joni told him was to join a group of people who had been wounded and who were now practicing the elves' secrets. They were committed to the discipline of love. That meant that they delayed gratification, were self-responsible, told the truth at any cost, and lived a balanced life.

Farquhar was accepted with open arms. Very soon he *saw* his elf self in the loving eyes of his fellow group members. He lived one day at a time and committed himself to the discipline of love. He reclaimed and championed his wounded inner child. Soon he began to teach the secret of the elves. As the years went by he became a famous teacher and transformer of Snamuh souls. He loved his life and lived for the day he could return to his true home, endlessly creating and basking in the vision of the Great I AM.

# PART

# 4

# REGENERATION

It is important to understand that the need to find the child is part of an ancient human longing. Behind our individual past lies our cultural past, contained in myths. In myths we see that the child is often the offspring of the union of the human and the divine. It is the mythical child ... that we seek as well as the child of our personal history.

—RACHEL V.

And the end of all our exploring
Will be to arrive where we started
And know the place for the first time.

—T. S. ELIOT
*Four Quartets*

Where there had only been fearful emptiness ... there is now unfolding a wealth of vitality. This is not a home-coming since this home had never before existed. It is the discovery of home.

—ALICE MILLER

# INTRODUCTION

As you allow your child to become an integral part of your life—dialoguing with him, listening to him, setting boundaries for him, letting him know that you will never leave him—a new power and creativity begin to emerge. You will connect with a fresh vision of your child, enriched and deepened by your years of adult experience.

The child who now emerges is your wonder child. As your championing work progresses, your wonder child will naturally flourish and move into expansiveness and self-actualization. The natural state of the wonder child is creativity. Getting in touch with your creativity is more than a homecoming: it is a discovery of your essence, your deepest, unique self.

Finding and reclaiming the *wounded* inner child is an *uncovery* process. In addition to developing your personal power, championing your wounded child leads to recovering his spiritual power. With his newfound spiritual power, your self-creation begins. This is your true homecoming. That which was hidden can now unfold. The urgings and signals from your deepest self can now be heard and responded to.

In this last section I will focus on the universal human need to find our wonder child. I will point out two of the ways our world mythologies have witnessed to the regeneration and transformative power of the wonder child. The first mythic pattern involves the *puer aeternus,* or eternal child, who ushers in the golden age. The second mythic pattern is the divine/hero infant who has been exiled and who comes to find his divine birthright. Both are symbols of the vital and ineluctable human urge continually to realize and transcend ourselves.

I will invite you to use your wonder child as a guide to your authentic self and to a new sense of your life's purpose.

Finally, I'll suggest that your wonder child is the core of your spirituality and your most profound connection with the source and creative ground of your being. In fact, I'll suggest to you that your wonder child is your *Imago Dei*—the part of you that bears a likeness to your creator.

# CHAPTER 13

# THE CHILD AS A UNIVERSAL SYMBOL OF REGENERATION AND TRANSFORMATION

> The "child" is all that is abandoned and exposed and at the same time divinely powerful; the insignificantly dubious beginning, and the triumphal end. The "eternal child" in man is an indescribable experience, an incongruity, a handicap, and a divine prerogative; an imponderable that determines the ultimate worth or worthlessness of a personality.
>
> —C. G. JUNG

The great psychologist Carl Jung saw clearly the paradoxical quality of the inner child. For Jung the child was the source of divinity, regeneration, and new beginnings, and at the same time a possible source of contamination and destruction. Jung clearly saw the *wounded child* as a part of the archetypal child. This was Jung's genius, for it is only in the last fifty years that human consciousness has focused on the wounded child. In fact, I believe that the wounded child has become a *modern archetype*.

An archetype is a representation of the cumulative and collective experience of mankind, a universal potential in every human being. Jung felt that when a certain pattern of human experience was clearly established, it became part of our collective psychic inheritance. He believed that the archetypes are passed on genetically like DNA.

Archetypes are like organs of our psyche, comparable to the skeletal structures of our body. Archetypes are congenital psychic predispositions derived from inherited patterns created in past generations. These patterns emerge when certain thresholds of human experience are reached.

Archetypes embody both positive and negative aspects of the patterns they represent. In the mother archetype the positive aspect is the nurturing and life-giving mother; the negative aspect is the mother who smothers, devours, and destroys her children.

In the father archetype, the positive aspect protects and sets limits for his children and passes on the laws and traditions of the culture. The negative father is the tyrant who, fearing the loss of his power, keeps his children in bondage and refuses to pass on the traditions.

In the child archetype, the positive child is vulnerable, childlike, spontaneous, and creative. The negative child is selfish, childish, and resists emotional and intellectual growth.

The negative aspect of the child is the wounded child. It is only in our century that the wounded inner child has received our attention. In times past, the abuse and subjugation of children were commonplace and often taken for granted. As late as 1890, there was no Society for the Prevention of Cruelty to Children, although there was a Society for the Prevention of Cruelty to Animals.

One of the great advances of our generation has been the exposure of child abuse. We have come to see that our prevailing rules for raising children shame and violate their uniqueness and their dignity. Such rules have been a part of our emotional endarkenment. Alice Miller has shown with painful clarity how our current parenting rules have aimed at making the child fit the projected image of the parent. They have also enforced the idealization of parents by the wounded child. Such idealization creates a fantasy bond that assures the wounded child of his parents' love for him. But it has also perpetuated the abuse of children for generations.

George Bernard Shaw coined a marvelous description of a child when he wrote:

What is a child? An experiment. A fresh attempt to produce the just man . . . that is to make humanity divine.

Shaw fully understood that this experiment cannot be toyed with or manipulated:

And if you should try to shape this new being into *your idea* of a
godly man or a godly woman, you will destroy its own holiest
expectation and perhaps create a monster.

It is this latter scenario that we've now come to understand. As we
begin to confront the ancient and pervasive tradition of child abuse,
we are giving new names to the demons of incest, battering, and
emotion violation. We see clearly the *soul murder* that constitutes the
spiritual wound that results from the violation of a child's I AMness.

The massive energy of the adult child movement has born witness
to this new understanding of the wounded child archetype.

Ours has been a time of catastrophe and dark destruction. There
has been nothing comparable to it in the history of humankind.
Millions have died in the struggle for freedom and democracy. I
believe that the catastrophe of Nazism was rooted in the structure of
the German family with its shaming and authoritarian parental rules.
However, while these rules were taken to their extreme in Germany,
they are not German rules. In fact, they are worldwide rules that have
wounded children for generations and still exist today. Because the
rules were considered normal, there was no awareness of how destructive they were. With the declaration of human rights in the
American and French revolutions—however flawed the revolutions—a
new and golden age slowly began emerging. Like the mythical phoenix, it has been rising out of the ashes. Our awareness of the wounded
child archetype has led us to heal and reclaim the child. This in turn
allows the wonder child to emerge.

## THE PUER AETERNUS

In all the world's great mythologies, creation recurs eternally and
cyclically. Periodically the world returns to chaos. The mountains
crumble, the plains are leveled by torrential rains of fire, the earth
quakes, the dead return. These events are the apocalyptic prefigura-
tion of the new and golden age. Everything must be reduced to chaos
before the new creation can begin.

In many myths, a new tree sprouts up out of the chaotic ruins. The
top of the tree reaches into heaven. Then a miraculous *child* appears
and runs up the trunk of the tree. It is the arrival of this miraculous
child, this *puer aeternus,* that marks the beginning of the golden age.

In some versions the child alters the structure of the cosmos. In other myths the child brings the wholeness that characterizes the golden age. With the coming of the child all opposites are reconciled. The old become young; the sick are made well; yams and potatoes grow on trees; coconuts and pineapples grow in the earth. There is an abundance of food and goods; no one has to work or pay taxes. In all these myths the child is the symbol of regeneration and wholeness.

Jung describes what this means to us personally:

In the individuation process, the child anticipates the figure that comes from the synthesis of conscious and unconscious elements in the personality. It is therefore the unifying symbol which unites the opposites; a mediator; a bringer of healing; one who makes whole.

It is this creative and regenerative aspect of the child that I'd like to turn to now.

## THE WONDER CHILD AS AUTHENTIC SELF

In Gail Godwin's novel *The Finishing School,* one of the characters says, "There are two kinds of people.... One kind you can tell just by looking at them at what point they congealed into their final self ... you know you can expect no more surprises from it ... the other kind keep moving, changing ... and making new trysts with life and the motion of it keeps them young." The latter type is a person in touch with his wonder child. Your wonder child is your truest self.

I remember it as if it were yesterday. I was 12 years old and was standing waiting for a bus when I had a very powerful experience of my I AMness. Somehow I experienced the realization that I was me and there was no one else like me. I remember being frightened as I recognized my aloneness. I remember thinking that my eyes are windows that only *I* can see out of. I realized that no one else could view the world from my point of view—from the windows that were my eyes. I also realized that no one else could ever really be inside me, that I was separate from everyone else. I was me and no one could change that, no matter what they did to me or tried to make me do. I was who I was, and I was unique.

At that moment, at that bus stop on Fairview Street, I had the intuition of my own being. That intuition born of wonder would be lost to me many times in the ensuing years. But it would lead me to study and teach philosophy, and it would lead me on a personal journey toward wholeness. I'm still utterly fascinated with philosophy. I am awed by a sense of *being,* what Jacques Maritain described as "the victorious thrust by which we triumph over nothingness." The wonder child is still awed by the question Spinoza asked, "Why is there something rather than nothing?" This same question, millennia earlier, had motivated Thales of Miletus, the father of ancient philosophy. Later, Aristotle wrote, "It is owing to their wonder that men both now begin and at first began to philosophize."

The early experience of my own beingness was the work of my wonder child. And forty-three years later that wonder child is speaking through me as I write this book. In the core of my awareness, nothing has changed. Although for many years my wounded child kept me from experiencing the sacredness of the present moment, I'm slowly coming back to that primitive sense of awe and wonder. I can again feel chills running down my spine when I truly touch the being of an ocean or a sunset or a starry night.

You may continually expand your awareness and broaden your horizons, but the core of your authentic self never changes. Francis of Assisi wrote, "Who we are looking for is who is looking." The transpersonal psychologists call it your "witnessing self"—the "I" that looks at me.

In your wonder child you will find your authentic feelings, needs, and wants. For most adult children this child was lost long ago. As you champion your wounded child, he comes to trust you and your nourishing protection; he knows you will not abandon him. That deep sense of safety and basic trust allows the wonder child to emerge. Then, to be yourself requires no work or effort. There is nothing to do. As Sam Keen puts it:

It may be that homecoming is the secularized or deparochialized equivalent of what Christians traditionally mean by justification by faith. . . . In divorcing salvation from achievement, the Christian had established the priority of *being* over *doing.*

My wounded shame-based child became a human "doing" in order to have significance and to matter to others. After forty years of being a

Star, Superachiever, and Caretaker, I had to learn that *I could not heal my being with my doing. To be who I am is all that matters.*

Your wonder child is your *essential self.* Transpersonal psychologists make a distinction between the essential self and the adapted self. The word which they often use to describe your essential self is the word *soul.* The word used to describe your adapted self is *ego.*

In their model your ego is the limited sphere of consciousness you use in order to adapt to the demands of your family and culture. Ego is limited by these survival needs. It is your time-bound self and is rooted in your family of origin as well as in the culture into which you were born. All cultural and family systems are relative and represent only one of the many possible ways that reality can be understood and interpreted. Even if your ego adaptation was *fully functional* in relation to your family and culture, it was still limited and fragmented in relation to your true self. In transpersonal theory, *your ego is always inauthentic compared to your soul.* This is why I identify the soul with the wonder child and the ego with the wounded child.

Still, your ego must be integrated and functional if you are to survive and cope with the exigencies of everyday temporal life.

A strong integrated ego gives you a sense of confidence and control. Reclaiming and championing your wounded inner child allows you to heal and integrate your ego. Once integrated, your ego then becomes the source of strength that allows you to explore your wonder child: your essential self. Paradoxical as it may seem, your ego needs to be strong enough to let go of its limited defensiveness and control. You need a strong ego to transcend ego. To give a crude example: the ego is like the booster rocket that puts you into orbit. Your soul takes over from there, operating in the unlimited expanse of outer space.

The relationship between your wonder child (soul) and your wounded child (ego) *must* be healed before you can connect with your essential self. Once you've done your ego work (your original pain work or legitimate suffering), you're ready for full self-actualization.

Actually, it is your wonder child who motivates you to do your ego work. The wounded child cannot do the work of recovery, since he is so busy defending and surviving. When all of life is a chronic toothache, one cannot transcend that pain to see that there are greener pastures. Since your wonder child is your authentic self, he has always been pulling at you to achieve self-actualization even when your ego has been closed and unaware due to its preoccupation with survival issues. Carl Jung sums it up beautifully:

> The child archetype is a personification of vital forces quite outside the limited range of our conscious mind.... It represents the strongest most ineluctable urge in every being, namely, the urge to realize itself.

Once you feel the connection with your wonder child, you begin to see your whole life from a larger perspective. Your wonder child no longer has to hide behind ego defenses for survival. He can see things from a different level of consciousness. The wonder child is not a better self; he is a different self with a much larger vision.


### MEDITATION FOR REFRAMING YOUR LIFE WITH YOUR WONDER CHILD

The Zen Buddhists have a traditional koan, or riddle, that says: "What was your original face—the one you had before your parents gave birth to you?"

Think about this as you approach the following meditation. I'm also going to ask you to adopt, at least temporarily, some beliefs that may not be usual for you. Do not get lost in a debate about whether you really believe these things. Simply allow yourself to think and feel as if your wonder child had a sense of destiny before you were born. Let yourself accept the belief of many religious traditions that you are an incarnate spirit. Entertain the possibility that you are more than your time-bound sociocultural personality; that you have an eternal divine inheritance. Let yourself believe with Thomas Aquinas and the great Sufi masters that you are a unique expression of God—The Great I AM. Let yourself believe further that the universe would be impoverished if you had not been born; that *there is something of God that can be expressed only by you and that can be experienced by others only through you.* Let yourself believe that your wonder child has known all of this all along. In this meditation you will make contact with your wonder child and experience your divine inheritance—the purpose of your incarnation. Once you experience this, you will be in touch with your authentic self and see your whole life differently.

I recommend that you either put the meditation on tape or have a friend read it to you. Remember that the dots mean a pause of ten to twenty seconds.

Begin by focusing on your breathing. Slowly observe your own process of breathing.... Become mindful of your breathing.... Be aware of the feeling of the air as you breathe in and out.... Begin to see the number five as you breathe out.... See a black number five on a white curtain or a white number five on a black curtain.... If you have trouble visualizing, imagine yourself finger painting the number five, or *hear* it in your mind's ear. If possible, do all three. See it, finger paint it, and hear it.... Now, the number four; see it, finger paint it, or hear it, or do all three.... Then do the same with the numbers three, two, and one. *(long pause)* ... When you see the number one, imagine it's a door. Before walking through this door, imagine that you are putting all your troubles and worries into a crystal ball. Bury the ball filled with worries.... You can have your worries back when the meditation is over.... Now walk through the door and see a set of three steps leading to another door. Now imagine that you are putting your disbeliefs and skepticism into a crystal ball. Bury the ball filled with your disbeliefs and skepticism. Now review your new belief system. Here is your "as if" myth:

> You are a unique and unrepeatable manifestation of the divine.
>
> You have a destiny that *only* you can express through your being.
>
> It is not dramatic or melodramatic.
>
> It is simply the difference your *being* here makes. It is a difference that makes a difference.
>
> Your wonder child has always known what it is.
>
> Your wonder child can lead you to discover your life purpose.

Now walk up the stairs and open the door.... You will find a porch with stairs leading up into the heavens. [You might want to play Steven Halpern's *Ancient Echoes* or *Starborn Suite* here.] Begin to see a figure surrounded in blue white light coming down the stairs.... As the figure comes closer, you experience it as a warm and friendly being. Whatever form it takes is okay as long as it feels warm and friendly to you. *If the figure frightens you, tell it to go away and wait for another figure to come.* This being is your inner guide. Ask its name.

Tell it you want to speak to your wonder child. . . . Let it take
you by the hand and begin ascending the stairs. . . . You will
come to a large temple. Your guide will lead you to the door. . . .
Walk in. See objects of exquisite beauty. Walk toward a high
altar where you see a statue of a beautiful and precious child—
this is your wonder child. . . . See the figure come alive. Take a
moment to embrace your wonder child. Ask him or her for a
statement of your life's purpose: Why am I here? *(long pause)*
. . . Take the answer in whatever form it comes. A symbol,
actual words, a strong feeling. Talk to your wonder child about
it. *(long pause)* . . . Even if you do not understand, take with
you what you've been given. Thank your wonder child and
walk back to the door. Your inner guide is waiting for you. Let
your guide take you down the stairs. . . . When you reach the
porch, pause. You are now going to review your whole life
from birth till the present, in the light of your new understanding. Even if your wonder child's message was not clear, review
your life with what you do understand about your life's purpose. . . . Now go back to the moment of your birth. Just as if
you could see yourself being born. From birth onward, review
every milestone or event you can remember, viewing it in the
light of your new knowledge. See the people who were there.
Do you see them any differently now? *(long pause)* . . . You
may see someone whom you thought was insignificant as much
more significant now. *(long pause)* . . . Certain events may take
on a new meaning. Can you find a new meaning in the traumatic events you have endured? *(long pause)* . . . Come to the
present moment of your life. Accept your whole life as perfect
from your soul's point of view. Now that you've done your
original pain and ego work, you can see from this higher
vantage point. Accept the past as perfect. Commit yourself to
your purpose. . . . Send love to all you know. . . . Realize that we
are all children struggling for the light. See your parents as
wounded children. See warm golden sunlight surrounding everyone. Imagine yourself touching and embracing the people in
your life. *(long pause)* . . . Think of everyone as a child in need
of friendship and love.

Now go back to the porch with stairs leading to the temple.
Open the door and walk down the three stairs. Take back any
beliefs, skepticism, and presuppositions you want. . . . Walk

through the next door and take back any worries or anxieties you want.... Take three deep breaths. Feel the life coming back into your feet and toes as you see the number one.... Then feel the seat you're sitting in; your clothes on your body as you see the number two.... Then feel the energy in your hands. Let it come up through your arms into your neck and shoulders.... Now see the number three. Feel your whole brain wide awake. Breathe in deeply. Tell yourself you'll remember this experience. Tell yourself you will stay with the images even if you don't fully understand them. Now see the number four and feel yourself fully awake as you see the number five.

It's good just to live with this meditation for a while. Sometimes the images will make more sense later. For some this meditation marked the beginning of a new awareness about themselves and their lives. One man's wonder child gave him a key with the word *antique* written on it. As a child, he loved to spend time at his grandmother's house. She had a large collection of antique watches. He loved to listen to his grandmother as she told him the history behind each watch. She was a wonderful story-teller and piqued his imagination. He started his own collection of antique watches. But he could never devote much time to his collection, because he was busy running his own insurance agency. I saw him a year and a half after he had done the meditation. I was at an antiques show. He had sold his agency and become an antique dealer. He specialized in antique watches and unusual antique keys! He seemed very excited about his new life. Other people have shared equally dramatic outcomes from this meditation. The inner guide and wonder child represent your soul's wisdom. The soul operates in a world of symbol and speaks the language of imagery. It is your soul that speaks in your dreams. The language of dreams is hard for the ego to understand. The images must be lived with and felt before their meaning can be fully grasped. Just accept what you get as right for you.

Be sure to share this meditative experience with a nonshaming and supportive friend.

I've had a wonderful regeneration with this exercise. Many others have also had powerful experiences with it. If you did not have a powerful experience, that's okay too.

## THE NONIDEALIZATION OF THE WONDER CHILD

At this point, let me make it clear that I do not believe in the wonder child as the *sole model* for authentic life. I believe, along with Sam Keen, that that would be destructive to the dignity of mature human existence. To be only a wonder child would be to live in exile in the present. I can tell you the horror of that. My grandfather completely lost his memory in the last years of his life. When I visited him, he would often ask me the same questions over and over again. He was a beautiful man who had created his life out of hard work, fidelity, and love. To experience him without a past or future was extremely painful. We need to live *in* the now, but *not for* the now. We need to "fill the unforgiving minute with sixty seconds' worth of distance run," as Kipling would have it. But the fresh vision of the wonder child needs the wisdom and experience of the adult you have become. In fact, your wonder child will become present only if your adult is there to support and protect him.

A child, no matter how wonderful, is no more a model for authentic adult life than an adult is an adequate model for what a child should be. Sam Keen writes:

> We become human only on leaving Eden, mature only in realizing that childhood is over. We come home to the fullness of our humanity only in owning and taking responsibility for present awareness as well as for the full measure of our memories and dreams. Graceful existence integrates past, present, and future.

Reframing my life with my wonder child helped me to see that everything in my childhood prepared me for what I'm doing now. The *purpose* I found in my meditation was that I am here to be myself and to proclaim my human freedom and to help others do the same.

In order to achieve that task, I need all my years of knowledge, all my work in recovery, all my experience as a therapist, and all the wisdom I've gained from my pain and my mistakes. With my wonder child as a guide, I can now see that my whole life is perfect. My dysfunctional family, my alcoholic dad and co-dependent mom, my poverty—all were perfect. *They were exactly what I needed to experience in order to do the work I am now doing.* Without my childhood I would never have done a TV series on dysfunctional families or written books on shame and shame-based families. And certainly I wouldn't be writing this book on homecoming, which calls you and me to reclaim and champion our wounded inner kids.

The wonder child urges us to continually expand. It calls us to more and more life. It says that life is growth, that to be human is to be overcoming. To be committed to life as growth and overcoming is to be willing to accept suffering and risk pain.

As the philosopher Karlfried Graf Von Durkheim wrote:

Only to the extent that man exposes himself over and over again to annihilation, can that which is indestructible arise within him. In this lies the dignity of daring.

When we make a commitment to the process of growing, we can see that we needed our wounded child to let us know we had a wonder child. Our wonder child endured and will endure. It is that which is indestructible. Our wonder child is our *Imago Dei*. Let us look at that now.

# CHAPTER 14

# THE WONDER CHILD AS IMAGO DEI

> God does not die on the day we cease to believe in a personal deity, but we die on the day when our lives cease to be illuminated by the steady radiance, renewed daily, of a *wonder,* the source of which is beyond all reason.
>
> —DAG HAMMARSKJÖLD

> The sense of wonder, that is our sixth sense and it is the natural religious sense....
>
> —D. H. LAWRENCE

> Except ye be converted, and become as little children, ye shall not enter into the kingdom of heaven.
>
> —MATTHEW 18:3

Whatever your personal religious beliefs, you cannot be in touch with your wonder child and not have a sense of something greater than yourself. Immanuel Kant, who was surely one of the greatest philosophical minds of all time, attested to the existence of God by gazing at the immensity of a starry night.

We can see that night follows day and seasons occur with predictability and regularity. There is cosmos: there is obvious and observable order. The earth is only one infinitesimal part of endless galactic ranges. One cannot fail to be awed by the *wonder* of it all! The wonder child is naturally religious. He is childlike and believes in something greater than self with an unwavering faith. The wonder child's poetic soul touches the heart of being itself.

Your wonder child is the part of you that possesses in a human way that power which is most godlike: creative regeneration.

## THE WONDER CHILD AS CREATIVE REGENERATION

The wonder child has all the natural ingredients necessary for creativity. Carl Rogers and a group of psychologists and artists studied the dynamics of creativity. They looked for the psychological conditions that are necessary in order for a person to be creative. They found that the following elements were essential in fostering creativity: playfulness; spontaneity; ability to live in the now; ability to experience wonder; ability to concentrate; and the capacity to be one's own locus of evaluation. The latter quality, being one's own locus of evaluation, means that one has a sense of satisfaction with himself. He is delighted with his own products. This amounts to having a sense of I AMness. All of these qualities are the qualities of the wonder child. They are *childlike* qualities. *Childlikeness* includes the following: To be spontaneous, able to live in the moment, concentrated, imaginative, creative, to play, to be joyous, to experience wonder, trust, sorrow, love, surprise, and hope.

The wonder child is the natural poet that Morley describes in the poem I quoted in part one. When we're in touch with this part of us, we have our creative power available. Most folks are not aware of their creative power, because they stay congealed in the frozen grief of their wounded child. "The mass of mankind live lives of quiet desperation," said Thoreau. Once we've done our reclaiming and championing work, the wonder child is clamoring for creative regeneration.

One way to help you get in touch with the creative power of your wonder child is for you to personalize the meaning of the myths that describe "the infant child in exile." *To discover a personal meaning involves your becoming aware of how the events of these myths have actually occurred in your life.* In these myths the child is usually either a divine being or a hero-leader who will usher in change and regeneration. In some cases the child will be the savior; in other cases, the founder of a new order. For Western minds the most familiar infant child in exile is Jesus. Leaving aside the question of the historical accuracy of this narrative, the story of Jesus's birth embodies the major pattern of the infant-in-exile motif. Different combinations of the same elements are present in the birth stories of Romulus and Remus, Sargon, Moses, Abraham, Oedipus, Paris, Krishna, Perseus, Siegfried, Buddha, Zoroaster, Hercules, Cyrus, and Gilgamesh, among others. Mythology is filled with the theme of the infant child in exile.

In all the mythical descriptions of the infant in exile, several elemental patterns are to be found. These patterns have been outlined by Otto Rank, one of the early fathers in the psychoanalytic movement, and also by the Jungian child psychologist Edith Sullwold. What follows is a synthesis of their work.

- The child to be exiled is the child of distinguished parents, the son of a king, or one who should legitimately inherit the throne. The child to be exiled is sometimes of divine origin.
- His birth is surrounded by unusual circumstances (barrenness, continence), an unusual pregnancy (virgin birth, born from mother's side, etc.).
- Often, during or before the pregnancy there is a prophecy in the form of a dream or oracle. The prophecy usually cautions against the birth, suggesting that it is in some way a threat (often to the father or his representative, often to the ruling power). The word gets out that something unusual is about to happen.
- The child is born in some unusual way and immediately surrendered to the elemental forces (put in a box and placed in the water, left on a mountain, born in a cave or manger). The child is sometimes born of elemental forces (the sea).
- The child is often saved by lowly people (sheperds), a humble woman, or suckled by a female animal. Basically the myth suggests that the child is thrown onto the mercy of elemental forces.
- The old order attempts to kill the child (the slaughter of the innocents). But the abandoned child is strong and able to survive. The child is extraordinary. That is why he is a threat.
- Slowly the child begins to recognize his own extraordinariness. When it is deemed that the child is strong enough, then the child's time has come. The child's strength comes from the gradual recognition of who he is.
- The new self-recognition lets the divine child (hero) know that there is something he has to teach the old order. He understands that at this precise moment in time, the old order can hear him and

be regenerated. Now, not only has a new child been born, but a new world order has been born. The child may have to find his distinguished parents. He may have to take revenge; sometimes he may have to kill them (Oedipus; Electra).

- Finally the child achieves the rank and honor that is his due. He accepts his divinity or his kingship or his leadership role.

Myths represent the collective stories of mankind. The elements of myths are archetypal in character. This means that mythical stories describe *patterns that are relived by each of us over and over again in our personal lives.*

What then does the archetypal infant in exile mean for us? Besides the memory of our childhood pain, *there may be the memory of a very particular creativity that is our unique and unrepeatable personal gift.* Each of us is a divine child, a hero or heroine, a leader, and a healer in exile. Our spiritual wound has so preoccupied us that we've failed to notice all the nudges and cues that our wonder child has been giving us along the way.

Many of us found ourselves in a bewildering place in childhood. We felt overcome by the forces around us. Only our elemental instincts allowed us to survive. We had to develop false selves in order to matter. We were lost; we didn't know who we were.

By reclaiming and championing your wonder child you can let your divine light shine. Again, it was Jung who said, "The child is that which brings the light into the darkness and carries the light before it."

## TELLING OUR STORIES

There are many ways we can get back in touch with our archetypal wonder child. Listening to each other's *stories* is one of the ways in which we find the deep strength of the wonder child. When I listen to people tell their stories in my inner child workshop, it touches something deep in me. This happens over and over again. Sometimes I'm overwhelmed at the inner strength and creativity people have used to survive their most sordid and dreadful beginnings. Mostly I hear very common patterns. I've listened to literally hundreds of people tell their childhood stories. What happens to me is that I am taken out of my own loneliness as a child. My own story begins to sound more common. Edith Sullwold has said, "The telling of our story begins to touch at a deep level who we are on an archetypal level." One of our greatest banes in childhood and adolescence was the feeling of a terrible loneliness, because we thought we were the only ones who had suffered our childhood pains. Most of us lived in families with "no talk" rules. Consequently, there was no one to tell our story to. In my workshops, when people sit in groups of six or eight and share their childhood stories with one another, there is *a healing that comes from the universality of our lives as children. In some way or another, we are all infants in exile.*

This is crucial for us to know. Adult children often believe that they are the *only ones* who suffered as children. Out of our hurt and pain, out of our lack of nourishment, we try to concretize things. We often concretize our wounded child and lose sight of the wonder child. We get bogged down in the literal and lose sight of the symbolic. To lose the symbolic is to lose sight of the spiritual. This creates what Marion Woodman calls the "materialization of consciousness." We see no world beyond the world of our actual historical wounded child. To be bogged down in your wounded personal history is *never to get beyond your wounds.* Never to get beyond your wounds is to explain everything that's wrong in your life as your wounded child's contamination. When we hear others' stories, they connect us with something larger. They connect us to our archetypal depths.

The wonder child archetype calls us to spiritual regeneration. It represents our soul's need for transformation. The wonder child opens us to the mythical divine child expressed in the infant-in-exile motif. It takes us beyond the literal child of our personal histories. All of our stories tell of a hero/heroine, a divine child who was exiled and who is on a journey to find his true self.


## ENERGETIC EMERGENCE

According to Jung, the archetypes are part of our collective unconscious. Therefore, they cannot be known directly. That's why we must learn to recognize the cues that mark the emergence of the child archetype. Hearing one another's stories touches archetypal depths. Another way your archetypal wonder child may be calling you to regeneration and creative change is through some kind of *energetic emergence.*

## Strong Feelings

The energetic emergence could be an unusually strong or all-pervasive feeling. It may manifest itself in a strong emotional attraction to something or someone, or it could appear as a strong bodily sensation that masks a repressed feeling. Some examples will help.

I once worked with a lawyer I'll call Norman. He was devoted to detail and had an astonishing knowledge of the law. He was one of the senior partners in a law firm founded by his father. The other lawyers often picked his brains. He sometimes spent hours helping his colleagues as they tried and won lawsuits. Norman rarely got credit for his help. When I questioned him on this, he shrugged it off with the disclaimer that it helped the entire firm become stronger.

One day Norman reported that he had awakened from a dream with immense sadness and that the sadness had persisted for six days. Sometimes during this post-dream period, Norman had sobbed for as long as an hour. This emotional energy was quite unusual for Norman's rather stoic lifestyle.

When I asked him about the dream, he told me a story focused on the loss of a number of animals, predominantly dogs and cats. This triggered a long-forgotten memory of a favorite childhood game in which Norman was an animal doctor taking care of his dogs and cats. Norman remembered that as a child he wanted to be a veterinarian, but his father had scoffed at this idea. It emerged that Norman's propensity for legal detail was a way to cover up his sadness over the loss of his true vocation. His sadness over this loss was so deep that Norman would not allow himself any feelings of sadness at all. The dream triggered the deep archetypal energy calling Norman to get in touch with his inner child's urging for change and transformation.

Norman was a man of some wealth. I helped him to listen to the urging of his wonder child, to go to veterinary college, and to open his own animal clinic. Norman was 36 when his dream occurred. Now, ten years later, he lives happily taking care of his animals. His dream had triggered overwhelming emotional sadness. This *energetic emergence* led him to hear the voice of his wonder child.

This regenerative change took a lot of courage. His father was aghast. His colleagues thought he had gone crazy. The *old order* rose up to defy the emergence of the wonder child's energy. His father called me a charlatan; he insisted that Norman was depressed and needed medication and hospitalization. All the archetypal patterns were present: the infant child wanting to be a healer in the natural order and his true self calling him to that life work; the constant opposition from the old order; the years of pain, hiding in the cave of his sadness; the years of struggle to find his true self. Finally, the child broke free. And Norman let his energy move him to creative transformation.

Energetic emergence in the form of strong emotional attraction to a person or thing has occurred often in my life. I have had strong emotional attraction to certain philosophical thinkers. I will describe this more fully when I talk about my seminary experience. Several of these thinkers were quite unusual considering my intellectual curriculum at the time.

On several occasions I have experienced an unusually strong attraction to unfamiliar books. While browsing in a bookstore a certain book will catch my eye. It may be the title of the book or it may be something about the cover of the book. Generally I have no conscious *reason* for being attracted to the book. However, I usually feel an urgency to buy the book and I almost always do so. When I get home, I look the book over and then lay it aside without clearly understanding why I wanted it.

Sometime later, almost always when I'm energetically involved in a new project, one of these books will pop into my awareness. On several occasions the book in question has been a catalyst for triggering a creative outpouring. The two most notable examples relate to my 1985 PBS series *Bradshaw On: The Family* and my book *Healing the Shame That Binds You.*

Several years after my first PBS TV series, I was asked to do another series on a different topic. I couldn't find a subject that really excited me. One day as I was looking through my own library, I focused on a book titled *The Family Crucible,* by Carl Whitaker and Augustus Napier. It had been sitting on my shelf for several years. The book presented the theory of family systems. It read like a novel, describing a family therapy using the family-system model. In the past, I had found the family-system material too clinical and dry, certainly not appropriate for a public service TV audience. The book moved me deeply and I was inspired to conceive a series based on an exposition of families as general systems. After the series was completed, I realized that the family-systems' material spoke to the deepest emotional issues in my personal life. The breakdown of my family of origin was a great sorrow to me. I came to see that my popularization of this vital material was an important part of my life's work: it was the work that led me to reclaim and champion my wounded inner child.

When I started to write *Healing the Shame That Binds You,* I felt stuck. I was dissatisfied with the way shame was presented in the available literature. No one had clearly differentiated healthy shame from unhealthy shame. One day when I was puttering around in my office I spotted a very thin red book titled *Shame.* It was published by Hazelden and the author was anonymous. I had bought the book several years earlier and had forgotten about it. I began to read it and found that the author touched me deeply. He saw healthy shame as the guardian of our humanness. Shame, he posited, is the emotion that signals our human finitude, our human limits. Unhealthy shame results when we try to be *more than human* or when we act *less than human.* This insight was what I needed.

Here were two books that triggered strong emotions in me that I bought for no good reason. They had lain on my shelf for years, then had caught my attention just when I needed them. Family systems and shame-based families were the doorways to my own divine child in exile. Working out these two issues has been a part of my personal spiritual journey and my life's work.

Another way that feelings can lead us to important discoveries concerning our divine child in exile is through *body memories.* Often when I lecture on physical or sexual violation, someone in the audience experiences strong bodily sensations—nausea, stomach-ache, headache, neck pain, feelings of being smothered, feeling a band of constriction around their head. These bodily sensations are energetic signals calling the person to an awareness that can lead to new life. Victims of physical and sexual violence dissociate from the pain of their traumas in order to survive. They literally leave their bodies. The wounding, however, remains imprinted in their bodies and can be revitalized in the form of bodily sensations when such violence is described, as in my lecture. The value of this energetic emergence is that it calls the victim back to the painful trauma. Until this original pain is embraced and worked through, the person cannot recover from the effects of the violation. Without doing their original pain grieving, they cannot find and reclaim their wonder child.

# TRAUMATIC EVENTS AND EMOTIONAL PAIN

The energetic emergence can also occur in response to a traumatic life event. You get a divorce, lose a friend, get fired from a job, and the energy of change calls you to regeneration and new life. I saw this happen many times when my clients decided to end very bad marriages. Often, abused women, when they found the courage to leave their abusers, found that within a few years their lives were transformed in ways they had never dreamed of.

I know of no formula that will predict whether a person will be broken by a traumatic event or energized and transformed by it. I can simply tell you that all of us need to be aware that trauma has a twofold potential: it can be the catalyst for creative change or the cause of self-destruction. It depends on your courage to embrace the unresolved pain you repressed at the time the trauma happened and the meaning you chose to give it.

It is important to look back on your own life and find the strengths that have resulted from your traumatic experiences. Many of my clients, while doing the meditation that I describe on p. 281, have found great strengths in past traumatic events. They understand the words of Leon Bloy:

> There are places in the heart which do not yet exist; pain must be in order that they be.

I have no true convictions as to why bad things happen to good people or why terrible abuse is the lot of some rather than others. None of the standard religious answers have convinced me.

## Transforming Trauma: A Personal Story

In my own life, the worst thing that happened to me was ultimately the best thing. I ended my seventeen years of alcoholism by being carried on a stretcher into Austin State Hospital. I was 30 years old. Alcohol was robbing me of my creative potential. Alcoholism was itself an energetic witness that I was longing for spirit. Marion Woodman has called addiction the "perversion of spirit"; literally, "our spiritual nature turned in on itself." Alcohol was the medicine I was taking to heal my wounded inner child, but the medicine was killing me. The addiction was a metaphor of my deep spiritual need.

After my father abandoned me and our family, we moved often, living mostly with relatives. I adapted by being a very obedient child. To cover my shame and to give my alcoholic family a sense of dignity, I became a superachiever, making straight A's in school and being class president every year of my elementary-school life. I was trying to be more than human—being overidentified with my role of good guy, people-pleasing superachiever. My natural child's wild instinctive energy was locked in the basement and was straining to get out. By my early teens my wild side had found several fatherless guys from broken homes. I began running around with them and letting out my wild side. Soon I became overidentified with it, covering my pain in wild orgiastic living. I begin drowning my hurt and sorrow in alcohol. My high school years were dominated by drinking, whoring, and carousing. I had become less than human. By 21 I felt trapped and alone. One day I saw a way out. I could solve all my problems by going to a seminary to study for the Catholic priesthood. Hadn't several nuns and priests told me they thought I had a vocation to religious life—a special calling to do God's work? I became a member of the Basilian order. Going to the seminary was clearly an attempt to heal my spiritual wound. Here was a place where I could find spiritual health. But I had not yet done my ego work. My soul thirsted for God, but my repressed emotional energy called me back to itself. In the seminary I became spiritually compulsive, often kneeling to pray for hours at a time and fasting to the point of exhaustion.

Nietzsche spoke of three transformations in our personal growth. "How the spirit becomes a camel, the camel a lion and the lion finally a child." Like a camel, I loaded myself with knowledge. I studied the great spiritual masters. I meditated and prayed.

Like many young men, I was on a spiritual pilgrimage, but I wasn't free to ask the right questions. I was unable to hear the signals my archetypal wonder child was giving me. I did not find inner peace because I did not find myself. I was wearing a black robe and a white Roman collar. People called me "Father," but I had no idea who I really was.

My archetypal child led me to study existential philosophy. First Jacques Maritain, the great Catholic Thomistic philosopher, became one of my fathers. Then I was emotionally attracted to the works of Dostoevski, Kierkegaard, Nietzsche, and Kafka. All of these men were

wounded children whose archetypal energy had broken out in spite
of themselves. They are magnificent examples of what the archetypal
wonder child can do. Their lives were pained and tormented. They
never reclaimed and championed their wounded child, but their
archetypal energy was so powerful that it moved them to the heights
of creativity. There was a tragic sense in these men's lives. They never
found an inner peace and were tormented till the end. Yet, their
wonder child still led them to produce great works of art. The
greatest artists seem to have this archetypal pattern. Many never
achieve the enjoyment I've described in the work of reclaiming and
championing the wounded child. There is something mysterious
about all this—something that I do not fully understand, which sets
the lives of genius and saints apart from the lives of the rest of us. I
think it has something to do with the wonder child.

In any case, I was drawn to these men, especially to Friedrich
Nietzsche. How ironic! There I was in a Roman Catholic seminary
where everyone was doing work on St. Thomas Aquinas and I was
studying the writings of Nietzsche, the philosopher who pronounced
the "death of God." I remember how moved I was when I first read
these lines from one of Nietzsche's letters:

> If these Christians want me to believe in their god, they'll have to
> sing me better songs; they'll have to look more like people who
> have been saved; they'll have to wear on their countenance the
> joy of the beatitudes. I could only believe in a god who dances.

A god who dances! A god who is joyous and celebrates life! What a far
cry from the seminary's lugubrious black robes, sacred silence, and
prohibition against any special friendships among the novices. Joyous
celebration and dancing were the last things my religious training was
about! I was being taught mortification of the flesh, custody of the
eyes, and denial of emotion. Custody of the eyes meant we were to
keep our eyes cast down so that we would not see anything that
would arouse our lust. I was in fact an absolute prisoner of the old
order. Dostoevski expressed it well in the "Legend of the Grand
Inquisitor." If Jesus had come back, they would lock him up. He came
to set us free. That is too much for the old order to handle. Jesus calls
us to creativity and our own unique I AMness. As our model, he said,
"Before Abraham, *I am*." They crucified him for this. The old order
crucifies all of us for expressing our I AMness and creativity.

In the seminary, obedience to authority was the rule we memo-
rized and read four times a year. I had a new mother (Holy Mother
Church) and a new father (my father superior), but I remained lost in
my spiritual wound.

But I was not totally lost. My wonder child was stirring. He led me
to write my master's thesis on Nietzsche. I called it "Philosophy as
Dionysian Knowledge." Nietzsche was intrigued by the god Dionysus—
the god of ecstasy, wine, and raw creativity. He struggled with the god
Apollo—the god of form and structured discipline. He knew they
were both necessary for art and life but had trouble balancing them
in his own life. In my thesis I grasped how inadequate philosophy
was without the Dionysian element. For Nietzsche, philosophy was
almost poetry itself. That was an overreaction to the frozen Apollonian
rationalism of his day. I felt the Dionysian power at the heart of
Nietzsche's work. I saw how important it was to find the balance
between the Apollonian and Dionysian. (The latter, the Dionysian,
being the wild creative energy of the wonder child, and the former,
the Apollonian, being the form and structure that incarnates that deep
poetic energy.) I saw it intellectually, but I did not know how to
balance it in my own life. I opted for Dionysus.

Now my camel became a roaring lion. I rebelled against the anti-
life forces of the old order. Mine was an intellectual revolt at first. But
my alcoholism helped me to act it out. The old order called me in. I
was reprimanded and scolded for my disobedience. My rebellion
continued, and in a night of Dionysian frenzy I ran drunkenly down
the monastery halls at three in the morning screaming curses at the
authorities and guardians of the old order. My wonder child was
kicking up a storm! I was exiled for a year of teaching. My ordination
was to be delayed. My class was ordained the day after my exile.
*Whew!* That's cutting it close! The old order almost won.

On the train from Toronto to Texas, I drank. The ale soothed my
tormented soul. I had no idea what was happening. My wounded
child ached with shame. Slowly over the next months I listened to my
wonder child. He came to me in Nietzsche's words: "You sought the
heaviest burden of all and found yourself." There was no one to
affirm my being. It took all the courage I had to leave the Basilians,
and they did not make it easy. They gave me four hundred bucks to
make my way. I was 30 years old; I had no car; no clothes; no shelter.
When I left, no one called me, encouraged me, or supported me in
any way. Men I had lived with for almost ten years, many of whom I

loved dearly, followed the unwritten rule of no talk and no contact with a departing brother. An uncle who had given parties when I left to be a priest told me he knew I "didn't have the guts to make it." I feel the old rage and pain as I write this.

Like the exiled child of the myths, I was alone in the elements of the world. My previous work experience was as an office boy and a grocery checker. I didn't know where to go or what to do. Deep inside, my wonder child pushed me on. When I look back on those days, I do not know how I made it. My alcoholism was reaching its apex. I felt totally lost and alone. Not only did I have no car, I didn't even know how to drive. I was terrified. The end of this road was Austin State Hospital.

When I left the hospital, I joined a 12 Step group dealing with alcoholism. Hands went out to me. In my shattered state, I saw myself in the eyes of my fellow wounded human beings. We are all "infants crying in the night," who need one another's support. The inner push that led me to escape the old order was verified in the eyes of my recovering colleagues. I began to truly see *myself* as I listened to others sharing their experience, strength, and hope—all recovering alcoholics. I stabilized; I found the space from which my wonder child has slowly emerged over the last twenty-five years.

Today I know at the deepest level that *I am I—a wondrous person!* I'm rageful, pouty, and selfish; but I am also loving, exciting, truly creative, and even amazing to myself at times. The greatest learning of my life is that creativity overcomes violation and is the answer to violence. It was much later before I could see how my wonder child had been guiding me all along. The energy for Nietzsche, Kafka, Kierkegaard, and Dostoevski was from my wonder child. I now see why I so identified with these men. I thank them. They are my fathers in the truest sense. They helped me to find myself.

## DREAMS

Earlier I mentioned Norman's dream. It was not his dream *per se* that led him to discover the transformative urges of his wonder child. For Norman it was the long period of intense and unusual sadness. But his dream began the process.

Sometimes the dream itself can be the energy from the archetypal wonder child. In his autobiographical work, *Memories, Dreams,*

*Reflections,* Carl Jung calls such life-shaping dreams "big dreams." Jung himself had a "big" dream when he was between 3 and 4 years old, a dream that was to preoccupy him all his life. Jung was amazed that a young child could have such a dream that symbolized problems "far beyond (his) knowledge." Jung asked:

> Who brought the above and below together, and laid the foundation for everything that was to fill the second half of my life with stormiest passion?

I presented an analysis of one of my own "big dreams" in my book *Bradshaw On: Healing the Shame That Binds You.* My dream, which came twenty years after I had left the seminary, called me back to the elements of that life. It especially called me to begin meditating in earnest. At that time I was on the board of an oil company, working as a psychological adviser in charge of developing their human resources program. The work was crushing my creativity. I was also involved in a damaging relationship with a woman and was becoming more and more obsessed with making a lot of money. As a board member, I was awarded stock options. This was the heyday of the oil industry. Everything we touched turned to gold. Then the crisis came. People were laid off. I lost all my options plus a six-figure income as a consultant. I felt devastated. I grew up poor and had obsessed on money all my life. My fear of poverty manifested itself as a low-grade chronic sense of impending doom. There was never enough. Someday the bottom would surely drop out. Now it actually had dropped out.

Shortly after this, I had three dreams that were clearly connected. They occurred over several days. In the first dream I was trying to fly to Toronto, but I couldn't get off the ground. In the second dream, I took off and landed near Niagara Falls in Buffalo, New York. In the airport I saw an abbot of a Trappist monastery whom I had met twenty-five years earlier. He had impressed me deeply at the time, but somehow I had not thought of him in all the ensuing years. His image haunted me for several days. In the third dream, I rented a car in Buffalo, New York, and traveled to Toronto. When I got to Toronto I was all alone. I went straight to 95 St. Joseph Street, where I had done my theological studies. I wandered around and finally came to the large chapel. I sat there for what seemed like hours. I spoke with several men whom I had considered very pious. They somehow just appeared to me. Each urged me to find my inner sanctum.

Toronto was where I had studied to become a priest, and these dreams brought me back to my spiritual center. They *moved* me to begin meditating daily. I had dabbled with meditation for years but had never really gotten serious about it. These dreams also brought a rather lasting peace about my money issues. Somehow I knew that I would be secure financially. I determined that what I needed to do was devote my energy to spiritual matters. For me, creativity is spirituality. So I began thinking about doing a new TV series. That series was the beginning of my present life. It all started to happen once I realized clearly that corporate life and financial issues were not where my creative energy belonged. My wonder child set me on a new course through my big dream.

## CHILDHOOD MEMORIES

Another way to stalk the archetypal unconscious is to look for significant childhood memories. Sometimes these memories are very clearly the seeds of our later creativity.

Georgia O'Keeffe, the celebrated painter, tells us in her autobiography that she remembered lying on a big carpet at five months old, being fascinated by the design and colors of a quilt in her aunt's house. This particular quilt design subsequently became a core pattern in many of her paintings. She reports telling her mother of this memory. Her mother told her that it was impossible for her to remember that far back. Georgia then described her aunt's dress in great detail. *Childhood seems to be a time when the inner quest is laid for many great creators.*

The great paleontologist Teilhard de Chardin tells in his childhood recollections that he was certainly no more than 6 or 7 when he began to be drawn to matter. He describes being fascinated by rocks and by iron. Einstein was 5 years old when he was given a magnetic compass. He was filled with a sense of mystery that moved him to seek out the answers to the secrets of the universe. That sense of mystery remained with him throughout his life. The paintings of Picasso and Chagall are dominated with childlike images. The seeds of their creativity resided in their childhood.

A leading Jungian child psychiatrist, Frances Wickes, states the matter rather well:

Experiences of timeless realities may come to the very young child.... As he grows older, problems ... press upon him. His ego must grow to meet the demands of greater consciousness and numinous experience may appear to be forgotten by the ego, but it is remembered by the self....

In *Memories, Dreams, Reflections,* Jung recalls an unexpected encounter with his wonder child. The experience came at a time when Jung's life seemed stalled. He felt so confused and disoriented that he feared he had a "psychic disturbance." In an attempt to find the root cause of his problem he began to search through his childhood memories. He wrote:

The first thing that came to the surface was a childhood memory from my tenth or eleventh year. At that time I had a spell of playing passionately with building blocks.... To my astonishment this memory was accompanied by a good deal of emotion. "Aha," I said to myself, there is still life in these things. The small boy is still around and possesses a creative life which I lack.

Deciding that he had to reconnect with this child's energy, Jung reestablished contact by taking up the "child's life with his childish games" and bought a set of building blocks. He experienced lots of resistance from his critical inner voices (old order), but he gave in and began building an entire village complete with castle and church. He worked on it every day after lunch and in the evenings. He was questioned by his own family. But he wrote, "I had only the inner certainty that I was on the way to discovering my own myth."

This experience played a crucial part in releasing Jung's extraordinary creative energies that culminated in the theories of the archetypes and the collective unconscious.

Years ago, while reading this section of Jung's autobiography, I was reminded of a similar incident in my own life. When I was around 10 years old I got interested in building model airplanes. I remember spending weeks working on one model. For the first time, I had painstakingly put the whole plane together. It was made of tiny pieces of balsa wood, very delicate and complex. All I needed was to glue on the outer paper and finish the paint job. One day when I came home I found my airplane crushed and broken. My little brother had tried to fly it and it had torn up. I was heartbroken, truly beside myself.

From time to time I thought about starting over, but I never did so. Thirty years later I still had energy to complete the task of building a model plane. It was very important to me in some strange way. At 39 I bought a model plane and laboriously built it. I sometimes worked on it half the night. I put it all together, painted it, and truly *finished* the job. I had great pride in this achievement, although I had no idea why I felt an urgency to build a model airplane.

I now look back on the period since age 39 as the greatest period of creativity in my life. There was some unfinished energy in me from not completing the model airplane. I needed to finish it in order to move on to other creative work.

## A PIECE OF GOOD NEWS

So many of us from dysfunctional families spend a great part of our lives recycling our wounded inner child's contaminations. We live defensively, so married to our delusional life myths that we have no idea that there is a piece of good news inside of us: the good news that each of us is highly creative. This shows up even in our neurotic adaptations. Each of us has a wonder child with creative potential. This applies to everyone, not just great painters or musicians. Our life can be our work of art. A mother can be unique and creative by mothering in a way that has never been done before. The same is true for any other vocation or role in life. Each of us is called to be unique and unrepeatable. If you will start looking for your creativity, you may find traces of it in some experience you had as a child.

Adult children need to realize that each element of their lives is significant in composing the unique story that is themselves. Co-dependent contaminations take us away from our unique I AMness, we no longer believe we are significant. What I'm telling you is that every element of your life is special and unique. There has never been another you. We could go back a million years and we'd never find anyone like you. Trust the specialness of your unique self. Learn to believe that your memories matter.

The following meditation is geared to help you get back in touch with a childhood memory or memories that may still be holding some creative energy. You might want to read or reread *The Little Prince,* by Antoine de Saint-Exupéry, before beginning this meditation. If you don't have time for that, I'll just remind you that the author describes how his budding painting career was destroyed by adults. He had drawn a picture of a boa constrictor who swallowed an elephant. The adults who looked at his drawing did not see a boa constrictor at all. They saw a hat. The author reports:

> The grown-ups' response ... was to advise me to lay aside my drawings of boa constrictors ... and devote myself instead to geography, history, arithmetic and grammar. That is why, at the age of six, I gave up what might have been a magnificent career as a painter.... Grown-ups never understand anything by themselves, and it is tiresome for children to be always and forever explaining things to them.

If your creativity was crushed by some adult early on, do the following meditation. It may help you get in touch with a memory that's still lurking there like a burning ember in the ashes of your mind.

### MEDITATION ON CREATIVE CHILDHOOD MEMORIES

Record the following on your tape recorder. A wonderful piece of background music is the cassette tape by Daniel Kobialka called *When You Wish Upon a Star*.

> Focus on your breathing.... Be aware of what happens in your body when you breathe in.... And out.... Slowly begin to exhale a white vapor which forms the number five on a black curtain.... If you can't see the five, finger paint it.... Then breathe out the number four or finger paint it.... Feel yourself letting go a tiny bit.... Also be aware of holding on as much as you need to.... Now breathe out or finger paint the number three.... Now you can let go a little more.... Remember when you first learned to hold on and let go.... You learn to hold on when you learned to walk.... When you learned to eat.... You learned to let go when you played on a swing and felt the air blowing your hair.... You let go when you first daydreamed or when you went to sleep at night.... So you really know how much to hold on and how much to let go.... And you can be completely aware of your voice, the music, the feeling of your clothes on your body.... Your back on the chair, the air on your face.... And at the same time go into a light and restful

*trance.* . . . You can feel your whole outer body becoming numb. . . . You may either feel your body as heavy . . . or as light as a feather. . . . Whichever you feel, heavy or light, you can let that feeling take you into a dream. . . . It will be a dream of discovery. . . . In it you will find a long-forgotten childhood memory of a most unusual kind. . . . It may be quite obvious or it may be extremely vague. . . . But it will certainly be a dream memory of a creative seed. . . . You may already be living it out or it may be a seed memory you need now. . . . You will know. . . . And what you know will be right for you. . . . Get ready to let yourself take two minutes of clock time, which is all the time in the world to the unconscious. . . . In that time you'll find another time. . . . So you can do it now. . . . *(two minutes' pause)* Whatever it is you are experiencing is right for you. . . . It is *exactly* where you *need to be.* . . . You can mull your experience over. . . . You may already know. . . . You may need to take what you got and live with it for several days. . . . Maybe weeks. . . . Only you will know. . . . You may be surprised. . . . You may be suddenly aware. . . . Looking at something, reading a book, as you walk. . . . It will *come* to you. . . . Now slowing see the number three and feel your hands and wiggle your toes. . . . Now see the number five and feel all your body fully awake. . . . Now let your mind be fully present, fully restored to your normal waking consciousness. . . . Now open your eyes.

You may or may not have gotten in touch with a creative memory. You may have touched an energetic memory but do not know what it means. Just trust that you'll know whatever it is you need to know.

If none of the experiences I've described in this chapter tap in to your wonder child's energy, here are a few other suggestions that may be clues to your inner child's presence:

1. Pay attention to anything that you seem unduly fascinated with. Maybe there is something you collect, but don't know why; maybe you are fascinated by some foreign country and its customs; maybe you're deeply attracted to some color or sound.

2. Pay attention to your intuition and hunches. Einstein often acknowledged the role of intuition in his work. He stated that long before he had worked out his famous equations, he knew them at

another, nonverbal level with an immediate certainty. While no one of us is Einstein, we all possess intuition. Intuition has been described as "felt thought." It is almost as if you feel it rather than know it. Intuition involves knowing something without reason. Many believe that intuitive knowing comes from the nondominant hemisphere of the brain. The dominant hemisphere knows logically and is the seat of linear thinking. The nondominant hemisphere knows intuitively and is the seat of holistic or "all at once" thinking. Few shame-based adult children with a wounded inner child trust their intuition. Our lives are so guarded, we operate in a state of hypervigilance focused solely on the danger outside of us. We are never relaxed enough to allow ourselves to listen to our inner intuition. We have an opportunity to experience this part of ourselves after we've reclaimed and championed our wonder child.

Once I worked with a woman who in spite of a seemingly stable marriage insisted that she needed a divorce. Her husband was well off, loved her, and wanted to work out their problems. They had six teenage children. My client spoke with a sense of urgency, saying things like, "If I stay in this marriage I know I'll never be what God created me to be. My life is on the line. I can't tell you why, I just *feel* it and I *know* that I am right." She filed for divorce. The old order went bananas. Her Baptist pastor was horrified. Her Bible-study group began a weekly prayer vigil. Her husband blamed *me!*

Five years later she wrote me. She told me how she had formed her own real estate company, something she had dreamed of as a little girl. She had an income that was crowding a half-million dollars a year. The kids were doing well. She had a wonderful friendship with a special man and was blissfully happy. She had followed her intuition against all odds, and her wonder child had won out.

It is not always easy to determine whether our inner voice is truly intuition. Sometimes it can be confused with desire. I know of no absolute guidelines that can tell you whether it's part of your higher intelligence or your egoistic desire. Allow yourself to listen and try out your inner voice in fantasy. We usually know the things we want or have wanted for a long time. Intuition is usually something unfamiliar—something fresh and new.

3. Pay attention to any persistent impulse. For example, you always wanted to go to Bali or the Far East; you've always wanted to go metal hunting; or you've always wanted to learn to play a musical instru-

ment or learn to be a sculptor or painter. This does not mean you should immediately drop everything and follow your impulse. But it is worth exploring. You might do this by going on an imaginary trip, seeing and feeling how this impulse is important to you. Or you can use the technique of free association. Say you've always wanted to go to Bali and you really don't know why. Ask yourself: What does Bali mean to me? Draw a circle and put the word Bali in the center of it. Then let your mind freely associate any words or phrases that come to you.

Look over all the associations and allow the one with the highest voltage to attract you. Once you have an association, live with it for a while. Let yourself be open to its meaning. Once you have a strong sense of its meaning, make a plan of action and follow it.

4. Pay attention to new persons who come into your life; who seem to call you in a new direction. Take the "as if" position that the more the person interrupts your familiar patterns, the more he may be offering you an opportunity to break out of the old order and find what is most original in you. The person may challenge your way of thinking and threaten your belief system. The person may be fascinating to you, touching places in you that have been dormant and frozen for years. It's good to be cautious rather than impulsive in developing a relationship with this new person. But see him as a possible metaphor for self-revelation.

Creative regeneration is the essence of life itself. Finding old memories, trusting your hunches and intuitions, and following your new energies may motivate you to risk new bursts of creativity.

## CREATIVITY

Creativity is the glory of being human. It is what distinguishes us from all other created beings. Our human destiny is to create our own unique lifestyle. You may do it as a parent who challenges the old order. Someone else might do it by refusing to play his designated cultural role. Creating your own life takes the courage to risk new ways of being. Creativity is closely related to success. As I see it, success is doing what you want with your one and only life. Joseph Campbell, perhaps the greatest teacher of the meaning of myth, called doing what you want with your own life *finding your bliss.* This also takes courage—to try new things and to stop and move on when they don't work for us. To do this, we need the spontaneity, resiliency, and curiosity of the wonder child. When we have the courage to wish upon our own star, we give the universe something new. In his poem "The Love Song of J. Alfred Prufrock," T. S. Eliot asks: "Do I dare distrub the universe?" Indeed, every unique lifestyle that is achieved creates the universe anew.

Being creative is not just our crowning human glory, it is our true Image of God. To create is to be *like* our creator in the truest sense of the word. Creativity gives us the chance to fashion our lives as our own work of art. In so doing we help create the patterns of all future human life. As James Joyce put it:

Welcome, O life! I go to encounter for the millionth time the reality of experience and to forge in the smithy of my soul the uncreated conscience of my race.

Creative choice is your birthright. Please own it.

# EPILOGUE

# "HOME, ELLIOTT, HOME!"

The movie *E.T.* was loved by millions. When masses of people exhibit such energy for something, there's often some deep archetypal pattern it has stirred up. One scene especially tapped our collective unconscious. When the abandoned E.T. whispers, "Home, Elliott, home," his words touch the exact symbol that evokes our deep archetypal longings. When E.T. whispered, "Home, Elliott, home," millions of every age in every culture wept.

We wept because *we are still divine infants in exile*. No matter how hard we work to reclaim and champion our inner child, there is a level of emptiness and absence in us all. I call it the "metaphysical blues."

There is surely rejoicing when we reclaim and champion our wounded inner child. For many of us, finding our inner child is like finding home for the first time. But no matter how secure and how connected we all become, there is a *dark journey we all still have to take*. As fearful as it is, there's a longing for it inside us all. For no matter how completely we fulfill our earthly goals and dreams, even when we arrive just where we have longed to be, we always experience a slight disappointment. So much so that even after Dante, Shakespeare, and Mozart, we say: Is that all?

I believe this sense of disappointment arises because we have another home where we all belong. I believe we came forth out of the depth of being, and being calls us back. I believe we came from God and we belong to God. No matter how good it gets, we still are not home. The wounded child Augustine said it well: "Thou hast made us for Thyself, O Lord, and our hearts are restless till they repose in Thee." That will be our true homecoming at last.

# REFERENCES

Alberti, Robert E. and Emmons, Michael L. *Your Perfect Right* (San Luis Obispo, CA: Impact Publishers, Inc., 1986).

Andreas, Connairae and Andreas, Steve. *Heart of the Mind* (Moab, UT: Real People Press, n.d.).

Armstrong, Thomas. *The Radiant Child* (Wheaton, IL: Quest, 1985). This stimulating book was a major resource for part 4 of this book.

Bandler, Richard and Grinder, John. *Frogs into Princes* (Moab, UT: Real People Press, 1979). ———. *Reframing* (Moab, UT: Real People Press, 1982).

Berne, Eric. *Games People Play* (London: Penguin, 1970). ———. *What Do You Say after You Say Hello?* (New York: Bantam Books, 1984).

Bettelheim, Bruno. *Surviving and Other Essays* (New York: Vintage, 1980).

Black Elk. *The Sacred Pipe* (Norman, OK: University of Oklahoma Press, 1953).

Bly, Robert. *Selected Poems* (New York: Harper & Row, 1986). I recommend everything that Robert Bly has written. He is one of the "earth fathers" of our time.

Booth, Leo. *Meditations for Compulsive People* (Deerfield Beach, FL: Health Communications, Inc., 1987). I used Leo's meditation "My Name is Shame" as the source of my meditation on Toxic Shame.

Cameron-Bandler, Leslie and Lebeau, Michael. *The Emotional Hostage* (San Rafael, CA: FuturePace, Inc., 1986). ———. *Solutions* (San Rafael, CA: FuturePace, Inc., 1985). Originally published as *They Lived Happily Ever After*.

Campbell, Joseph. *The Hero with a Thousand Faces* (Princeton: Princeton University Press, 1968).

Capaccione, Lucia. *The Power of Your Other Hand* (North Hollywood, CA: Newcastle Publishing Co., Inc., 1988). Read this wonderful book as an enrichment for learning to dialogue with your inner child.

Carnes, Patrick. *Contrary to Love* (Irvine, CA: CompCare Publishers, 1988). ———. *Out of the Shadows* (Irvine, CA: CompCare Publishers, 1985). Carnes' work is a must. He is the leading light in understanding sexual addiction.

Cashdan, Sheldon. *Object Relations Therapy* (New York: W. W. Norton & Co., 1988).

Cermak, Timmen L. *Diagnosing and Treating Co-Dependence* (Minneapolis: Johnson Institute Books, 1986).

Clarke, Jean Illsley. *Self-Esteem: A Family Affair* (New York: Harper & Row, 1980). ———. and Dawson, Connie. *Growing Up Again* (New York: Harper & Row, 1989). Jean is a gifted T. A. therapist. She has made a major contribution in the area of teaching reparenting skills.

Coudert, Jo. *Advice from a Failure* (Chelsea, MI: Scarborough House, 1965). This book is a treasure. The line stating, "Of all the people you will ever know, you are the only one you will never lose or leave" has touched me deeply.

DeMause, Lloyd. *Foundations of Psychohistory* (New York: Creative Roots, Inc., 1982). DeMause's work is crucial in understanding how the wounded child is archetypal of our time.

Dreikurs, Rudolf and Vicki Stolz. *Children: The Challenge* (New York: E. P. Dutton, 1987).

Eliade, Mircea. Winks, Robin W. ed. *Cosmos and History* (New York: Garland Publishing, Inc., 1985). ———. Cohen, J. M. tr. *The Two and the One* (Chicago: University of Chicago Press, 1979).

Elkind, David. *Children and Adolescents* (New York: Oxford University Press, 1981). ———, ed. Piaget, Jean. *Six Psychological Studies* (New York: Random House, 1968).

Erickson, Milton H. Erickson's works are very technical. My favortie work describing his genius is *Phoenix* by David Gordon and Maribeth Meyers-Anderson. (Cupertino, CA: Meta Publications, Inc., 1981).

Erikson, Erik H. *Childhood and Society* (New York: W. W. Norton & Co., 1964).

Fairbairn, W. Ronald. *Psychoanalytic Studies of the Personality* (New York: Routledge, Chapman & Hall, 1966).

Farmer, Steven. *Adult Children of Abusive Parents* (Los Angeles: Lowell House, 1989).

Fisher, Amy. Without any collaboration, Amy and I have arrived at many similar places. I wholeheartedly recommend her audiotapes. Write: Amy Fisher, 4516 Lover's Lane, #206, Dallas, TX 75225.

Forward, Susan with Buck, Craig. *Toxic Parents* (New York: Bantam Books, 1989).

Fossum, Merle A. and Mason, Marilyn J. *Facing Shame* (New York: W. W. Norton & Co., 1986). This work is especially good in describing the shame based rules which wounded the wonderful inner child.

Fromm, Erich. *The Heart of Man* (New York: Harper & Row, 1964).

Fulghum, Robert. *All I Really Need to Know I Learned in Kindergarten* (New York: Villard Books, 1988).

Goulding, Mary and Goulding, Robert. *Changing Lives Through Redecision Therapy* (New York: Grove, 1982).

Horney, Karen. *Neurosis and Human Growth* (New York: W. W. Norton & Co., 1970).

Isaacson, Robert L. *The Limbic System* (New York: Plenum Press, 1982).

Jackins, Harvey. *The Human Side of Human Beings* (Seattle: Rational Island Publishers, 1978).

Jung, Carl G. Adler, G., ed. Hull, R.F., tr. *Four Archetypes* (London: Ark Publishers, 1986). ———. *Memories, Dreams, Reflections* (London: Collins, 1983).

Keen, Sam. *Apology for Wonder* (New York: Harper & Row, 1969). ———. *To A Dancing God* (New York: Harper & Row, 1970).
Kirsten, Grace and Robertiello, Richard C. *Big You, Little You* (New York: Pocket Books, 1978).
Kurtz, Ron. *Body-Centered Psychotherapy: The Hakomi Method* (Mendocino, CA: LifeRhythm, 1990).
Levin, Pamela. *Becoming the Way We Are* (Deerfield Beach, FL: Health Communications, Inc., 1988). ———. *Cycles of Power* (Deerfield Beach, FL: Health Communications, Inc., 1988). These works have been a major resource for this book. Pamela Levin gives powerful workshops in reparenting for both laypeople and professionals. For more information, write her at: Box 1429, Ukiah, CA 95482.
Lidz, Theodore. *The Person* (New York: Basic Books, 1983).
Melzack, Ronald and Wall, Patrick. *The Challenge of Pain* (London: Penguin, 1988).
Miller, Alice. *The Drama of being Gifted Child* (London: Virago, 1987). ———. *For Your Own Good* (New York: Farrar, Straus & Giroux, 1983).
Miller, Sherod, *et al. Alive and Aware* (Minneapolis: Interpersonal Communications Programs, Inc., 1975). This book is the best one I know of for helping you teach your inner child good communication skills. I took the "awareness model" from this source.
Mills, Joyce C. and Crowley, Richard J. *Therapeutic Metaphors for Children and the Child Within* (New York: Brunner/Mazel, Inc., 1986).
Missildine, W. Hugh. *Your Inner Child of the Past* (New York: Pocket Books, 1983).
Montagu, Ashley, *Growing Young* (Westport, CT: Bergin & Garvey Publishers, Inc., 1989).
Morpugo, C. V. and D. W. Spinelli, "Plasticity of Pain, Perception," *Brain Theory Newsletter,* 2 (1976).
Napier, Augustus Y. and Whitaker, Carl. *The Family Crucible* (New York: Harper & Row, 1988).
Oaklander, Violet. *Windows to Our Children* (Highland, NY: Gestalt Journal, 1989). This book is filled with a variety of beautiful exercises for you to do with your inner child.
Pearce, Joseph Chilton. *The Crack in the Cosmic Egg* (New York: Crown, 1988). ———. *Exploring the Crack in the Cosmic Egg* (New York: Pocket Books, 1982). ———. *Magical Child* New York: Bantam Books, 1981).
Peck, M. Scott. *The Road Less Traveled* (London: Arrow Books, 1990).
Pelletier, Kenneth R. *Mind as Healer, Mind as Slayer* (New York: Delta/Dell, 1977).
Perls, Fritz. *Gestalt Therapy Verbatim* (Moab, UT: Real People Press, 1969).
Piaget, Jean and Inhelder, Barbel. *The Growth of Logical Thinking from Childhood to Adolescence* (New York: Basic Books, 1958).
Pollard, John K., III. *Self-Parenting* (Malibu, CA: Generic Human Studies Publishing, 1987).
Rank, Otto. *The Myth of the Birth of the Hero and Other Writings* (New York, Vintage, 1964).
Robinson, Edward. *The Original Vision* (New York: Harper & Row, 1983).
Rogers, Carl R. *On Becoming A Person* (New York: Houghton Mifflin Co., 1972).
Simon, Sidney B., *et al. Values Clarification* (New York: Dodd, 1985).
Small, Jacquelyn. *Transformers* (Marina del Rey, CA: De Vorss & Co., 1984).
Smith, Manuel J. *When I Say No, I Feel Guilty* (New York: Bantam Books, 1985).
Stern, Karl, *The Flight From Woman* (New York: Noonday Books/Farrar, Straus & Giroux, n.d.).
Stone, Hal and Winkelman, Sidra. *Embracing Our Selves* (Marina del Rey, CA: De Vorss & Co., 1985).
Sullwold, Edith. Taken from an audiotape entitled "The Archetype of the Inner Child" (GS2-388-87). Order from Audio Transcripts, Ltd., 610 Madison Street, Alexandria, VA 22314.
Tomkins, Silvan S. *Affect, Imagery, Consciousness,* I, II (New York: Springer Publishing Co., 1962, 63).
V., Rachel. *Family Secrets* (New York: Harper & Row, 1987). Contains a powerful interview with Robert Bly and an interview with Marion Woodman, which includes the story of the woman who tried to see the Pope.
Weinhold, Barry K. and Weinhold, Janae B. *Breaking the Co-Dependency Trap* (Walpole, NH: Stillpoint, 1989). The Weinhold's work is rooted in developmental psychology. I am indebted to them for their division of childhood into the stages of co-dependence, counter-dependence, independence, and interdependence.
Weiss, Laurie and Weiss, Jonathan B. *Recovery from Co-Dependency* (Deerfield Beach, FL: Health Communications, Inc., 1989). I consider the Weisses to be the best representatives of a handful of T. A. therapists who use a true developmental approach. I am indebted to them in many places.
Wickes, Frances. *The Inner World of Childhood* (Boston: Sigo Press, 1988).
Woodman, Marion. *Addiction to Perfection* (Toronto: Inner City Books, 1982).
Wright, Chris. *Repression: The Gated Brain* (unpublished paper).

## Addresses you may find useful

Al-Anon Family Groups, 61 Great Dover Street, London SE1 4YF 0171–403 0888

Alcoholics Anonymous, PO Box 1, Stonebow House, Stonebow, York YO1 2NJ 01904 644026; London Service Office 0171–352 3001

Co-Dependents Anonymous (CoDA), Ashburnham Community Centre, Tetcott Road, London SW10 0SH 0171–376 8191

Families Anonymous, The Doddington & Rolo's Community Association, Charlotte Despard Avenue, London SW11 5JE 0171–498 4680

The National Association of Children of Alcoholics, PO Box 64, Fishponds, Bristol, BS16 2UE 0800 289 0611 or 0117 9573432